T0278213

SECRET
MEXICO CITY

Mario Yaír T.S.

JONGLEZ PUBLISHING

Travel guides

We have taken great pleasure in drawing up *Secret Mexico City* and hope that through its guidance you will, like us, continue to discover unusual, hidden or little-known aspects of the city.

Descriptions of certain places are accompanied by thematic sections highlighting historical details or anecdotes as an aid to understanding the city in all its complexity.

Secret Mexico City also draws attention to the multitude of details found in places that we may pass every day without noticing. These are an invitation to look more closely at the urban landscape and, more generally, a means of seeing our own city with the curiosity and attention that we often display while travelling elsewhere …

Comments on this guidebook and its contents, as well as information on places we may not have mentioned, are more than welcome and will enrich future editions.

Don't hesitate to contact us:
  Jonglez publishing,
  info@jonglezpublishing.com

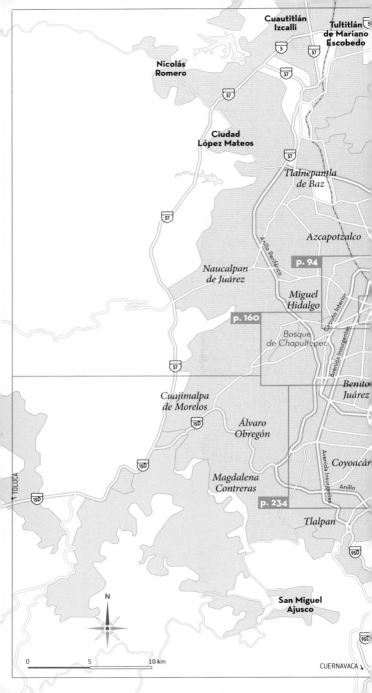

Cuautitlán
Izcalli

Tultitlán
de Mariano
Escobedo

Nicolás
Romero

Ciudad
López Mateos

Tlalnepantla
de Baz

Azcapotzalco

Naucalpan
de Juárez

p. 94

Miguel
Hidalgo

Bosque
de Chapultepec

p. 160

Cuajimalpa
de Morelos

Álvaro
Obregón

Benito
Juárez

Coyoacán

Magdalena
Contreras

p. 234

Tlalpan

San Miguel
Ajusco

N

0   5   10 km

CUERNAVACA

TOLUCA

p. 14
p. 280
p. 314

PACHUCA ↗

TULANCINGO ↗

Coacalco
de Berriozábal

Ecatepec
de Morelos

Sierra de
Guadalupe

Texcoco

Anillo Periférico

Gustavo
A. Madero

Centro
Histórico

Venustiano
Carranza

Aeropuerto Internacional
Benito Juárez

Chimalhuacán

Chicoloapan

Cuauhtémoc

Nezahualcóyotl

Iztacalco

CIUDAD DE MÉXICO

La Paz

Iztapalapa

Ixtapaluca

PUEBLA

Anillo Periférico

Valle de Chalco
Solidaridad

Tláhuac

Chalco de Díaz
Covarrubias

Xochimilco

San Bartolomé
Xicomulco

Milpa Alta

CONTENTS

Centro Histórico

From la Narvarte to Coyoacán

CONTENTS

From Chapultepec to la Doctores

From Tacuba to Peñón de los Baños

To the North

CONTENTS

To the South

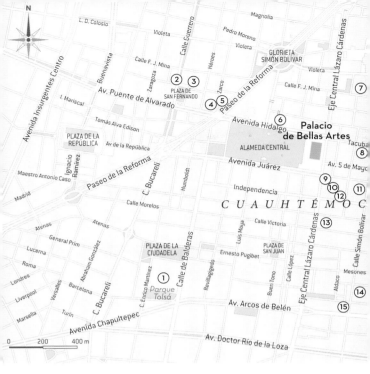

Centro Histórico

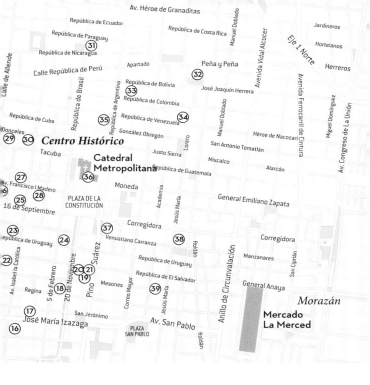

BIBLIOTECA
DE CARLOS MONSIVÁIS

A library built to reflect the chaos of Mexico City

Plaza de la Ciudadela 4
Colonia Centro
(+52) (55) 4155 0830
Daily 9.30am–6pm
Guided tours by appointment
Admission free
Metro: Balderas

Among the five private libraries housed in the Biblioteca de México, that of Mexican writer, intellectual and political activist Carlos Monsiváis is perhaps the most intriguing because of the hidden meaning of its architecture.

The premise was that each private library would reflect the personality of its previous owner. In the case of Monsiváis, there was no better approach than 'order in chaos', or anarchy as the principle of all creation.

Monsiváis' house was defined by his bookshelves of all shapes and sizes and his love for the chaos that is Mexico City. The 27,000 books of his collection are stacked on multiple rows of shelves, all of different sizes, forming labyrinthine corridors like the streets of the city.

From the rear of the library dedicated to his memory, the shelves represent (from left to right) an apartment block, a house, private homes, a skyscraper, alleyways, neighbourhoods, to the extent that you could lose yourself in it.

The designers were Javier Sánchez and Aisha Ballesteros, with the assistance of the writer's artist friend Francisco Toledo.

Toledo's finishing touch was the wall hangings showing Monsiváis in profile next to his books, a reminder that books and hangings have something in common: use inevitably leads to wear and tear. Toledo also laid out the floor as a tribute to the writer's cats.

This ordered disorder ends with a display of objects that Monsiváis kept in his house, regularly changed in the showcase at the exit.

NEARBY

The private libraries of Antonio Castro, Jaime García, Alí Chumacero and José Luis Martínez are also worth a visit because they reflect the personalities of these intellectuals, as well as exhibiting their finest books, designs and artworks. The librarians at the entrance to each library are happy to explain the wealth of detail that gives it such significance.

In 2010, on the death of Carlos Monsiváis, many people affectionately remembered the names he'd given to the 13 cats that lived with him (as shown by Toledo in the library floor mosaic). Among the cats were Miau Tse Tung, Fray Gatolomé de las Bardas, Voto de Castidad (Vow of Chastity), Catzinger, Peligro (Danger) para México, Fetiche de Peluche (Plush Fetish) and Miss Oginia.

DE GÁLVEZ TOMBS

The only viceroys buried in Mexico as the result of a plot?

Templo de San Fernando
Ribera de San Cosme, junction with Guerrero
Entrance usually through side door
Monday to Saturday 9am–7.30pm, Sunday 7.30am–7pm
Closed during mealtimes, which may vary

The mortal remains of Matías and Bernardo de Gálvez lie in two niches on the right of the main altar of San Fernando church. They were the only viceroys of New Spain who wished to be interred in Mexico. The plaque commemorating Matías (on the right, dated 1783), and that of Bernardo (on the left, dated 1786), are tributes from the United States for their help in the cause of North American independence.

Matías de Gálvez was appointed viceroy in 1783 through the influence of his brother, Minister José de Gálvez. Matías began his tenure with urban improvements, while his son Bernardo was appointed governor of Cuba after serving in Louisiana: the Gálvez were the most influential family on the continent at that time.

Matías initiated the construction of Castillo de Chapultepec and a gunpowder works in Santa Fe. In July 1784 he contracted a strange illness and no human contact was allowed. He died in mysterious circumstances on 3 November.

His successor, Bernardo, carried on building the castle – which people thought looked like a fortress. His popularity grew when he bought corn with his own money to alleviate the shortage of 1785, and amnestied all condemned prisoners. Rumours grew that he supported the independence of the New World from Spain. Then in 1786 he apparently caught the same disease as his father and died at Tacubaya.

Many deny that this was a plot by the Spanish court, although the disease that carried off the viceroys was never named. Bernardo's widow, Felícitas de Saint Maxent, pregnant and alone, is said to have shed bitter tears inside the church of San Fernando before returning to Spain. Here, she was accused of spreading revolutionary ideas during meetings at her home. Despite rejecting all such accusations, she's said to have been poisoned, and died in 1799 at Aranjuez.

A horse that wasn't a horse

Bernardo's rebellion is reflected in his portrait in the history museum at Chapultepec castle.

Although only the King of Spain officially had the right to be shown on a horse, Bernardo demanded that the artist-monks Pablo and Jerónimo paint him on horseback.

The pair improvised with a sgraffito representing the horse in a single continuous line, so that nobody could say that it wasn't a horse … or indeed that it was a horse.

*How were Isadora Duncan's remains transported from
Paris to a Mexican cemetery closed 55 years earlier?*

*Museo Panteón de San Fernando
Plaza de San Fernando 17
Colonia Guerrero
(+52) (55) 5518 4736
Tuesday to Sunday 9am–5pm
Metro: Hidalgo*

The last official burial to take place in San Fernando cemetery, in the Guerrero district, was that of President Benito Juárez in 1872. After his funeral it was decreed that the site would no longer be used as a cemetery (it became a museum in 2006). However, an interesting funerary plaque in the small courtyard bears the name of famous American dancer Isadora Duncan, who died in 1927 – 55 years after Juárez.

Isadora Duncan died in Nice and was buried in Paris the same year. But two years later her name appeared one morning in funeral niche 19 of the abandoned Mexican cemetery, with the wrong date of death.

Some said that a millionaire Mexican banker, Isadora's lover, had brought over her remains with her family's permission; others that a poet in love with her was responsible; but the commonly accepted version involves the then president, Plutarco Elías Calles. Calles was reputedly in love with Isadora, and secretly ordered her remains to be moved from Paris. According to the neighbours, he brought her a white rose every Saturday at 6 o'clock sharp. Time passed and Calles was sent into exile in 1936. After he was pardoned, he lived in Cuernavaca from 1941 until his death in 1945, during which time the story goes that he was never seen again at San Fernando.

The rumours surrounding the funerary niche were so persistent that it was finally opened in the mid-20th century. The marble plaque was removed with great care, but only dust was found inside. Even today, the mystery of niche 19 is unresolved …

A surrealist ending – Isadora Duncan

Known as the 'goddess of modern expressive dance', she performed barefoot, dressed in Greek robes, breaking with ballet conventions as very few dancers of the early 20th century would have dared to do. Such was Isadora Duncan, the woman whose organic choreography was inspired by Greek vases and the music of Mozart and Chopin. But Isadora hated cars because in 1913 a car had rolled into the Seine and claimed the lives of its passengers – her two children and their governess. Dance did nothing to alleviate her grief and her only escape was with her lovers. Among them was a mechanic who invited her to come for a ride one day in a French-made Amilcar sports model, which she called the 'Bugatti'. Flamboyantly dressed as ever, she was wearing a long silk scarf that became entangled in the back wheel as they drove through Nice, strangling her.

IGLESIA DE SAN HIPÓLITO
HIGH-RELIEF SCULPTURE

④

Legend of the Indian carried across the sky by an eagle

Church cornice, junction of Reforma and Hidalgo
Metro: Hidalgo

St Hippolytus church is surrounded by street vendors selling thousands of likenesses of St Jude Thaddeus (the most popular saint at the church). On the cornice over the entrance is a high-relief sculpture of an eagle gripping an Indian in its talons.

The image is a reference to the text of *Historia de las Indias de Nueva España e Islas de Tierra Firma* (History of the Indies of New Spain), completed by Dominican friar Diego Durán in 1581, and based on chronicles and stories of the indigenous peoples who had survived the colonial conquest.

In Chapter LXVII, Brother Diego relates that before the conquistadors arrived, an Indian was ploughing his land when an eagle suddenly seized him and bore him away to the chambers of the Aztec emperor Moctezuma. There, a man gave him a flaming torch and told him that Moctezuma was so consumed with pride that if his thigh was burned with the torch he wouldn't feel anything. Boldly, the Indian did so. The man then told him to return to his land and warn Moctezuma that he had displeased God. This was achieved with the help of the eagle, and while the Indian was speaking, Moctezuma remembered a dream in which his thigh was burned. He looked for his wound and on finding it ordered the Indian to be sent to prison until he starved to death.

This was also the site of the flight of the Spaniards after their defeat at the battle of Noche Triste (Night of Sadness). A plaque above the eagle records the event. The sculpture was probably placed there to justify the colonial conquest by depicting Emperor Moctezuma as the proud tyrant of legend.

NEARBY
Reminders of the 1985 earthquake
The first blocks of Calle Juárez still show signs of the 1985 earthquake. Plaza Solidaridad, which commemorates the event, is on a slope formed by the rubble of Taberna del Greco, which was in the basement of the Hotel Regis, destroyed by the quake. The former entrance to the hotel is a landmark along the alley that leads to the memorial. Opposite, at number 70, stood the Hotel del Prado, demolished because of the extensive damage it suffered. Only a plaque remains to tell the Prado's story, and a few little circles on the ground to mark the site.

VIRGIN OF HIDALGO METRO STATION

A random Marian apparition

Paseo de la Reforma, junction with Francisco Zarco
In front of entrance to Hidalgo metro

On 1 July 1997, in the middle of the rainy season, water seeping into the corridors of Hidalgo metro station caused a strange apparition to appear on the mosaic floor. During her break, one of the street vendors recognised the image of Our Lady of Guadalupe and spread the news to all and sundry.

According to some reports and press articles, the priest of the nearby San Hipólito church collected 11,000 pesos' worth of alms in 20 days. Some 70,000 people passed by this spot to venerate the image and leave flowers, while the incident was given wide publicity on television.

In spite of all this excitement, the Mexican archdiocese declared that the image had no theological attributes that could confirm a divine presence, which didn't stop the metro authorities from sealing it off with signs and barriers.

The image of the Virgin was not allowed inside any of the churches, so believers eventually removed the section of mosaic from the metro floor and set it behind reinforced glass in a metal frame, like an altar in the street.

Nowadays the image has almost been forgotten. Although some people cross themselves when walking past, most are unaware of its existence. The space is also used for overnight storage by street vendors. The glass plates and grilles make it difficult to see the image, but if you happen to arrive while the stallholders are packing up, they'll let you in for a closer look. The spot where the curious apparition was originally discovered is in the underground corridor before the gates, although there's no longer any trace of it.

RUTH LECHUGA COLLECTION

Fantastic strongroom protects Ruth Lechuga's folk-art collection

Museo Franz Mayer
Avenida Hidalgo 45
Guided tours on reservation
(+52) 5518 2266 Ext. 252, 254
ruthlechuga.franzmayer.org.mx; mruthdlechuga@gmail.com
Fridays at 10am and 3pm
Admission free
Metro: Bellas Artes

Ruth Lechuga's folk-art collection is only open to visitors once a week as part of a guided tour, but it's well worth seeing.

The Centro de Estudios de Arte Popular Ruth D. Lechuga (Ruth D. Lechuga Center for the Study of the Popular Arts) opened in 2016 in the renowned Franz Mayer Museum, which houses his extensive collections of decorative arts. The space has been turned into an amazing red strongroom with movable sections. A crank mechanism is used to turn the display panels around so they can be seen one by one.

All the objects are categorised by theme and each is unique. A horse-drawn coach made entirely from glass in the glassware section; a dish covered with *chaquira* pearl beads among the utensils; a doll's house made from palm leaves and straw in the toys section; and a *güiro* (traditional percussion) fashioned from a donkey's jawbone with the musical instruments.

The star attraction is the miniatures section, so ask to see inside each drawer. You'll find typical indigenous masks no larger than a finger, stones cut in the shape of animals, and a series of finely carved bone figurines. Most of them represent corpses. The tiny cupboard with its scaled-down utensils, and a pile of skeletons in a walnut shell, are very popular.

The collection includes some of Lechuga's personal belongings, such as spectacles and hair ornaments. Also two plaster casts like boots that she wore after an accident and covered with dedications to her friends and close relatives. The objects from the so-called pink room, where she slept, are on a special shelf: they all evoke death, and among them are examples of sugar art, cardboard dolls, clay corpses, and even a skull.

Ruth Lechuga (1920–2004) was an Austrian-born, naturalized Mexican citizen whose interest in folk art led to her anthropological studies on indigenous cultures. Anyone who knows her work will be interested in her collection of masks. This is in another room, where around 1,200 masks from the walls of her Condesa home (where she stored and exhibited her artefacts) are hung on screens. There are masks of sirens, ocelots, devils, gazelles, corpses and imaginary characters (ask to see the masks that close their eyes).

When Lechuga started her collection, it filled just one shelf. In 1995 she turned her home into a museum, but planned a new site for her artefacts when in 1999 she was diagnosed with pulmonary emphysema. Before she died in 2004, she left her collection to the Franz Mayer Museum, which has done justice to it with such innovative display and conservation methods.

LA MANO DE DIOS

Expressionist vision of the Hand of God

Templo de San Lorenzo
Belisario Domínguez 28
Colonia Centro
Thursday to Tuesday 9am–1.30pm and 4pm–7pm
Metrobus: República de Chile

The impressive high-relief altarpiece entitled *La mano de Dios* (The Hand of God) in the church of San Lorenzo represents the hand of Christ – the mark in the centre is the hole left by the Crucifixion.

This work, carried out between 1954 and 1955, was based on an Expressionist wooden sculpture made by German artist Mathias Göeritz in 1952, *La mano divina* (The Divine Hand).

The background to all this was the arrival of Spanish refugee Ramón de Ertze Garamendi, who became a priest in the San Lorenzo parish in 1954. Years before, Garamendi had become aware of the relationship between art and religion during a stay in Assy (France), where experimental sacred art had been commissioned for a modern church.

Garamendi's main aim was to renovate the church of San Lorenzo (which had been extensively damaged by fire in 1940) in a modern style. He asked Göeritz, who had moved from Spain to Mexico in 1949, for help.

The restoration was completed in October 1955 – a plaque inside pays tribute to all those involved. The design of the altarpiece and the stained-glass windows in the dome, also by Göeritz, gives the interior a luminous glow.

The only ornament was the hand, as Garamendi wanted the church to be sober and elegant. But many parishioners thought the altarpiece failed to meet their conservative standards, so after Garamendi's death in 1974 Baroque tableaux were hung over Göeritz's strange relief, relegating it to second place.

Windows à gogo

As Garamendi was pleased with Göeritz's work at San Lorenzo, he backed him for the Catedral Metropolitana (Metropolitan Cathedral) stained-glass windows commission in 1966. The irregular shape and red and amber tones of the finished windows were considered an aberration. Critics said they were 'excellent for a cabaret' while the architect Dreinhofer called them 'windows à gogo', but the cathedral fire 18 months later put an end to the debate. These stained-glass windows, along with those that Göeritz designed for the convent at Azcapotzalco, are still in situ today – the ones in San Lorenzo are considered the most beautiful.

CASINO METROPOLITANO
UPPER FLOOR

A miniature Versailles, open on rare occasions

Tacuba 15
Centro Histórico
Open only during the Feria del Libro de Ocasión (Second-Hand Book Fair, whose venue may change; various dates between February and March)
Metro: Allende

Although the ground floor of the Casino Metropolitano houses a museum, the upper floor, topped by a spectacular Art Nouveau cupola, is rarely open to the public. The doors are open only occasionally, for art exhibitions or special events, and since 2013 for the Second-Hand Book Fair – the ideal time to check out the building.

The hall at the top of the staircase is decorated with friezes of infants dancing to flutes and violins, or enjoying a feast. The rear section is very plain because it lost much of its ornamentation in 1925, when the site was converted into a gymnasium. The magnificent coffered ceiling is still there, however.

On one side is the Salón de los Espejos (Hall of Mirrors), a sumptuously decorated space also known as 'Pequeño Versalles' in reference to the Palace of Versailles (France). But perhaps the most beautiful room is the one overlooking the balcony, which can be glimpsed through the glass of the foyer doors. Its lavish decoration includes scarcely discernible tapestries, one depicting a couple painting in a garden, another with young men seducing courtesans. Although not all the furniture is original, it has been chosen to fit in with the period – proof of the good taste of those who restored the splendour of this multi-purpose building, which in addition to the gym has been home to the Aladdin Cinema, the Spanish Republican Centre, a casino and a billiards hall.

Annual guided tour of the Hebrew past of Casino Metropolitano (including two secret rooms)

Once a year, during the Second-Hand Book Fair at Casino Metropolitano, the Synagoga Historica Justo Sierra (Justo Sierra Historical Synagogue, at number 71 of the street of that name), in partnership with booksellers, organises a guided tour to discover the building's Hebrew past.

According to researcher Mónica Unikel-Fasja, in 1925 the casino became a leisure centre for Yiddish-speaking Jews. Ceremonies, festivals and gymnastic classes were held here at the time, and the Hall of Mirrors was a library with books in Yiddish, Hebrew, Spanish, English, Russian and Polish.

These tours are the only chance to see around the whole building, including two secret rooms whose ceilings are covered with frescoes of flying cherubs. There's also a Morisco (Spanish Muslim) living room in the fashion of the 19th century, with complex *ataurique* (stylised plant-themed) designs on the ceiling and walls.

CAPILLA DE BALVANERA

Where prisoners had to pass before being sentenced by the Inquisition

Francisco I. Madero 7
Colonia Centro
Monday to Saturday 9am–12pm
Avoid visiting afternoons and Sundays, out of respect for churchgoers
Admission free
Metro: Bellas Artes

Tucked in between the Latinoamericana tower and a neo-Roman temple, the former monastery of San Francisco el Grande (St Francis the Great) still has its Baroque chapel. Access is via the side entrance of the church, as the main entrance has been demolished. The vestibule, known as the Balvanera (or Valvanera) chapel, contains a curious archaeological relic.

The present church of St Francis is actually the third to be built on this site, the earlier two having been demolished to allow for modifications. The remains of an older chapel seem to be emerging from the walls. Among them is an entrance door set between two columns. There is also an image dating back to the 17th century of Christ carrying the Cross helped by Simon of Cyrene.

It was here that the Mexican Inquisition performed the public ceremony known as the *auto-da-fé* (act of faith). This took place when a certain number of prisoners awaiting sentence had been reached. Prisoners and clergy marched in a great procession from Santo Domingo to the Plaza Mayor (Zócalo) before heading for the gallows near the Alameda Central, where their sentences were read out. In order to beg forgiveness for their sins, the condemned men passed through a series of chapels along the route. The entrance to one of these can still be seen.

The chapel's main altar has a painting of the Virgin of Guadalupe. The story goes that when the painting was taken down for restoration, it was found to consist of five assembled boards bearing the following inscription: 'Board of the table of Ilmo. Sr. Zumárraga, on which the fortunate neophyte placed the *tilma* (indigenous cape) stamped with this marvellous image.' According to some studies, the table is made of cedar wood and the image is the work of one of the first Spanish painters to arrive in Mexico, Echave (Baltasar de Echave Orio, c. 1558–1623).

NEARBY

Next to the church is the courtyard of the Latinoamericana tower. At its base are the ruins of the side wall of San Francisco monastery, notable for its *tezontle* (volcanic rock) construction and large windows.

VIRGEN DE LA MACANA

The strange cult of a miraculous figure

Francisco I. Madero 7
Colonia Centro
Monday to Saturday 9am–12pm
Avoid visiting afternoons and Sundays, out of respect for churchgoers
Admission free
Metro: Bellas Artes

On the side wall at the back of the church of San Francisco (St Francis) is a modest altar with a copy of a statue of Nuestra Señora del Sagrario de Toledo (Our Lady of the Tabernacle of Toledo, in Spain). The Mexican statue was vandalised and a strange story grew up around it, as the object of a cult that is now dying out in the city.

At the time of the Viceroyalty of New Spain, before the indigenous rebellions against the Spanish colonisers, the Roman Catholic Church tried to impose its teachings.

This led to a local rebellion in 1680 during which indigenous people demanded the release of prisoners of war and slaves from various tribes. It culminated in the murder of 21 Franciscan priests and the destruction of several churches, until finally the Spanish government decided to intervene.

One of the surviving Franciscans, Agustín de Vetancurt, published an account of these events in 1698 in his book *Teatro mexicano* (Mexican Theatre), and also mentioned a miracle that apparently really happened.

It appears that the statue, worshipped at the church of St Francis since 1524, was split in two by an Indian wielding a club during the 1680 rebellion. De Vetancurt also recounts that, six years earlier, this very statue had miraculously cured the governor's daughter and told the child that it would be destroyed because of the lack of veneration shown towards it.

This story aroused a degree of interest in neo-Hispanic society and the 'Virgen de la Macana' (Virgin of the Club) soon became a cult object in Mexico City, just as important as Our Lady of Guadalupe, but at a local level.

The cult is now disappearing, although some people still celebrate Mass in the Virgin's honour on 10 August, her feast day. The odd thing is that most of those attracted to the cult use batons in their work, such as the police. This celebration began in 1949, when the statue was again put on display – La Reforma (The Reform laws, 1854–76) had had it removed in 1861.

MUSEO DEL CALZADO
EL BORCEGUI

Neil Armstrong's space boots

Zapatería El Borcegui
Bolívar 27, Colonia Centro
(+52) 5510 0627
elborcegui.com.mx/museo.htm
Monday to Friday 10am–2pm and 3pm–6pm, Saturday 10am–6pm
Admission free

To see the impressive but little-known collection of El Borcegui Footwear Museum, just climb the narrow stairs up to the first floor of the famous shoe store and use the intercom.

The exhibition is divided into six sections. The first displays historical footwear such as Egyptian, Greek and Chinese sandals, an Inca shoe from the 15th century, and even an Aztec shoe found in a 1309 tomb. You'll also find the most up-to-date protective footwear, even a reproduction supplied by NASA of the boots Neil Armstrong wore in space.

In the sports section, note the impressive size of Shaquille O'Neal's basketball boots and a pair of ice skates dating from 1800. Two other sections are particularly popular: one displays different types of Mexican *huaraches* (sandals with woven leather uppers), representing the various regions of the Mexican Republic; and the other has the largest collection of miniature shoes from both Spain and Mexico.

The shoes of some well-known personalities are also on display, notably those of writer Carlos Monsiváis, journalist Cristina Pacheco, Queen Isabella, astronomer Julieta Norma Fierro Gossman, a shoe signed by former Brazilian president Lula da Silva, and even a painted shoe belonging to artist Martha Chapa.

Don't leave without admiring the paintings on footwear themes, as well as various themed articles such as keyrings, and shoes carved in chalk or made from a banknote, not to mention the visitor's chair in the form of a slipper.

TEMPLO DE LA SANTÍSIMA TRINIDAD

The great cloister of St Francis converted into a Methodist church

Gante 5, Centro Histórico
(+52) 5512 5304
Monday to Friday 8am–6pm
Admission free
Metro: San Juan de Letrán / Bellas Artes

To visit the Methodist Church of the Holy Trinity, just ring at the entrance. The large gate inscribed 'Templo' gives access to the church. The vast hall is surrounded by Baroque columns and arches with a protective grid below the vaulting. Until the 19th century, this was the main cloister of the monastery of St Francis.

The Methodists adapted the space for their form of worship without altering the decor, and even added an engraved stone pulpit as if it were part of the original construction. Offices were set up on the first floor, and a neoclassical atrium was built on the ground floor in 1873, when the Methodists acquired the building.

The cloister has been repurposed several times and was put to the most varied uses in the span of just 10 years. In 1866 architect Luis G. Carrillo opened up the passage that communicates with Calle de Gante at the request of Giuseppe Chiarini, who converted the cloister

into a circus. It's said that Emperor Maximilian brought Chiarini a wild horse and bet that he wouldn't be able to break it in, but the newly docile animal took part in the opening of his cloister-circus. During the restoration of the Republic a year later, President Benito Juárez was invited to a dinner in what was now a banqueting hall. In 1870 the then owner, Jean Perrot, set up the Gran Circo Nacional as a theatre. The Chamber of Deputies met there in 1872 after a fire in their premises. The Methodists opened the church for worship on 24 December 1873, the year they took over.

The cloister was on the site of Moctezuma's wild beast zoo. Human beings with strange deformations or diseases were also to be found in his collection. It is said that the dwarves, hunchbacks and albinos were treated better than the warriors.

CASA 8 1/2

The city's narrowest façade?

Venustiano Carranza 9
Metro: San Juan de Letrán

A few years ago, El Malecón restaurant boasted the city's narrowest façade. Although the plaque announcing this disappeared along with the restaurant, the strange building on three levels, 2.5-metres-wide, is still standing.

Some say that the French-style building was meant to be a hotel, since the 'G.H.' in the shield high up on the building could stand for 'Gran Hotel'. However, the true meaning of these initials is a mystery.

In the 1990s, the number 9 on the building was changed to 8½ in a humorous reference to its narrowness. The sloping roof is supposed to prevent snow accumulating. This is very odd as it's only snowed twice in Mexico City in the last 500 years, but can be explained by the strong influence of Parisian architecture on the Porfirian regime in the late 19th century.

Although the building – in a plaza occupied by cellphone retailers – is connected with the premises at the rear, it still has a tiny staircase leading to the upper floors, now office space.

Other narrow façades

- Berna 18, Zona Rosa

2.23 metres wide, this one's easy to spot: it's actually the back of a slightly larger building divided into apartments in Hamburgo (a blind alley).

- Francisco Sosa 32, Coyoacán

The entrance to this house is 1.45 metres wide. A passageway with a decorative iron lighthouse leads to a larger property at the rear.

- Venustiano Carranza 97, Centro Histórico

The winner of the narrowest façade contest (at 25 centimetres wide) is between numbers 97 and 99, Venustiano Carranza. This is all that remains of an old building saved from demolition for the sake of some 19th century architectural details.

MUSEO DE SITIO DEL ANTIGUO HOSPITAL CONCEPCIÓN BÉISTEGUI

A mummified ovarian cyst and other delights ...

Regina 7
First floor of Fundación para Ancianos Concepción Béistegui
(+52) 5709 3124
Saturday and Sunday 10am–5pm
Guided tours: Saturday and Sunday 11am–4pm (every hour on the hour)
If gates are closed, wait for them to be opened, as the institution is still in operation
Metro: Isabel la Católica

The Concepción Béistegui Foundation for the Elderly, which is still open as an old people's home, is housed in a property that is half-colonial and half-Porfirian in design. It has a sensational museum hidden on the first floor, open only at weekends.

The museum is in what used to be the meeting room of Concepción Béistegui Hospital, which was open from 1886 to 1984. María Concepción Máxima Béistegui y García was a rich young lady who, mindful that her heirs were aristocrats, donated her fortune to found the hospital before she died. Her portrait dominates the room.

If you take the guided tour, you can explore part of the Regina convent, which was later converted into a hospital: you can see some of the confessionals installed in 1876, a little garden with an old aqueduct, the remains of murals and the areas used as sickrooms and an operating theatre.

In the museum, three huge wooden dressers hold ancient ceramic apothecary's jars, each with different powders that the pharmacists mixed together to make their treatments. The only name on a jar that you might recognise is '*píldoras purgativas*' ('purgative pills').

Two shelves under the windows display old surgical equipment. Another has posters dating from 1954 that were stuck on the walls. One poster from a campaign against polio says: 'Large numbers of visitors are not allowed, nor are children.' Another warns: 'Doctors must not charge fees to in-patients.' And don't miss this one: 'It is forbidden to bring in refreshments for the patients.'

The strangest objects in the museum collection are two mummified tumours of unknown origin, preserved like trophies. The hospital was the first to perform an abdominal hysterectomy for fibroids in 1887, when the uterus was removed from a woman who had a cyst. One photo shows the woman before the operation, another the 15 doctors in action, but the most impressive sight is the huge mummified cyst that was removed, now kept in a velvet box.

EL JUEGO DE UN NIÑO GRAFFITI

Four styles, one artwork

Calle Bolívar, junction with San Jerónimo
Metro: Isabel la Católica

I t all began in 2008, when the French artist Fafi, known for the female caricatures she calls *Fafinettes*, arrived in Mexico City. A few days before the Day of the Dead celebrations, Fafi was intrigued to discover the etching by Mexican illustrator and lithographer José Guadalupe Posada entitled *La calavera catrina* (Elegant Skull). The *calavera* (skull / skeleton image) has been a popular motif in Mexican culture since the turn of the 20th century.

Taking advantage of the Federal District Government's plan to make the streets in the city centre more attractive, Fafi painted her version of the *calavera catrina* with her arms around a *Fafinette.*

The intention was to regularly replace the artwork with a new

one. However, when Spanish street artist Spok discovered the graffiti, he decided to reinterpret it instead. Known for experimenting with three-dimensional forms, Spok created the monstrous black character enveloping and devouring the *Fafinette*.

The following year it was the turn of Italian Ericailcane, who expresses social criticism through animal forms, to add her touch. In defiance of Spok's monster – or perhaps just taking the game a step further – she painted a huge lynx-like beast clawing at the other three characters.

Finally, Minoz and Meiz, two Mexican hyperrealist artists, added the monumental image of a child wearing a *huichol* shirt, based on a photo taken nearby. This mural, called *El juego de un niño* (A Child's Game), hasn't been altered since.

> The streets of San Jerónimo and Regina (between Isabel la Católica and 5 de Febrero) take part in the *Murales Artísticos Temporales* (Temporary Artistic Murals) programme, which commissions artwork addressing topical social issues.

MUSEO DE LA CHARRERÍA

Riding out against hardship and injustice

Isabel la Católica 108, junction with Izazaga
(+54) 5709 4823 / 5709 5032
fmcharreria.com
Monday to Friday 10am–2pm and 4pm–6pm
Admission free
Metro: Isabel la Católica

The Charrería Museum, located in the former church of Monserrat, tells the story of the Mexican 'national sport' of rodeo (*charrería*) in great detail, as you'll see from the first display case opposite a huge collection of beautifully designed saddles.

Over the years, what had just been a means of moving cattle around in colonial days became a sport and an entire way of life. The artefacts on display include personal possessions of the best-known Mexican *charros* (cowboys).

You'll find saddles that belonged to Emperor Maximilian (who encouraged the traditional *charro* outfit) and Vicente Fernández (made from python and crocodile skin), and another one made entirely from silver wire. Don't miss the showcase containing Francisco Villa's charro saddle, whip and 45-calibre handgun.

The museum's gala section counts itself lucky to possess one of film star Jorge Negrete's charro costumes. Another room has the clothes women wore for the Escaramuza, a female-only event. Workwear, spurs, embroidered sombreros: each article reveals the personality of its owner. Some are outlined in gold thread, others have pre-Hispanic motifs.

Another showcase contains three 19th-century *chinaco* (Mexican guerrilla) outfits: when Mexico had gained its independence and North American intervention was testing the nation's mettle, the *charro* ranchers were becoming poverty-stricken. Three of them tried to make a living through the sale of tobacco leaves, inventing their own code of honour to evade customs. Known as *charro* smugglers, they were immortalised in the novel *Astucia, el jefe de los Hermanos de la Hoja* (Astucia, Chief of the Brothers of the Leaf) by Luis G. Inclán, a printer who started the tobacco smugglers legend.

The Brothers of the Leaf were the epitome of the Mexican *charro*: men confronting hardship and injustice on horseback, with the sole aim of a quiet life with their families down on the farm. As their motto says: '*patria, mujer y caballo*' (homeland, wife and horse). This is why one of the three brothers' outfits is displayed in the *chinaco* showcase.

Another outfit belonged to one of the Plateados, charro bandits who worked the roads leading to Mexico City and were known for their silver buttons.

SECRETS OF THE UCSJ

Secrets of the convent where Sor Juana Inés lived

Izazaga 92
Inside the Universidad del Claustro de Sor Juana (UCSJ)
(+52) 5130 3300 – ucsj.edu.mx
Guided tours on reservation: difusioncultural@elclaustro.edu.mx
Monday to Friday 10am–5pm, Saturday 10am–2pm
Admission free
Metro: Isabel la Católica

In 1976, during restoration work to house the University of the Cloister of Sor Juana (UCSJ), the excavations brought to light part

of the former San Jerónimo convent. This convent was the home of the best-known intellectual of Baroque Mexico: Sor Juana Inés de la Cruz. While the UCSJ organises guided tours given by students, they don't always reveal all its secrets.

The spaces open to the public are three semi-hidden museums: the Museo de la Indumentaria Mexicana Luis Márquez Romay (Luis Márquez Romay Museum of Mexican Attire), with temporary exhibitions of traditional costumes belonging to photographer Márquez Romay; Sor Juana's cell (although not her original one), where the life story of the 'Tenth Muse', as the nun was known, is mapped out; and the so-called Celda Contemporánea (Contemporary Cell), for temporary exhibitions of modern art, which is perhaps the most impressive of all and has the largest archaeological window (glass viewing floor) in all of Latin America.

Don't miss the chapel converted into an auditorium, the Auditorio Divino Narciso (from the title of an allegorical play by Sor Juana), which has a showcase with a coffin supposedly containing the nun's remains.

Losing yourself in this labyrinthine building, you might discover that the library has frescoes on sections of its walls, the patio has a colonial-era fountain that had been buried, and the confessionals are now used by students as a recreational area. If you're curious enough, you'll find the water tank in front of the School of Gastronomy, the offices among the remains of cells, the nuns' laundry, and the only positive short-octave organ in Mexico still in working order.

The least-known features even go unnoticed by the students: a miniature engraving of a Virgin on a column in the main cloister; the piano with bronze signatures that belonged to Carmen Romano, First Lady of Mexico 1976–82; engravings from colonial days in a door frame on the first floor; and a staircase where the 'pure hands' of children used to carry holy images up to the church altar.

Don't forget to check out the programme of events, such as book launches or concerts of experimental music. Although these are mainly aimed at students, visitors are always welcome.

A restaurant managed by gastronomy students

You could also try the Zéfiro Restaurante Escuela (Restaurant School) on the nearby Regina campus. This exclusive restaurant is located in the cell where the Marquise of Selva Nevada lived. The students on the university's gastronomy course cook and serve the menus under the supervision of their tutors – an excellent opportunity to try Sor Juana's *manchamanteles* ('tablecloth stainers' stew) recipe.

MUSEO·CASA DE LA MEMORIA INDÓMITA

A bitter cry in memory of 'the disappeared' and victims of political assassinations in Mexico

Regina 66, Centro Histórico
(+52) 5709 1512
Opening times vary and sometimes differ from the café
Metro: Isabel la Católica

The House-Museum of Indomitable Memory, on the first floor of an old house in the city centre, is a bitter cry in memory of 'the disappeared' and victims of political assassinations in Mexico in 1968.

Through a series of spaces designed by various artists, visitors are invited to reflect on social movements in Mexico. In a small pink-painted room, for example, several televisions show the country in a good mood, celebrating its victory in the 1970 World Cup. In the next room, which is plunged into darkness, a spotlight is trained on a chair to recreate the atmosphere of an interrogation. Testimonies of people tortured at the time of the so-called 'dirty war' play in the background.

Another room in the house is lined with portraits of missing politicians.

The museum, which has a café, organises cultural events and temporary exhibitions on the social movements theme.

Perhaps the most important of these movements is the Comité Pro Defensa de Presos Perseguidos, Desaparecidos y Exiliados Políticos de México (Committee for the Defence of Persecuted Prisoners, Missing Persons and Political Exiles of Mexico), better known as the 'Comité ¡Eureka!'.

After the disappearance of Jesús Piedra Ibarra in 1975, his mother Rosario Ibarra de la Piedra went in search of him. While on her mission, she met other mothers demanding that their missing children be brought back alive, and in 1977 they set up the Comité ¡Eureka!. The following year, the committee organised a hunger strike at the entrance to the cathedral, as can be seen in the blown-up photograph on the house doors.

HOSPITAL DE JESÚS
DIRECTOR-GENERAL'S OFFICE

Portraits, a coffered ceiling and a table carved from a solid block of wood

20 de Noviembre 82
Colonia Centro
(+52) 5542 6501
hospitaldejesus.com.mx/
Monday to Friday 8.30am–3.30pm, Saturday 9am–1pm
Admission free, request permission from management office
Metro: Zócalo; Metrobus: Museo de la Ciudad

Inside the Hospital of Jesus, the director-general's office is a large yellow room containing a series of stunning portraits and ornaments. Although the room is private, visitors are always welcome: just ask for access at the management office.

The first thing you'll notice is the coffered Renaissance ceiling carved by Spanish cabinet maker Nicolás de Illescas in 1582. Unique in Latin America, the ceiling is composed of 153 octahedrons carved in wood and covered with gold, as well as a series of Maltese crosses.

The most interesting of the paintings is perhaps the altarpiece on the left wall which depicts how, in 1584, the Virgin of the Immaculate Conception (patron of the hospital) appeared here, accompanied by Mary Magdalene and St Catherine, to feed a sick Indian woman.

The most impressive piece is the central table, carved from a solid block of wood just over 2 metres in diameter. After the Spanish conquest, the new inhabitants of Mexico used wood for much of their furniture. A quick look at the table gives a good idea of the girth of the *ahuehuete* (Mexican cypress) trees at the time. The relics of Hernán Cortés were studied in 1946–47 to verify their authenticity. The table itself, still in perfect condition, is over 450 years old.

FACES IN THE FRIEZE
AT THE HOSPITAL DE JESÚS

Portrait of Cortés between the beams?

20 de Noviembre 82
Colonia Centro
(+52) 5542 6501
hospitaldejesus.com.mx/
Daily, 24/7
Admission free

On the first floor of the Hospital de la Purísima Concepción y Jesús Nazareno (Hospital of the Immaculate Conception and Jesus of Nazareth) is a 1940s mural by Antonio González Orozco tracing the history of pre-Hispanic medicine. Above the mural is a frieze dating from the viceroyalty (16th century) and attributed to Juan de Arrúe, which features religious and symbolic motifs on the Passion of Christ. In addition, peeping out between the beams, is a series of faces unrelated to the main theme of the frieze.

The Hospital of Jesus, the first hospital in Latin America, has been continuously in operation since 1524. It was founded by none other than Spanish conquistador Hernán Cortés, which is why colonial relics such as this frieze have been conserved.

The characters between the beams are miniature portraits of the conquistadors, identified as Friar Bartolomé de Olmedo, chaplain Juan Díaz, explorer Cristóbal de Olid, soldier Pedro de Alvarado and of course Hernán Cortés himself … or at least this is what is believed. Olid betrayed Cortés during his expedition to Honduras, leading to a war between the two. After an attempt on his life, Olid escaped to the Honduran jungle, where he was found and executed for treason in 1524. As for the faces, they can't be expected to be accurate portrayals, although thought to correspond to the earliest images of such personalities in Mexico, including Cortés – unless he wanted to engage with his old enemy again. This only adds to the strangeness of the frieze.

As well as the faces in the frieze, the Hospital of Jesus houses other curiosities, such as a pre-Hispanic stele found during excavations and a bronze replica of a bust of Hernán Cortés by Manuel Tolsá.

On the ground floor, a plaque records that the first human dissection performed for teaching purposes in Latin America (or at least in Mexico) took place in this hospital in 1643. This is strange, as classes in anatomy and surgery had started 23 years earlier. The hospital also took in people tormented and flogged by the Inquisition after they had served their sentences.

TOMB OF HERNÁN CORTÉS

A forgotten alcove in a simple church

Templo de Jesús Nazareno
20 de Noviembre, junction with Pino Suárez
Colonia Centro
(+52) 5542 7908
Monday to Saturday 10am–6pm, Sunday 11am–3pm
Admission free
Metro: Zócalo; Metrobus: Museo de la Ciudad

A modest plaque on the side wall of Jesus of Nazareth church is the only indication of the little-known last resting place of conquistador Hernán Cortés.

In 1823, anti-Spanish feeling born of the independence movement was still running high, especially among those who wanted to desecrate the Cortés mausoleum at the Hospital of Jesus.

This mausoleum had been inaugurated in 1800 with so much pomp that the Roman Catholic priest and preacher Fray Servando himself conducted the ceremony. Inside were Cortés' remains, which were to be cremated in San Lázaro following a presidential decree on 16 September. However, on the night of 15 September, government minister Lucas Alamán (see box) and the chaplain of Joaquín Canales Hospital removed the bones from the mausoleum and hid them under the floorboards, to save them from being burned. The mausoleum was dismantled and a bust of Cortés sent to Palermo (Italy), to make people believe that his remains were no longer in Mexico.

The conquistador's bones were hidden beneath this floor for 13 years until Alamán removed them to change the urn and winding sheet, which had deteriorated in the humid conditions. This time, he hid them next to a copy of the Gospels in Jesus of Nazareth church. He then sent a secret document to Spain in which he revealed the hiding place.

This document was found in 1946 by Spanish exile Fernando Baeza and Cuban historian Manuel M. Franginals. With the help of Francisco de la Maza and Alberto M. Carreño, they searched the church to find out if the story was true. After 110 years of anonymity, the remains of Cortés finally emerged from the darkness and he now has a plaque bearing his name.

NEARBY

The church choir has a fresco by master muralist David Alfaro Siqueiros on the post-apocalyptic theme, as the Virgin of the Apocalypse is worshipped here. The carved wooden figures date from the colonial era.

Lucas Alamán was a Mexican historian, politician and writer. Despite his conservative leanings, he was respected for his work as a minister until he died of pneumonia. His mortal remains lie in Jesus of Nazareth church, near those of Cortés.

CAPILLA DE LA BIBLIOTECA LERDO DE TEJADA

⑫

The Sistine Chapel of Revolutions

República del Salvador 49
Centro Histórico
(+52) 9158 9837 / 9158 9833
Monday to Friday 9am–5.30pm
For events and exhibitions, see cultural agenda of Secretaría de Hacienda y Crédito Público (SHCP – Ministry of Finance and Public Credit)
hacienda.gob.mx/cultura/museo_virtual_biblioteca_lerdo/index.htm
Admission free

The former chapel of San Felipe Neri houses the spectacular SHCP library, featuring a huge mural by Russian-Mexican painter Vladimir Rusakov, better known as Vlady.

He and his father, essayist Victor Serge, fled the Stalinist regime and arrived in Mexico in 1941, accompanied by French intellectuals Claude Lévi-Strauss and André Breton.

In 1972, President Luis Echeverría attempted to give a new impetus to Mexican muralism by commissioning work for the Palacio Nacional. Instead, Vlady suggested painting the interior of the Lerdo de Tejada library. Echeverría agreed, and gave him carte blanche for the entire space to depict the various revolutions throughout history. Vlady named his fresco *La Revolución y sus elementos*, affectionately referring to it as 'The Sistine Chapel of Revolutions'. The work was carried out between 1974 and 1982.

Part of the mural is inside the library chapel and the gallery, which are closed most of the time. To visit, just ask permission at the visitors' desk or security.

The chapel that was never used

The chapel of San Felipe Neri encountered many difficulties and was never used for worship. The Marquise de Villa del Villar and Don Pedro Romero de Terreros, whose houses still stand nearby, were opposed to the construction. When it was completed, the congregation preferred La Profesa church, and the chapel was abandoned.

In 1875, Porfirio Macedo opened the Teatro Arbreu – the first theatre to be lit by hydrogen lamps – in the chapel. Anna Pavlova and Enrico Caruso performed there. Blakamán, a magician-hypnotist from Peru, is said to have left a crocodile in the basement after presenting a wild animal show. The staff found it dead and made belts and wallets from its skin. The last artist to perform at the theatre was an illusionist called Cleopatra.

'Governor Juan José Baz's Collection of Prostitutes'

While the library's archives include newspapers from the 18th century to the present day, the collection of books is still more impressive, with works by Vitruvius, Newton, Athanasius Kircher and Carlos de Singüenza y Góngora.

There is even a photograph album entitled *Collección de prostitutas del gobernador Juan José Baz*, based on a 19th century census of prostitutes.

On presentation of an ID you can consult this heritage, but for the oldest works further authorisation is required.

PLAZA CAPUCHINAS ALTARPIECE ㉓

A Baroque altarpiece made from papier-mâché

Plaza Capuchinas
Accessible by Venustiano Carranza and República de Uruguay
Between Bolívar and Isabel la Católica
Metrobus: Isabel la Católica

Asuperb Baroque altarpiece with cherubs at the top and a little stained-glass window with an image of the Holy Spirit is concealed in a shelter in the middle of Plaza Capuchinas (which connects Calle Venustiano Carranza with República de Uruguay). The only figure is a Virgin of Guadalupe, in the centre of the altarpiece, while the other niches stand empty.

Although this looks like a classic altarpiece in gilded wood, it's entirely made from papier-mâché, and the protective grille that seems to be wrought iron is really cardboard.

The site used to be part of a huge department store that specialised in craft objects. The decoration consisted of several religious altarpieces, and even fonts of holy water, all made from papier-mâché. This example was made in the store over three to four months by students of master craftsman Martín Rentería. Several of the pieces were for sale. But when the store closed in 2009, this papier-mâché altarpiece and cardboard grille were kept as the final vestiges of the enterprise.

NEARBY
La Faena mosaics
Venustiano Carranza 49
Sunday to Thursday 11am–11pm, Friday and Saturday 11am–2am
In one of the corridors of La Faena canteen (and bullfighting museum), founded in 1954, are mosaics captioned by phrases typically heard in Mexican canteens. These range from the sayings of historical figures to popular word games. One of them reads: '*Para el catarro, el jarro. Y si no se quita, la botellita* …' ('For catarrh, a little jar. And if that's no cure, it's the bottle for sure …').

AZULEJOS AT THE CASA DE LA MARQUISA DE ULUAPA

Viceroyalty staff immortalised in Talavera ceramics

5 de Febrero, No. 18
Centro Histórico
Guided tours on reservation
(+52) 5339 1092
Metro: Zócalo

Despite the name of the house, the Marchioness of Uluapa never had any connection with number 18 Calle 5 de Febrero in her lifetime. Now the private property of a textile company, this 18th century mansion only opens its doors on request.

A tour of the deserted offices of the labyrinthine dwelling reveals the decorations added between 1762 and 1766 by Lieutenant Nicolás Cobián y Valdés. The profusion of azulejos features characters rarely depicted in colonial days: the staff.

Portraits of these various characters can be found in their rooms at the back of the house: the housekeeper welcoming visitors, a maid carrying some cups for hot chocolate, a black cook setting about her work, three laundresses doing the washing, the water carrier bringing in a couple of pitchers, a servant with a plate of soup, the gardener with his shovel and flower pot at the ready, and even an American Indian chicken seller.

On the top floor, all around the inner balcony, there are small azulejos that look like Chinese vases. Each shows a different oriental artist: a juggler on a tightrope, a guitarist, a horse trainer, a rider and even a circus dwarf. Finally, the Quetzalcóatl plumed serpent climbs up a column to the top of the house (an effect only seen from the first-floor balcony at the back).

The house has also kept its decorative stonework, including majestic projecting arches and some small kitchens.

NEARBY

Staircase designed by Leonardo da Vinci

Venustiano Carranza 60

The former palace of the Counts of San Mateo Valparaíso, at number 60 Venustiano Carranza, now belongs to the Bank of Mexico. From an inside corridor you can admire two interlaced flights of steps, the work of Mexican Baroque architect Francisco Antonio de Guerrero y Torres. These were probably inspired by a sketch attributed to Leonardo da Vinci for the Château de Chambord in France. Each flight begins and ends on an opposite side, one for use by the staff and the other by the lords, so that their paths would never cross.

EAGLE AT THE EDIFICIO BOKER

Archaeological artefacts and other curiosities

Isabel la Católica, junction with 16 de Septiembre
Colonia Centro
Metrobus: Isabel la Católica

The Boker building was commissioned by German merchant Roberto Boker during the Porfirian regime (1876–1911), and built by New York architects De Lemos and Cordes, who drew up the plans in Chicago style. The four existing buildings on the site were demolished, and during the excavation work to lay the new foundations two archaeological artefacts were discovered. The first was a headless eagle, of unknown provenance, which was donated to the Museo Nacional de Antropología at Chapultepec; and the second was a *cihuateteo*, one of the deified spirits of women who died in childbirth, depicted on a strip of cloth which is now in the Museo Nacional de Arte. A replica of the eagle is displayed in the lobby of the building (entrance on 16 de Septiembre).

Inside, the photographs attributed to renowned photographer Guillermo Kahlo (father of Frida) featured in his first documentary, which traces construction work on the building from 1898.

NEARBY
Site of the plaque melted down for bullets

There used to be two huge bronze plaques fixed to the wall at the main entrance, bearing the name Edificio Boker. They were taken away by the Mexican revolutionaries and melted down to make bullets. You can still see the hollow left by one of them.

Architects who'd never been to Mexico!

The architects who designed the Boker building had never been to Mexico.
That's why some features are more suited to the cold climate of Chicago, such as the huge double-glazed timber-framed windows on the first floor, which can be seen from the street.

The first hotel in Latin America, known as the Hotel de la Gran Sociedad, used to stand on this site. Founded in 1818, it witnessed the assassination of Mexican statesman Juan de Dios Cañedo in 1850 – one of the most widely reported crimes of the time. Despite the fact that this had been an inn for so long, the premises were closed down to make way for the commercial building, just as it was taken over during the Second World War because it belonged to Germans.

LION'S HEAD

High-water level during the 1629 flood

Junction of Motolinia and Francisco I. Madero
Metro: Allende

Very few of the thousands passing through the Madero pedestrian area every day know that at the junction of Madero and Motolinia is a stone lion's head dating from colonial days fixed to the wall of a modern building.

There is nothing to indicate that this lion's head marks the high-water level during the great flood of 1629. Even though the building doesn't belong to that period, it was decided to relocate the head on the façade in memory of the time when the city was under water for years.

Despite the tunnels dug into the hillsides to drain the brackish water from the vast Texcoco lake, torrential rain flooded New Spain one night in September 1629.

Only two-storey buildings and large churches were spared. People got around in *trajineras* (see p. 366) and Masses were said on the boats as solace for the afflicted. There was even a floating procession to transport the image of *Our Lady of Guadalupe* from La Villa to the Metropolitan Cathedral.

According to a letter from Archbishop Manso y Zúñiga, the city was home to around 20,000 families in 1629. By 1635, when the flood waters had finally receded, there were only 400 people left.

Some of the higher parts of the city attracted animals seeking refuge. This explains old place names such as Isla de los Perros (Isle of Dogs) and Callejón de las Ratas (Rat Lane).

27

PINACOTECA DE LA PROFESA

*Colonial art treasures in the secret galleries of
La Profesa, open two hours a week*

Isabel la Católica 21
(+52) 5521 8362
Saturday 12pm–2pm
Admission free
Metro: Allende

While the convents and monasteries still governed Mexico City in the 19th century, many of them contained magnificent religious art from the colonial era. But, as Frances Calderón de la Barca (wife of the first Spanish ambassador) remarked during her visit to the city, 'La Profesa [church of San Felipe Neri] is where the most beautiful paintings are to be found ... but nobody can get in to see them!'

In the 19th century women were banned from visiting La Profesa, as it was a monastery, but nowadays anyone can see the collection: the doors are open for two hours a week.

All these paintings are masterly. Although virgins, saints and portraits predominate, the most imposing and mysterious are allegories of the underworld.

Las penas del infierno (The Trials of Hell) is an impressive 18th-century work based on passages from the Bible describing torture by demons, dragons and serpents, imprisonment, fire, pain and despair – to remind sinners that they are condemned for eternity.

La boca del infierno (The Jaws of Hell) is another monumental oil showing a monster opening its jaws to reveal the Catholic hell. Alongside is the legend of a woman who pretended to be dying to confess a terrible sin, but then decided to keep quiet about it and, by divine judgment, died without receiving salvation. Below is a highly realistic painting of a decomposing body, the corpse covered with ticks and maggots.

In another painting, two figures can be seen at the confessional: the first is guided by an angel and the second, claimed by a demon, spits vermin because he has refused to repent.

The art gallery possesses three unique portraits: a pastel profile of neoclassical architect Manuel Tolsá in later life; a portrait of Matías Monteagudo, who ordered the conspiracy that led to Mexican independence; and the only known portrait of the notorious Archbishop Francisco de Aguiar y Seijas, a patron of Baroque art whose only fault was to be a misogynist (see p. 73). It's said that he never left home for fear of meeting women and that he had violent arguments with the poet Sor Juana Inés de la Cruz.

Strangely enough, the best-known and most mesmerising painting dates from 1856 rather than the viceregal days: *Alegoría de la muerte* (Allegory of Death) by Tomás Mondragón shows a woman divided by the thread of life. The right half of the picture shows her overflowing with life in lavish surroundings, and the other half as a corpse in a cemetery. She is popularly referred to as 'the mirror' because Mondragón inscribed at the foot of the portrait: '*Este es el espejo que no te engaña*' ('Here is the mirror that does not lie').

CALLE PALMA CLOCK

28

Automated soldiers mark time

Palma 33
Colonia Centro
Can be seen Monday to Friday 11am–7pm, Saturday 10am–4pm
Metro: Zócalo

Passers-by fortunate enough to be in Calle Palma at certain times of day will hear the little-known *Espíritus del tiempo* (Spirits of Time) monumental clock. The spectacle can be viewed through the small doors, which are easily missed, on the façade of number 33 Palma. Wooden model soldiers operate a mechanism linked to a recording of music from Tchaikovsky's *Nutcracker*. Finally, another soldier rings some little bells and a large bell chimes the hours.

The doors of the *sonería* (chimes) open every 15 minutes, and the whole show takes place every hour. To fully appreciate it best arrive 5 minutes early as, ironically, it doesn't start exactly on the hour.

The clock, which was made in England in 1895, ended up in a church in Xochimilco. Clockmaker Luis Hernández bought it as scrap in 1998 and managed to get it working again. But it wasn't until 2003 that someone suggested installing it on this façade: it's been here ever since, together with the automated soldiers made by Mexican cabinetmakers.

The first and second floors of the building house the Centro del Reloj (Clock Center), Mexico's first shopping centre specialising in clocks and watches. Despite its impressive entrance, the building isn't very well known. Browse through the different boutiques and have a look around the internal courtyards, where you'll find a Mexican clock mechanism dating from 1942, an AC control for an OTIS elevator from the 1940s, and a mural by local artist Daniel Manrique entitled *La humanidad y el tiempo* (Humanity and Time). Manrique's entertaining explanation of his mural on a nearby plaque is worth reading.

Not only does the clock have an automated movement, it also indicates the phases of the Moon.

FACES ON THE DOORS OF THE FORMER HOSPITAL DEL DIVINO SALVADOR

Deranged women of the 17th century

Donceles 39, junction with Bolívar
Colonia Centro
Metro: Allende

At the headquarters of the Archivo Histórico de la Secretaría de Salud (Historical Archive of the Health Ministry) in the old Calle de Donceles, an inscription on the entrance door reads: *Real Hospital del Divino Salvador. Para Mujeres, Dementes* (Royal Hospital of the Divine Saviour. For Women, Deranged).

To understand the significance of this inscription, have a look at the six doors of the building on which a series of distressed faces have been carved. Each door represents a different mental condition in the order: senile, stupid, deranged. One of the doors has lost its original design but the face of a suffering woman can still be seen.

The hospital was founded in 1687 by José Sáyago, after coming across a mentally ill woman wandering in the street. He took in more and more such women because at the time no asylum would do so. When Archbishop Aguiar y Seijas heard about this, he donated a plot of land on the site of a house dating back to colonial days, whose huge quarry stones – still visible at the base of the walls – were used to shore up the hospital building.

After Seijas died, the hospital was run by the Jesuit Order of the Divine Saviour and the Pía Obra de la Buena Muerte (Religious Foundation of the Good Death) as the Hospital del Divino Salvador del Mundo. Although it only catered for mentally ill women, there are some men's faces engraved on the doors. It was rumoured that the misogynist Seijas commissioned the male characters because he couldn't accept the idea of only women on the façade. The melancholy woman and priest-like man on the main door are also said to represent Seijas and his wife, although this can't be true as the doors were part of the restructuring when the building was converted into a museum.

Although in the 19th century this hospital was considered to be one of the best of its kind, it closed in 1910 when the Manicomio General (General Asylum) was opened.

Ghost stories and tales of horror

The building's rich historical past is fertile ground for ghost stories and tales of horror.

One of these tells how the place was exorcised in the mid 1990s, another that numerous apparitions emanate from the niches built to shelter virgins.

You can't check out these stories because the site is off-limits to tourists, but you only need to glance at the façade to see where they all come from.

HEAD OF AN ANGEL

The day the Angel tried to fly

Archivo Histórico del Distrito Federal building
República de Chile 8, Colonia Centro
(+52) 5510 8582
Monday to Thursday 9am–6pm, Friday 9am–2pm
Admission free
Metro: Allende

The battered head with scarcely recognisable features that stands at the entrance to the Federal District's Historical Archive is, unbelievable as it may seem, the original head of the *Victoria Alada* (Winged Victory), a statue better known as *El Ángel de la Independencia* (The Angel of Independence), icon of Mexico City.

The story goes that in the small hours of 28 July 1957, while the dance halls and cinemas were still open, people were out on the town and families were asleep in the city's newly-built housing complexes; in the Anzures neighbourhood the zoo's lions could be heard desperately roaring.

At 2.45 in the morning, an earthquake struck the vulnerable Mexico City and disaster unfolded. The Encanto cinema collapsed, as did a building that had opened just three months earlier. The dancers fled into the streets and, in the city centre, shards from the Latinoamericana tower flew through the air. In Paseo de la Reforma not many people realised what was happening: the Angel of Independence broke free from its pedestal and (as was said at the time) tried to fly.

The huge 7-tonne bronze sculpture plunged to the ground, almost destroyed. The federal government was soon called upon to restore the monument and, after a year, the completed work was returned to its site. But as the head had been ruined in the fall, it was remade rather than restored. The original heavily damaged head is now kept at the Historical Archive in memory of the tragedy.

An urban love story

It's said that curious neighbours who came to see the angel lying on the ground discovered a love letter inside the statue's head. This had apparently been hidden by a young builder who was too shy to send it to his beloved.

They say that, with the neighbours' help, the intended recipient was given the letter and finally met this man after almost 60 years. Some even say that the couple were married in a church in the nearby Zona Rosa.

NEARBY

The building that houses the Historical Archive is the former palace of the Counts of Heras y Soto. At the corner, the sculpture of a child carrying a basket of fruit is a replica of a silver statue made for a colonial merchants' parade. The resident count liked the image so much that he had it reproduced on the façade. The fate of the original is unknown.

MARÍA EGIPCÍACA STATUE

The viceroyalty's gloomiest sculpture

Parish of Santa Catalina Mártir
Junction of República de Brasil 69 and Nicaragua 12
Colonia Centro
Tuesday to Sunday 8am–7pm; times may change
Metro: Lagunilla

Under the subdued lighting of its niche, the spectacular 17th-century sculpture of María Egipcíaca (Mary of Egypt) shows an elderly woman draped in a cloth and seated on a rock. Her arms scarred and bloodied, she seems to be in a pitiful state of repentance.

The small gloomy niche is reminiscent of the way Mary of Egypt is shown in some medieval paintings (such as the frescoes in the Basilica of St Francis in Assisi, Italy).

In Mexico she is customarily revered as the patron saint of prostitutes, as well as penitents and those sick with a fever.

Although there is a legend that most of the saint's remains brought to New Spain were hidden inside the statue, this has never been proved.

When Mexican playwright Miguel Sabido came across the statue and heard the legend, he wrote in 1967 *Las tentaciones de María Egipcíaca* (The Temptations of Mary of Egypt).

It's said that the woman known as Mary of Egypt embarked for Palestine at the Feast of the Exaltation of the Holy Cross in order to satisfy her curiosity. She paid for the voyage by prostitution and while on board lived a life of debauchery. On arrival at the Church of the Holy Sepulchre in Jerusalem, she felt excluded by an unknown force and, lamenting the error of her ways, promised to give up her life of sin if the Virgin would let her enter. Once permission was granted, she crossed the Jordan river and retreated into the desert, living alone for 40 years. She was found by a monk named Zosimas, to whom she told her story in exchange for a cloak. The following year, 421, Zosimas went back to meet her, but all he found was her corpse.

NEARBY
Relics of St Celestine
Templo de Santa Teresa la Nueva, Loreto 21
Tours daily, 10am–7pm
Metrobus: Teatro del Pueblo

At the rear of Santa Teresa church is a wax statue of a prone woman. At her feet is a mirror where remains of the saint can be seen beneath a sandal and through a small opening in the left hand. She's known as Santa Celeste but her real name is Celestina. Her mortal remains were brought to Mexico between 1701 and 1715 thanks to Manuela Molina, heroine of Mexican independence. People here believe that, as they couldn't find the appropriate vestments to cover her, someone used a wedding dress – ever since, she has been a patron saint of women about to marry.

TORRE DEL PARQUE TORRES QUINTERO

Remains of a Porfirian observatory

Plaza Torres Quintero
Calle José Joaquín Herrera, junction with Callejón Torres Quintero
Metrobus: Teatro del Pueblo

Although some people say this was a clock tower and others a cemetery steeple, the neo-Gothic building in the middle of Parque Torres Quintero is the remains of what was, at the end of the Porfirian regime just before the First World War, the Observatorio Popular Francisco Díaz Covarrubias.

The observatory was opened on 21 March 1905 by the founder of the Sociedad Astronómica de Mexico (Mexican Astronomical Society), engineer Luis G. León. Inspired by *Nova Persei*, a star that briefly became one of the brightest in the sky in 1901 and was visible from Mexico, León promoted astronomy in the city, writing booklets and opening several community observatories.

The tower, which had a rotating roof and a stone mast inside, was equipped with a telescope with a 160-millimetre lens and a 2-metre focal length. Lack of money and the Mexican Revolution forced the observatory to close.

Halley's Comet in the skies above Mexico City: enough to drive you crazy

Journalist Héctor de Mauleón recounts in one of his columns that when Halley's Comet was about to overfly Mexico City in 1910, the newspapers warned that it would release a toxic laughing gas that would drive people crazy, and that phone lines would be disrupted. To guard against the effects of the comet, bottles of agua Cruz Roja (Red Cross water) were offered for resale, and many people sealed up their doors and windows. On 18 May 1910, the day the comet passed over the city, the churches stayed open all night to comfort the superstitious, and the police stations were full of tearful drunks lamenting that 'the end of the world was nigh'. But next day, everything was back to normal. De Mauleón later wrote: 'It was just four years later, with the assassination of Archduke Franz Ferdinand and the arrival of 9 million soldiers in Europe's trenches, that the real end of the world began.'

CASA DE *EL HIJO DEL AHUIZOTE*

*Extra! Extra! The ferocious anti-Porfirian weekly
has its own museum!*

República de Colombia 42
(+52) 5702 1988
Monday to Friday 11am–5pm, Saturday 11.30am–5.30pm
Admission free
Metrobus: República de Argentina

Ensconced between market stalls, the first floor of the house at
number 42 Colombia used to be the editorial offices and the last

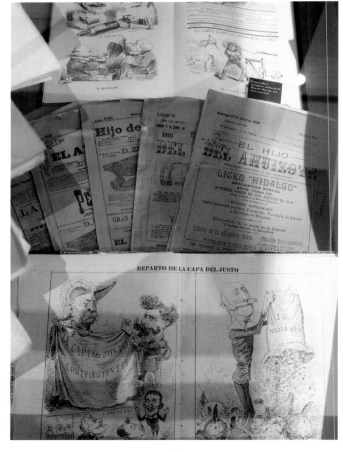

home of *El hijo del ahuizote*, a satirical political weekly founded in 1885.

The newspaper presented itself as the renegade son of the Mexican press, a 'ferocious weekly, but of noble instincts … and like its father, cunning and cadaverous (it has no mother)'.

The museum documents part of this heritage: huge wooden boxes contain photos, newspaper cuttings, contemporary objects and lots of copies of the paper. The documents tell the story of the weekly, founded as a harsh critic of the Porfiriato (the years when Díaz and his allies ruled Mexico). The key to its success was the publication of political cartoons charged with satirical humour. However, this editorial strategy was not to the taste of the Porfirian dictatorship. A diagram on the wall gives the names of 38 journalists employed there who were imprisoned. Only six of them walked free. A selection of photographs shows the harsh conditions the journalists endured in Belén prison.

The personal diary of Daniel Cabrera, the paper's founder, is also on display, in addition to the Archive Enrique Flores Magón, named after its last proprietor (one of three brothers associated with the anti-capitalist and anti-imperialist ideology known as *magonismo*). The second floor houses part of the collection and is where workshops are held. From the roof terrace you can enjoy a panoramic view of the Centro Histórico.

On 5 February 1903 (46th anniversary of the 1857 Constitution), *El hijo del ahuizote* organised a funeral on the premises. Backed up with flags, garlands and wreaths, the paper's supporters decorated the front of the building with the message: 'The Constitution is dead …'. The policies of Porfirio Díaz, elected for a second time, were systematically violating all the articles of the Constitution. The regime tightened up its censorship and raided the house. The Flores Magón brothers went into exile, but some of the journalists were again imprisoned – sounding the death knell for the paper.

Paradoxically, the photograph of this mythical funeral was used to identify the house a hundred years later. This meant it could be faithfully restored and the Museo y Acervo Documental (Documentary Heritage Museum) set up. There's a copy of the picture on the ground floor, together with the review published on that February day in 1903.

A red cart equipped with a printer, known as '*el ahuizote móvil*' and used at outdoor markets, can occasionally be seen distributing leaflets around the streets. A unique design for a district that lives by street vendors and casual traders!

MURALS ON THE NORTH-EAST STAIRCASE OF MERCADO ABELARDO RODRÍGUEZ

Socialist murals between the meat, fruit and veg stalls

República de Venezuela 72
Colonia Centro
Daily 7am–6pm
Admission free
Metrobus: Teatro Del Pueblo

The hidden treasure of historico-political murals on the first floor of the former Abelardo Rodríguez market is well worth seeking out. The best preserved but least known are on the north-east staircase, which is freely accessible. Others can be seen on the west side (one heavily damaged and another hidden by a grille), in the centre aisles and at the corners of the market, between the fruit stalls, butcher's shops, cables and tarpaulins (damaged by the dust and grease of this commercial site).

In 1934 a market large enough to accommodate a theatre, crèche and cinema was planned as a workers' educational and cultural centre. Diego Rivera was in charge of the interior decoration, but pressure of work meant that it was actually carried out by his pupils Pablo O'Higgins, Miguel Tzab and Antonio Pujol.

On O'Higgins advice, Rivera invited New York artists Grace and Marion Greenwood to paint the north-east staircase: Marion chose to condemn the conditions of workers in the sugar fields, while Grace worked on a scene of miners extracting ore to make coins (showing the stock exchange with money stashed in large bags while local children scrabble for food among the garbage).

These two artists' mastery of colour produces optical effects that transform windows into gear wheels and concrete pillars into metal beams.

The central section was given over to the North American / Japanese artist Isamu Noguchi, who carved *La historia de México* (The History of Mexico) in a brick wall covered with red, white and grey cement. You can see the Nazi swastika, ploughed fields, battlefields represented by a skeleton, picket lines as a symbol of socialism, and even a reference to the microcosm along with Einstein's formula $E = mc^2$.

Signature of authenticity

When the murals were completed, Rivera signed off one of O'Higgins' works as supervisor, but his signature has not yet been identified.

CROWNED NUNS

When nuns were crowned …

Secretariá de Educación Pública (SEP) museum
República de Argentina 28
Centro Histórico
Monday to Saturday 9am–5pm
Admission free
Metrobus: República de Argentina

Near Diego Rivera's mural *La entrada a la mina* (Entrance to the Mine), the small site museum has a collection of archaeological artefacts found between 1989 and 1991 during restoration work on the building.

Apart from the pre-Hispanic remains linked to the Earth god Tlaltecutli, the most striking pieces recall an unusual episode of monastic life in colonial days. In a Baroque ritual common at the time, sisters entering the novitiate were crowned at a grand ceremony in celebration of their virtuous life. The sisters wore large crowns decorated with flowers and carried candles or palm leaves. Their portraits were painted so that the family could display the image at home, demonstrating that one of its members had taken holy orders. It was also a way of showing that she was forever cloistered, dead to the outside world.

The nuns were also crowned when they were named abbesses, and if they completed 25, then 50, years of monastic life. Finally, when they died, they were buried along with their crowns.

Although only the framework of the crowns is left, the details of the flower fixings are worth seeing in themselves – a unique opportunity, as no other place in Mexico City has such treasures on display.

As well as these crowns, the museum's colonial section displays fragments of crockery from the convent, including a piece of Ming Dynasty porcelain – which gives some idea of the nuns' purchasing power.

Before becoming the SEP headquarters, this had been the site of the Convento de la Encarnación (Covent of the Incarnation) since 1594, which explains why the nuns were buried here, still wearing their crowns.

HOLY RELICS IN THE CATHEDRAL

Saints and crypts on display only twice a year

Catedral Metropolitana
Plaza de la Constitución
Open to visitors 1 and 2 November only, 9am–4pm
Metro: Zócalo

The Metropolitan Cathedral's Capilla de las Reliquias (Chapel of the Relics) is open only two days a year, during the Día de Muertos (Day

of the Dead) festivities. The rest of the year, however, you can admire the vast painted altarpieces and the closed funerary niches jealously guarding Roman Catholic holy relics. On 1 November, Día de Todos los Santos (All Saints' Day), and 2 November, Día de los Fieles Difuntos (Day of the Faithful Departed / All Souls' Day), these niches are opened to display the relics certified by the Church. The tradition arose with the Council of Trent (1545–63), which ordered the veneration of the bodies of martyrs, and in New Spain this gradually became the occasion for great celebrations to be held outside the cathedral.

The names of the saints and martyrs are marked on little cards to identify the relics: wax sculptures of St Vincent and St Catherine of Hungary with part of their preserved remains, a stone from the Mount of Olives, the tombstones of Gregorio López and Juan González, a fragment from the Crown of Thorns, another from the Holy Cross, and the remains of St Peter, St Hippolytus, St Pio, St Vitus, St Hilaria, St Cordula, etc. There are also huge reliquaries holding fragments from other saints, and a piece of cloth from Juan Diego's cloak (see p. 309) preserved in the painting of the Virgin Mary on one side of the chapel.

The Cripta de los Arzobispos (Crypt of the Archbishops), beside the west gate, also only opens twice a year. It contains funerary niches with the remains of all the cathedral's archbishops. In the centre is a life-size sculpture of the first archbishop of Mexico, Fray Juan de Zumárraga, on top of his tomb. The most spectacular sights in the crypt are the Byzantine Jerusalem Cross embellishing the roof and two pre-Hispanic pieces: the skull under Friar Juan's sarcophagus and the sacrificial stone with two snakes below the altar. Admission to the crypt includes a guided tour where the meaning of the religious symbolism of the site is explained.

MURALS OF THE SUPREMA CORTE DE JUSTICIA DE LA NACIÓN (SCJN)

A heartfelt plea for justice inside the Supreme Court

Pino Suárez 2
Colonia Centro
(+52) 4113 1100, Ext. 5810, 5811, 5820
scjn.gob.mx
Information on guided tours by email: visitas@mail.scjn.gob.mx
Monday to Thursday 9am–5pm, Friday 9am–4pm
Admission free (ID required)
Site visit includes free audio guide
Metro: Zócalo

The SCJN (Supreme Court of Justice of the Nation) is generally thought to be closed to the public. But visitors are in fact welcome and a free audio guide is available. Guided tours and admissions to the plenary sessions of the SCJN are also organised. It's worth a visit to see such features as the so-called *escalera de los ministros* (staircase of the ministers) with its spectacular mural *La historia de la Justicia en México* (The History of Justice in Mexico) by Rafael Cauduro.

The mural, which has seven panels, illustrates seven new sins and crimes associated with the judicial system: corruption, torture to obtain a statement, homicide, rape, kidnapping, incarceration and repression. On the upper windows are a series of 'angels', who turn out to be riot police intimidating people. The chillingly hyper-realistic style, brutally denounces the excesses in this vision of Mexico.

The mural project was approved by ministers in 2006 ... surprisingly, because the discussion of such matters was taboo in Mexico until the year 2000, when the Partido Revolucionario Institucional (PRI – Institutional Revolutionary Party) lost the elections after 70 uninterrupted years in power.

The guided tours, along with social statements like this mural, are just a tiny indication of the slow change that has begun within the complex machinery of justice.

There is another impressive hyper-realist mural (dating from 2010) on the third floor of the SCJN: *Caminos de palabras y silencios, de hombres y mujeres, de recuerdos y de olvidos* (Paths of Words and Silences, of Men and Women, of Memories and Forgetfulness) by Santiago Carbonell. Look out for the huge faces representing the tough personality of the north of the country and the mystery of the south.

As well as the Carbonell and Cauduro murals, the SCJN has four by José Clemente Orozco. At various points around the premises you can also see works by George Biddle, Héctor Cruz, Carlos Bracho, Ernesto Tamariz, Luis Nishizawa, Ismael Ramos and Leopoldo Flores. You just have to search through the labyrinthine corridors to find them.

LA MERCED'S AMPUTATED HAND

The most sinful hand

Junction of Calle Jesús María and Venustiano Carranza / Manzanares
Centro Histórico
Metro: Zócalo

At the entrance to La Merced convent, a strange hand is nailed to a stone conch below a niche with a statue of St James of Compostela.

One rainy night in 1823, José María Salinas broke into the convent at number 170 Uruguay. José had planned to steal the chapel jewels with his friends, but when they turned him down he decided to go it alone. So he stole the jewels himself, and found a new group of accomplices to sell them on to. The local people were furious and demanded that the culprit be found. José's hideout was soon discovered, and his brazenness led to his capture.

Although José was condemned to death for his crimes, the mob demanded that his hand should be cut off with an axe and nailed up at the entrance to the chapel. They wanted it to be the right hand because that was 'the most sinful'. The hand was left in the care of a religious order, who preserved it with so much loving care that, when only the bones were left, they had a bronze replica made. A witch is even said to have taken away the bones for use in a mysterious potion.

The strange bronze hand attracted the attention of a wealthy gent, who used it to decorate his mansion. The bronze version was lost during the expropriation of property under La Reforma (The Reform laws, 1854–76).

NEARBY
Casa de Los Lobos
Uruguay 42

When the city's first Spanish houses were being built, it was customary for their sewers to be in the shape of cannons or animals. The aim was not to scare away the spirits, but to drive away any rebellious locals who had remained after the colonial conquest. One of these curious culverts in the shape of a series of attacking wolves or dogs can be seen at the entrance to the 'House of the Wolves' at number 42 Uruguay.

RED HOUSES OF THE *GALLAS*

A necessary evil

Mesones, junction with Las Cruces
Centro Histórico
Metro: Pino Suárez

A little plaque on the wall of the colourful house at the junction of Mesones and Las Cruces marks the site of the city's first *casas de tolerancia*. The red paint on the buildings overlooking the street is not there by chance, but indicates a brothel. They were colloquially known as the houses of the *gayas* or *gallas* (meaning happy or joyful women).

The house on the corner isn't the only former brothel: along 7a Calle de Mesones some still have their colonial-style interior, perfectly suited to establishments such as restaurants or cafés.

Make your way through the maze of corridors at number 40 Calle de Las Cruces (the building with the plaque) to reach a small hostelry that serves food. Another restaurant, at 171 Mesones, which has an inner courtyard along an ancient corridor, also used to be a brothel. Most of the buildings on this street still have their narrow entrances, with doors next to each other. In colonial days, many Spanish men travelled to the New World without their wives. For this reason, in 1538 the Spanish Queen authorised the establishment of a brothel that was to be run by recently arrived Spanish sex workers.

In order to avoid worse sins, the Church tolerated these establishments as a 'necessary evil', while the state regulated and confined them to this neighbourhood, far from the colonial districts of the city.

The branch of a tree used to be placed above the entrance so that customers could identify these 'houses', and the prostitutes came to be known as *rameras* (from *ramo*, Spanish for branch). However, it wasn't long before there was trouble: Zumárraga, the first archbishop of Mexico, denounced before the king the fact that two priests were coming here at night on the pretext of destroying idols.

So from 1572 there were rules: first, each establishment was placed under the responsibility of a pimp or a madam, known as *padrote* and *madrota* respectively. In addition, only orphans and abandoned girls were allowed to join the *gayas*, who were generally detested by other women because they were often showered with gifts – gold jewellery, pearls, silks and shoes, which they flaunted in the street.

Spanish ecclesiastic Francisco Tello de Sandoval, responsible for the enforcement of the Leyes Nuevas (New Laws), forbade the women from wearing these ostentatious gifts outside, so there could be no mistaking them for society ladies.

From la Narvarte to Coyoacán

MUSEO DEL TATUAJE

Prison-designed tattooing machines, made from coins, hooks, insulating tape and ballpoint pens

Avenida Insurgentes 221
Colonia Roma
Tatuajes México, 3rd floor
Monday to Saturday 10am–8pm, Sunday 10am–6pm
Admission free
Metrobus: Durango

There's no better introduction to the history of tattooing in Mexico than through Tony Chacal's collection on the third floor of a building on Avenida Insurgentes. Ranging from early specialist magazines to business cards and flyers, all the displays have something to do with the art of injecting ink into the skin.

You can browse this museum at your leisure, but to grasp the detail it's better to ask for a guided tour. Among all the publicity materials, note particularly the hand-made business cards and the leaflets advertising the first exhibitions and tattoo parlours in Mexico City.

One showcase traces the history of tattooing and its ritual use in ancient and contemporary communities. Two of the various photographs and objects stand out. The first is a *khem sak*, a long metal rod sharpened to a point, used in South Asia for tattooing yantras (mystical diagrams that protect against physical dangers, diseases and phantoms) bequeathed by the late tattoo artist Crazy Ace Daniel. The other is an original *kanji* (Japanese character) by Horiyoshi III, a renowned artist who practises the Tebori technique of applying a traditional Japanese tattoo by hand rather than machine.

In Mexico, tattoos are looked down upon because they were so popular in prisons. But that's where a group of talented artists improvised their own tattooing machines. The most interesting showcases contain some of these ingenuous contraptions, acquired by donation or purchase. The Spike machine, for example, used a mixture of water and salt to power a device made from a pen, two bottle caps, a piece of foil, sticky tape, a magnet, a screw and a bit of wire. Other machines are made from coins, plastic clothes pegs, needles, pencils, keys, buttons, cell-phone chargers and even a bicycle gear. One of them uses a lighter spring, which has simply been straightened out and its tip sharpened on the ground, as a needle to inject the ink.

Not all the machines on display came from prisons, but many of them were invented inside – a genuine tattooing machine would not only have been very expensive but could hardly have been taken into a penitentiary.

In the words of tattoo artist 'El Chino': 'To be creative in prison is a way to free yourself from anxiety and the crushing weight of confinement. It's an escape from the reality of incarceration.'

PASEO DE LAS ESTRELLAS

Stars of 20th-century Mexican cinema

On the sidewalk of Antonio Maceo, near number 67
Colonia Tacubaya
Metro: Tacubaya; Metrobus: Antonio Maceo

On the façade of the abandoned Ecocine Ermita cinema are the words 'Paseo de las Estrellas' (Sidewalk of the Stars). On the sidewalk are the names and handprints of the great motion picture personalities of the second half of the 20th century, in the style of Hollywood's Chinese Theatre.

Among the handprints are those of comic actors like Gaspar Henaine 'Capulina', Antonio Espino 'Clavillazo' and José René Ruiz 'Tun-tun'; actresses like María Victoria, Silvia Pasquel and María Rojo; photographers like Ismael Rodríguez; film directors like Alfonso Arau; and exotic dancer and actress Yolanda Montes 'Tongolele'.

Near the entrance to the former cinema are the prints of actress María Elena Velasco, who has the distinction of being the only film star to have left footprints – a gesture worthy of 'La India María', the character she created.

The handprints, though passers-by walk over them without a second glance, were designed to recall the great movie roles of that era. Some of them are no longer identifiable because the nameplates are illegible or have disappeared, while others are remembered with nostalgia for the early days of colour cinema in Mexico.

NEARBY
A section of tramway track

In Calle Antonio Maceo, in front of the Paseo de las Estrellas, a section of track from the first tramway lines has been preserved. Arriving at Tacubaya from the Centro Histórico, the route forked, one branch heading towards La Venta and the other towards Mixcoac–San Ángel.

Capilla Mier y Pesado

It's practically impossible to get into the chapel of the Fundación Mier y Pesado, across the street, as the building is now a residential home for the elderly, run by the foundation. But the capitals, pediment and dome can be seen through the railings. The chapel was built in 1887 by Lauro Rosell, modelled on the Pantheon in Rome. The bell towers were added later. The land belonged to Don Antonio Mier and Doña Isabel Pesado, whose profusely decorated gardens have disappeared – all that's left of their legacy are the chapel and the foundation.

PLAZA DE ETIOPÍA

Mexico: the only country that opposed Italy's invasion of Ethiopia

Inside Etiopía metro station, Plaza de la Transparencia
Accessible during metro opening hours: Monday to Friday 5am–12am, Saturday 6am–12am, Sundays 7am–12am

In 1954 Haile Selassie I, Emperor of Ethiopia, arrived from East Africa. Diplomatic visits to Mexico had tended to be seen as a pretext for opening up a new market to foreign goods. So when the emperor seemed to have no such intentions, the entire diplomatic corps was impressed, even in the capital.

The reason for the emperor's visit was to express his sincere thanks to Mexico for its condemnation of the Italian government, under Benito Mussolini, for having invaded Ethiopia in 1935.

In fact, Mexico was the only country to oppose this invasion, and it even withdrew from the meeting of the League of Nations in protest. Haile Selassie made known the reasons for his visit in his speech of 21 June 1954. The following day the Plaza de Etiopía was inaugurated at that site, where the emperor unveiled a plaque.

During his visit, Haile Selassie was invited by the then President Ruiz Cortines to a reception at his official residence, Los Pinos (The Pines), where the emperor's punctuality – a rare attribute in Mexico – was remarked on. He also visited the Teotihuacán pyramids, the Bosque de Chapultepec, the Guadalupe basilica, the UNAM rectory and even the Plaza de Toros (bullring), where he greeted all who were present that day. He was quoted in the press as saying: 'This is an unforgettable day in my life as a great friend of Mexico.'

The Plaza de Etiopía was demolished when the metro was constructed in the 1960s, but it was reopened on a much smaller scale alongside the platform on the Indios Verdes line. The plaque that Haile Selassie unveiled is there, as well as a series of photos and framed articles about him. In one of the press cuttings, the 'Lion of Judah' can be seen wearing a *charro* sombrero during his visit.

IGLESIA DE LA MEDALLA MILAGROSA

④

Spectacular modern architecture

Ixcateopan 78
Monday to Saturday 8am–8pm, Sunday 8am–1pm and 7pm–8pm
Times may vary
Admission free
Metro: División del Norte

The Church of the Miraculous Medal, consecrated in 1957, is a little-known but exceptional example of Mexican modern architecture.

Inside the church, the roof seems to melt into the supporting columns. It uses a double-curved shape known as a hyperbolic paraboloid or *hypar*, which resembles a saddle. This architectural technique is the hallmark of the Cubiertas Ala company and its founder Félix Candela, who experimented with the conjunction of four *hypars* to create a kind of umbrella. This technique minimises materials so that in this case the church walls are only 4-centimetres-thick and were built at a relatively low total cost. The church has around 21 different *hypars*.

The commission covered everything, including the furnishings and interior decoration. All this is preserved as it was in 1957, including the refined Way of the Cross carved in cedarwood by Antonio Ballester, and the cell-like windows by José Luis Benlliure surrounding Our Lady of the Miraculous Medal. The Ritter brothers were responsible for the azulejo frescoes in the chapel of Our Lady of Guadalupe (don't miss the concealed stained glass that illuminates the roof vault). The candelabras, straight out of a sci-fi film, were designed by Pedro Miret and Félix Candela. The ensemble is an example of complete integration of the plastic arts, from the spiral staircases of the choir where the steps and banisters don't touch each other, to the benches and wrought-iron gateway. Although the Rayos Cósmicos pavilion (in University City, see p. 150) made Cubiertas Ala's name, the Church of the Miraculous Medal showed Candela was a contractor who could take on major projects. This church attracted so much attention that it was even featured in an issue of *LIFE* magazine.

Candela repeated the *hypar* construction around the world: at the entrance of the Great Southwest Industrial Park in Texas, in Madrid's Church of Our Lady of Guadalupe, in the Mexico City Palacio de los Deportes (Sports Palace), and in Valencia's Oceanográfic (Oceanographic Museum). His 'Concha Candela' (Shell Candle) for the Oslo Flower Festival inspired Norwegian Gunnar Hauguen's design for Tromsø Public Library.

Towards the end of his life, and after a long and prolific career, Candela admitted that the only work that he really appreciated, and that he liked most and considered his own, was this church in Mexico City.

Our Lady of the Miraculous Medal is said to have appeared in Paris on 27 November 1830 to novice nun Catherine Labouré. Rays of light streamed from the Virgin's fingers and she gave Catherine a medal, telling her that whoever wore it would receive grace. Pope Pius IX accepted the doctrine of the Immaculate Conception of the Virgin Mary in 1854. Construction of the church began exactly 100 years later.

PARQUE ARQUEOLÓGICO LUIS G. URBINA

Feel free to touch the archaeological remains

Avenida de los Insurgentes, junction with Porfirio Díaz
Colonia Extremadura
Metrobus: Parque Hundido

Everybody knows Parque Hundido on Insurgentes, an ideal place to run, take a walk around one of the largest dog-friendly spaces in the city, or visit the audio-visual show. However, its real name is Luis G. Urbina Archaeological Park, because of the archaeological remains.

Hidden among the greenery you'll find stone reproductions of pre-Hispanic sculptures from various regions of the country. Concrete lines mark the trails you can follow: blue for the Totonac route, violet for the Altiplano, red for Oaxaca, green for the Olmec route and yellow for the Mayan route.

The reproductions are of altars, steles, sculptures, a colossal head and several ancestral deities, ranging from the panel from the Temple of Kukulkán at Chichén Itzá to the base of the Temple of Quetzalcóatl at Teotihuacan. There are 51 pieces scattered around the park, most of which have lost their explanatory bronze plaque, although the descriptions were not exactly comprehensive. One, for example, bore the caption: 'Sculpture of a fat man. Protoclassic period 200 BC–200 AD.'

Some of these artefacts seem made for selfies. When visitors come across them, they take pictures of the altars or of themselves embracing the deities, without running the risk of damaging any ancestral remains.

The entrance to the archaeological park is composed of several snake-shaped columns like those found at Chichén Itzá.

Although the park has existed since 1893, the sculptures were placed here in 1972, under the nationalist government of Luis Echeverría, who tried to promote traditional Mexican culture. The park is well worth a visit, especially for sculptures that you'd rarely be able to study in so much detail at their original sites.

Mixcoac was known for its brickworks. The ground was ripped open to find the precious materials. When the Nochebuena works closed, trees were planted in the hollow to create Parque Nochebuena, although it was popularly called Parque Hundido (Sunken Park) as it was several metres below ground level. Other quarries have now become the Estadio Azul (Blue Stadium) and the monumental Plaza México, also below ground level.

CASA GAUDIANA

Gaudí-style house in Mixcoac

Empresa 83
Metro: Mixcoac

Strolling along Calle de Empresa in the Mixcoac neighbourhood, you'll come across a strange-looking house that borrows features from Spanish architect Antonio Gaudí.

Although only the upper part of the house is clearly visible from the road, recognisable Gaudí-like elements include the four-armed cross on top of a little tower, the bone-shaped columns on the windows, blocks of concrete that look like tree trunks, and the wavy roofs that are typical of Catalan modernism.

The house was originally Functionalist in style (like most of those nearby), but its owners, admirers of Gaudí, redecorated in 2005 as a curious homage to his Art Nouveau style.

NEARBY
Casa de Irineo Paz

Plaza Gómez Farías 8
Tuesday to Saturday 9am–6pm
Metro: Mixcoac

The Porfirian home of Mexican General Irineo (or Ireneo) Paz, now converted into a convent for Dominican nuns, is open to the public. You can visit part of the house as well as the chapel inside. It was the childhood haunt of 1990 Nobel Literature laureate, Octavio Paz, who was his grandson. As he writes in *Silueta de Ireneo Paz* (Outline of Ireneo Paz): 'One of my first childhood memories is that of a large rectangular terrace. The floor was made of carefully laid, diamond-shaped slabs of white and blue. There were rooms on three sides of the terrace: the dining room, a small circular sitting room with a skylight, the library, the fencing hall and other outbuildings.'

The Venetian mosaics at the entrance, and the outlines of the library and dining room, have been preserved. The fencing hall is now a chapel and features two devotional sculptures dating from the 18th century.

EL MONOLITO DE 1968

The university marched to this point

Central reservation of Avenida Insurgentes, junction with Eje 7 Sur Félix Cuevas
Metro: Insurgentes Sur; Metrobus: Félix Cuevas

Every day, crowds pass by the stone monolith on its plinth standing on the central reservation of Avenida Insurgentes. However, not many people are aware that it commemorates the site where *'La marcha del rector'* (The rector's march) ended, and what it represents.

It all began on 22 July 1968, during a street football match in which a foul led to a dispute between rival gangs – students at Vocational School #5 against the Isaac Ochoterena preparatory school. The riot police intervened with force, leading to a series of strikes, blockades and demonstrations that were severely repressed and resulted in the occupation of the city's main educational institutions.

The rector of the Universidad Nacional Autónoma de México (UNAM – National Autonomous University of Mexico), Javier Barrios Sierra, led a protest march from the south of the city against the military occupation. This is said to be the source of the slogan *Únete pueblo!* (People Unite!), as the march was joined by more followers along the way. The protesters were heading for the Zócalo, the city's main plaza, but were warned that riot police were waiting for them at Parque Hundido. To avoid a confrontation, they turned back on Eje 7 Félix Cuevas and returned to UNAM, where the rector had the flag lowered to half-mast and addressed the crowd.

The day after this march, the university campuses were deserted. The peaceful protests continued until the night of 2 October, the date of the infamous Tlatelolco massacre, when government forces were used to suppress opposition.

Some 30 years later, social rights activists had this monolith erected with a plaque at the point where the rector's march turned back. An inscription reads: 'On 1 August 1968, the university marched to this point, led by its rector, Javier Barrios Sierra.' Marcelino Perelló, leader of the student movement throughout 1968, explained that this demonstrated that the year's events 'weren't confined to just one night'.

NEARBY
Art Deco fountain

On the roundabout of Avenida Santander stands an Art Deco fountain-lighthouse, built in 1935 by architect Leonardo Noriega and engineer Javier Stavoli. Both men were involved in the design of Mexico City's 1930s Art Deco street furniture, including Reloj Radio in Parque México which signifies the links between the ancient village of Mixcoac and the modern district called Colonia Mixcoac.

ROOF GARDEN AT INFONAVIT

The largest roof garden in Latin America

Avenida Barranca del Muerto 280
Instituto del Fondo Nacional de la Vivienda para los Trabajadores headquarters
(+52) 9171 5050
Monday to Friday 6am–8pm
Access restricted; for guided tours, email eperez@ciceana.mx
Metro: Barranca del Muerto

On the roof of the Institute of the National Fund for Workers' Housing (INFONAVIT) building, designed in 1975 by renowned architects Teodoro González de León and Abraham Zabludovsky, is a spectacular display covering an area of 2,500 square metres – the largest roof garden in Latin America.

This educational project, aimed at both professionals and visitors, has scientific data sheets giving each plant's characteristics and cultivation methods.

On leaving the elevator, you're greeted by a vegetable plot filled with lettuce, potatoes, blackberries, oregano, tomatoes, etc.

There are two ways to visit the terrace. The first is to follow the small path leading to the three well-being zones and the shaded space for practising yoga, surrounded by mulberries, everlasting flowers and guava trees. The second is via the running track around the terrace, which features three different ecosystems: highland forest, desert and tropical.

The dominant species here are cacti such as yellow agave, blue or tequila agave (which blooms only once in its lifetime), dwarf prickly pear, golden barrel (an extremely rare plant threatened with extinction) and different varieties of biznaga cacti. You'll also find mango, American black cherry, apricot, lemon, cherry and hazelnut trees.

On one side of the stretch of water, complete with fish, medicinal plants such as fennel, arnica, lemon balm and aloe vera grow.

The terrace has been awarded Roof Point certification for its environmental benefits without recourse to herbicides, agrochemicals, pesticides or hormones. In addition to the leisure facilities, heated showers have been installed for the runners, as well as toilets and a greenhouse.

The resulting space is a major boost to urban ecology and, although it remains a beautiful secret garden, guided tours are organised for small groups. Best book your visit on a clear day, for a distant view of the Popocatépetl and Iztaccíhuatl volcanoes that dominate the city skyline.

TOMB AT TLACOPAC

The only known tomb from St Patrick's battalion

Tlacopac, junction with Callejón Corregidora
Purísima Concepción Tlacopac parish churchyard
Daily 8am–7pm
Metrobus: Olivo

A well-known anecdote about St Patrick's battalion (batallón de San Patricio) concerns the fate of deserters during the North American invasion of Mexico. The executed men were buried, but where?

The story goes that after the battle of Churubusco in 1847, 68 deserters from the US army who'd joined the Mexican ranks were condemned as traitors and sentenced to death by hanging. However, 18 of them were pardoned by US General Winfield Scott. At the very moment that the US flag was being hoisted at the Palacio Nacional in Mexico City, 34 men were being hanged at Mixcoac and 16 more from the trees of Plaza San Jacinto in San Ángel. The pardoned deserters received 50 lashes and were branded on the cheek with the letter 'D'. Finally, they dug the graves of their hanged comrades.

All the graves have disappeared except this one, in the courtyard of Tlacopac parish church. Seven of the 16 men hanged at San Ángel also lie here: the monks who heard their confessions took pity on them and buried their bodies in the churchyard.

A monument in memory of the heroic battalion, complete with plaque and Celtic cross, was erected on one side of the courtyard near the last remaining grave.

Commemorative stone plaques engraved with the names of the 70 prisoners from the battle of Churubusco have been erected at both San Ángel and Churubusco. A heraldic royal eagle surmounts a Celtic cross (alluding to the Irish roots of most of the battalion). The San Ángel stone also has a bust of Captain John O'Reilly, said to have been branded with a D on both cheeks because the first scar was barely visible.

St Patrick's battalion consisted of around 450 American soldiers (immigrants from Europe, mainly Ireland). Although some of the men deserted shortly before the start of the Mexican-American war because they saw the US invasion as unjust, most did so after hearing that López de Santa Anna (Mexico's commander-in-chief and president) had promised to reward them if they switched sides. At the court-martial, most of the prisoners claimed to have been drunk when the Mexican army captured and recruited them. In spite of pleas for mercy from both sides, General Scott only pardoned those who'd deserted before the declaration of war, and two others because of their youth.

TREES IN THE VIVERO DE COYOACÁN

Poets turned into trees

Avenida Progreso 1 - Colonia Del Carmen
Inside Parque Nacional Vivero de Coyoacán
Daily 6am–6pm
Metro: Viveros

f you leave the main paths of Vivero de Coyoacán (Coyoacán Tree Nursery) National Park and take the Palmas trail, you'll find a rather special installation. Tree trunks with spiral shapes, human forms or floating spheres are part of the *Nace, Crece y Permanece* (Born, Growing and Staying) exhibition which has been tucked away in Coyoacán since 1999.

One of the tree trunks bears the impression of human hands, another is formed from sections of trunk held together by wires and nails. Some are interwoven and others are formed into perfect circles and squares. A few of the artists' nameplates have survived at the base of the trees – students from the Escuela Nacional de Artes Plásticas (National School of Plastic Arts).

When the exhibition opened, it consisted of 36 dead tree trunks scattered around the park, of which only 15 are still standing. A popular legend says that if five joggers enter the park, five will leave; and if five tourists enter, five will leave; but if five poets enter, only four will leave, because one will be bewitched and turn into a tree. So are these the lost poets?

The sculptural trail continues along a path lined with acacia trees and dotted with stone statues. You'll need to squat down to appreciate the details. A closed fist, a stripped woman's torso, a seated cat and a human skull are all part of the *Infancias Botánicas* (Botanical Childhoods) exhibition, which also dates from 1999. For this event, the sculptors commissioned by the Japan Foundation carved their names on little plaques of green marble.

One of the pieces in this series, scattered around the palm plantation, is made up of small friezes depicting mythical animals. The sculpture at the park entrance – *Un solo mundo* (One World) by Japanese artist Mizuo Ishida – stands out from the rest as it's made from marble. These two schemes date from 1999, when the National Reforestation Programme was planning a makeover of the tree nursery's image.

The park has other secrets to divulge: to the side of one of the two guards' huts, dating from 1913, bullfighters and their apprentices have installed plaques with poems dedicated to the tree nursery. On the Celtis trail, joggers have named a luxuriant tree the Santuario de la Salud (Sanctuary of Health), as carved on the trunk.

CASA DE LOS DELFINES

Colonial monsters and medieval guardians

Callejón de la Cita 2, junction with General Marcial Lazcano
Metrobus: La Bombilla

Concealed in the alleyways of San Ángel is a very unusual house – the last vestige of the community of Rancho de la Palma. It has a pink façade adorned with mysterious sculptures. The long frontage starts at the garden gate and follows a white wall with four windows as far as the main door, with the sculptures on each side.

On this recently made door, 12 monks' faces are arranged in a triangle – a common motif among the local artisans. Six medieval Crusaders hold shields and standards (two more mounted Crusaders stand at the entrance to the garden). On one side is a carved frieze with features from a colonial landscape: it shows a gentleman standing in a cobbled street and a woman with her face covered, walking through a Baroque arch in the company of an Indian. The scene alludes to the name of the street, Callejón de la Cita (Alleyway of the Meeting).

The Catholic references include a Virgin and Child supporting the world and Christ accompanied by two angels – this one is damaged and covered with azulejos. Two picturesque little lions on slender columns guard the entrance.

But the best pieces are two intertwined marine serpents dating from the 18th century. Little would be known about them if it wasn't for the legend in the doorway: 'Casa de los Delfines – Año d 1786' (House of Dolphins – Year 1786). Another less obvious monster can be seen over the door.

Visitors' horses were tied to the stone rings laid out like a pre-Hispanic ball game on the wall. There are three rings, each with a face and a dolphin sculpture. The first two are probably of pre-Hispanic origin as they are carved in volcanic rock. Their meaning is unknown, but some people have hazarded the guess that they are the faces of an Indian, a Black and a Spaniard.

HOSPITAL DE NATURALES FAÇADE

A façade saved from demolition and relocated

Plazuela de los Licenciados 3
Junction of Juárez and Reyna
Metrobus: La Bombilla

he pretty old house at number 3, at the junction of Juárez and Reyna, dates back to the 19th century. Its façade was added in 1934 but it had previously belonged to the Hospital Real de San José de los Naturales, built in the 18th century.

In the 1920s, when the Dirección de Bienes Nacionales (National Heritage Authority) was set up as part of the Treasury, an exhaustive inventory of the country's churches was carried out with the help of local architects such as Manuel Ituarte, Federico Mariscal and Vicente Mendiola. One man in particular was closely involved – the Treasury Secretary himself, *Licenciado* (lawyer) Luis Montes de Oca.

In 1932, Abelardo Rodríguez became president and dismissed Montes de Oca. The inventory was stopped and the information already compiled was lost. A year later, the extension of Avenida San Juan de Letrán in the Centro Histórico began and several old buildings were demolished, including the Hospital de Naturales.

To avoid losing the building completely, Montes de Oca asked Mendiola to save the neoclassical façade and reintegrate it into his own house in San Ángel. He wanted it to overlook the adjoining plaza, which

neighbours had dubbed Plazuela de los Licenciados because as well as Montes de Oca, Licenciado Rafael Martinez de la Torre (who defended Emperor Maximilian I when he was condemned to death in 1867) had lived there.

It's said that when the façade was in place, a monk began to haunt the area. Floating around in the night, he pointed out the hiding place of a treasure: it was later discovered by the new residents when they knocked down an internal wall.

During the San Ángel Fiesta de las Flores in July, some of the neighbours still take part in the 'floral balcony' contest. They decorate their balconies with flowers and open the windows to display pictures of saints or scenes from everyday life. These floral balconies were originally made for the street processions in the 17th century. The Flower Festival dates back to 1857.

O'GORMAN'S FIRST MURAL

The project of a nation

Junction of Santísima, Galeana and Gral, Aureliano Rivera
Colonia San Ángel
Metrobus: La Bombilla

At the junction of Calles Santísima and Galeana, in Tlalpan, on the walls of the estate where Mexican architect and muralist Juan O'Gorman lived, are little niches containing heavily damaged paintings – his first mural.

O'Gorman lived here in his youth, marked by the Mexican Revolution. Despite his communist leanings, this work was meant as a gift for his Roman Catholic mother and an offering to a saint in the central niche. A stylised Mexico landscape is unveiled between blue curtains. Mexican architect Carlos González Lobo referred to it as 'the project of a nation'.

In the foreground is a little village with plaza, church and harbour. In the centre, the Virgin of Guadalupe is depicted with an archangel on her right, and on her left what appears to be an eagle (though this miniature has almost completely disappeared). The Sun, the Moon and the representation of the Eye of God adorn the upper section.

The work is reminiscent of the optimistic vision of this transgressive artist's mural *Paisaje d'Azcapotzalco* (Azcapotzalco Landscape), painted a few years later for the Biblioteca Fray Bartolomé in Azcapotzalco.

Juan O'Gorman: a suicide in three acts

Painter and muralist Juan O'Gorman (1905–1982) is also considered the father of modernist Mexican architecture. His group paintings contrast with the sobriety and elegance of the Functionalist houses he designed for friends Diego Rivera, Frida Khalo, Manuel Toussaint and Enrique Erro.

In the 1980s, disenchanted with the human race and depressed by the disappearance of most of his murals and architectural works, a feeling of bitterness appeared in his artwork. An unfortunate mix-up over letters involved him in a marriage with a woman he didn't love, and suicide became a recurrent topic of conversation with his friends. During an interview with journalist Cristina Pachero, he confided: 'Her pink dress disturbs me, it keeps me from dying.' A week later, on 18 January 1982, he made his final decision. The Mexican author Guadalupe Loaeza noted that this was a suicide in three acts: first he took cyanide, then tried to hang himself, and finally got hold of a pistol and shot himself.

CHILDREN'S GAMES AT UNIDAD INDEPENDENCIA

So innovative that it was praised by Charles de Gaulle and John F. Kennedy

Periférico Sur 3400
Anillo Periférico (ring road), San Jerónimo junction
Microbus: Line 2–24 from Chapultepec metro station to Unidad Independencia
(Recorre Periférico – line serving the ring road)

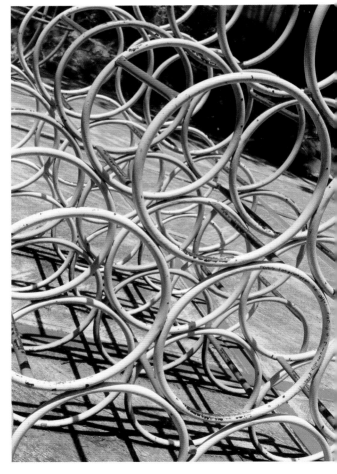

Unidad Independencia, a housing complex that combines architecture, design and art, was built between 1959 and 1960 as part of the infrastructure projects of the Mexican Social Security Institute (IMSS), then directed by Benito Coquet.

Three neighbourhoods of apartment blocks were built on land on the southern outskirts of the city, which had belonged to the Matsumoto family (Japanese emigrants to Mexico, who introduced jacaranda trees to the city in the Porfirian era). The layout retains some of Tatsugoro Matsumoto's original woodland design.

Inspired by Le Corbusier's 1933 Athens Charter on urban planning, architects Alejandro Prieto and J.M. Gutiérrez designed a vast modernist development of mid- and high-rise buildings integrated with shops, schools and a medical clinic. Between each building are frescoes by Mexican artist Francisco Eppens made from coloured stones. Some represent shells, pelicans, corn cobs, eagles and lizards; others pre-Hispanic glyphs (carved image of a sound, word or idea) and figures. There are also giant stone sculptures by Luis Ortiz Monasterio and Federico Garza, the most striking of which is Quetzalcóatl in the main plaza.

Open spaces and gardens played a vital role in community life. Take a look at the concrete paths inset with pebbles in op art designs. Pedro Miret's children's games are the highlight of the residence: although the little cement truck is the most obvious, there's also a kind of fish, and a podium that at first glance doesn't seem to be meant for games. The podium was designed by anarchist punk Roger Miret for children to meet and play together. Metal climbing frames trace incredible psychedelic shapes in the sunlight. One of them, composed of 50 metal rings, was built by the residents themselves and is the only one that has been copied around the country.

Housing complex visited by John F. Kennedy and Charles de Gaulle

The design of Unidad Independencia was so successful that even the diplomatic dignitaries visiting Mexico praised it. Indian Prime Minister Indira Gandhi, Marshal Tito of Yugoslavia and Queen Juliana of the Netherlands were received there, but also (as commemorated by two statues at the entrance) John F. Kennedy in 1962 and General Charles de Gaulle in 1964.

In his speech, Kennedy said that he'd never seen such a project before; he was so impressed by the integration of the various elements that he took the idea back to the USA.

OPTICAL ILLUSION IN PLAZA RUFINO TAMAYO

Deceptive perspective

Avenida Insurgentes Sur, between Copilco and San Jerónimo on Eje 10 Sur
Metrobus: Dr Gálvez

Plaza Rufino Tamayo, named after the famous painter from Oaxaca, was built in 1990. The architects, Teodoro González de León and Abraham Zabludovsky, have created a striking optical illusion that plays on perspective. You can see it from a bridge, on a slope facing the plaza: just look towards the fountain and its seven arches, which give the plaza a deceptive depth.

On the base of the fountain is a mosaic reproduction of a Tamayo watercolour initially painted as a backdrop for a London ballet company. This painting maintains the illusion because it follows the lines of the architecture.

In 1991, the plaza won an International Honorary Mention at the Xth Pan-American Architecture Biennial in Quito (Ecuador), even though it hadn't been planned for the occasion.

According to the Biennial catalogue, the plaza has four distinct features: the foliage-covered embankment, a background in perfect harmony with the magnificent Panteón de Atizapán woods just behind; the pergola, which provides a winding walk of light and shade leading to a little fountain; the series of square garden bench/planters, filled with flowering plants; and the monumental fountain with seven independent arches that create the optical illusion.

At the plaza's opening ceremony, water cascaded over the mosaics and ran down through the seven arches to a mirror of water in the centre, creating the illusion that it was flowing along a horizontal surface. The plants bore yellow, orange, red and mauve flowers – the colours Tamayo always used in his paintings. Lack of maintenance has led to the disappearance of the water feature, not to mention the flowers.

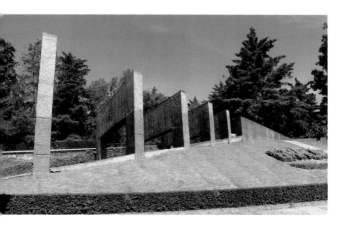

PARQUE MARGÁIN POOL

Emperor Maximilian's stopover on his trips to Cuernavaca

Inside Parque Hugo Margáin
Eje 10 Sur, junction with Odontología
Metro: Copilco

Even those who think they know every nook and cranny of Margáin park are unaware of this pool, which dates back more than a hundred years. The ruggedly finished basin, now a planter, has a well at one end that has been filled in and covered with flowers. An almost illegible metal plaque on one side reads: 'Here was the first stopover on the Mexico City–Cuernavaca road.'

Between December 1865 and July 1866, the Emperor of Mexico Maximilian von Habsburg and his wife Carlota of Belgium took a restful break in their isolated residence at Cuernavaca. The emperor also wanted to recover from his repeated head colds, which is why he spent more time in the sunny climate of Cuernavaca than in the capital. No wonder then that the plaque goes on to say: 'The water trough was regularly used by Maximilian's horses and the existing well was built at that time.' He did indeed use this road regularly.

It is perhaps here that the lunch took place as described by royal gardener Wilhem Knetchel in a letter he wrote at New Year 1866.

According to leading experts on Maximilian and the Second Empire, Konrad Ratz and Amparo Gómez Tepexicuapan, the emperor was in Cuernavaca when he received a telegram announcing that Carlota had been examined by Dr Riedel in Vienna. The emperor asked his doctor, Samuel Basch, if he was acquainted with Dr Riedel, and the latter, without knowing the reason for the question, simply replied: 'He's the director of the lunatic asylum.' On learning that his wife had been interned in the asylum, Maximilian never returned to Cuernavaca or to this stopover point.

In the 19th century, one of the most dangerous routes was between Mexico City and Cuernavaca. Some sections of the road were very narrow and it was little used for fear of attack by *Los Plateados* (The Wealthy Ones), a band of outlaws who used their loot to buy eccentric clothing and ostentatious silver jewellery. Travellers had to make frequent rest stops if they wished to reach their earthly paradise.

PEARS ON THE FOUNTAINS OF CHIMALISTAC

Two fountains marking the site of the former Carmelite orchard

Junction of Fresno and Pimentel; junction of Rafael Checa and Del Carmen
Metrobus: La Bombilla

In the quiet streets of Chimalistac, two fountains mark the site of the former orchard belonging to the Roman Catholic Order of Discalced (Barefoot) Carmelites, whose convent is now the Museo de El Carmen.

The first fountain, on Plaza de los Arcángeles, was paid for by donations from the neighbours and designed by architect Juan Carlos Villalon in 1992. Pears and oranges have been carved on the back of the fountain in memory of the orchard. On the four upper stones, three different names are inscribed:

'Fray Andrés de San Miguel 1577–1652': Friar Andrés, an architect and hydraulic engineer who became a Carmelite as he'd vowed after divine intervention saved him from shipwreck, designed the Convento del Carmen and adjoining aqueduct.

'Fray Antonio Vázquez de Espinosa 1570–1630': this Discalced Carmelite friar is known to have travelled from New Spain to South America. In 1629, he narrated his discoveries in *Compendio y descripción de las Indias Occidentales* (Compendium and Description of the West Indies).

'IV Centenario de San Juan de la Cruz 1991': the Spanish monk who became St John of the Cross was the co-founder of the Discalced Carmelite Order, along with St Teresa of Avila.

The second fountain, on the Josefina roundabout, dates from 1986. It was dedicated to St John and Brother Andrés. Its exquisite neo-Baroque ornamentation is complemented by a plaque at the corner that gives a literary account of the story of the orchard.

The orchard and monastery covered much of the Chimalistac neighbourhood. The Magdalena river irrigated the fruit trees and an aqueduct on the side of the buildings channelled the water of the reservoir (now Centro Cultural Jaime Sabines) to the vegetable gardens. When the crop was good, the friars sold their produce in San Ángel.

The Ermita del Secreto (Chapel of the Secret) stood at one end of the orchard and the three bridges of Chimalistac led to the stony area where the monks meditated. The gardens had their own internal paths that disappeared when the building was deconsecrated, but their central point was used to create the Josefina roundabout, where the second fountain now stands.

The total area of the monastery and gardens is believed to be exactly that of Vatican City.

BRIDGES OF CHIMALISTAC

Three bridges with no river

Camellón del Paseo del Río
Colonia Chimalistac
Metrobus: La Bombilla

Along the quiet and pleasant Paseo del Río, running from Río Chico to Oxtopulco, are three ancient bridges that were all used to cross the Magdalena river to reach the Convento del Carmen (see p. 129). Each bridge is in a different architectural style and all were built at different periods of the 17th century.

Travelling from south to north, the first bridge is formed by a semicircular arch. The Magdalena river ran 6 metres below, and there was also a small waterfall, which is why the Carmen friars installed a pulpit on one side of the bridge. The novices had to practise their oratory and diction down there, preaching a sermon and making themselves heard over the roar of the river. This is how the name Puente del Púlpito (Bridge of the Pulpit) came about, although the pulpit disappeared in 1962 during restoration work.

The second bridge, with its segmental 'humped' arch, is known as Puente del Camello, or Camellito (Bridge of the Camel, or Little Camel). Apart from its distinctive shape, this is the only bridge that doesn't have steps, probably in order to take the carriages and carts on their way to and from the convent orchard. The third bridge, Puente de la Presa Grande (Bridge of the Large Dam), is now known as Oxtopulco. Not only was this the largest bridge, but it also marked the boundary of the property on one side. At the centre is a *garitón* (turret) that may

have been a niche for the statue of a saint. The bridge has four arches, two semicircular and two segmental, suggesting that it was built in two stages.

The Magdalena river still runs below the bridges, but was encased in 1962 at the neighbours' request because of its high level of pollution.

A few steps from Oxtopulco bridge are some mosaics showing the Magdalena river landscape as it used to be. The original work on which the mosaics are based is an 1855 oil painting by Eugenio Landesio, entitled *Puente de Chimalistac, el puente de San Antonio en el camino de San Ángel*. Behind the chapel of San Antonio de Padua (Francisco Sosa, junction with Universidad, Coyoacán) you can still see the river and the bridge shown in the mosaics.

JUNCTION OF CALLE DEL SECRETO AND PROGRESO

⑲

Coyoacán's best-kept secret

Colonia Chimalistac
Metro: Miguel Ángel de Quevedo

Hidden in the quiet, picturesque streets of the Chimalistac neighbourhood, this little rectangular building protected by railings is known as the Ermita del Secreto (Chapel of the Secret).

Despite the barrier, you can still view the chapel from all angles as it stands in the middle of the road. Although there is no public access, a Cross can be seen inside the chapel. There's an information panel at the entrance.

Historically, the Chimalistac lands were part of an orchard belonging to Juan de Guzmán Ixtolinque, then *tlatoani* (mayor) of Coyoacán, who had been an ally of Cortés during the colonial conquest of Mexico. One day he saved Cortés' life, and to thank him the kings of Spain granted him extensive lands in the newly conquered territory. When he died, Ixtolinque 'the younger' then became owner of the Coyoacán lands.

On his own death, he bequeathed them to the Carmelite convent, whose construction began in 1615.

It was not until 1620 that the Chapel of the Secret was built, in the grounds of the former kitchen garden of the convent. According to some chroniclers, the soil was so fertile that the Carmelites not only had enough garden produce for themselves, but could also sell their surplus. The chapel used to have murals of the Sermon on the Mount, but they've been obliterated by the passage of time.

The Chapel of the Secret owes its name to the remarkable acoustics of its architectural design. Something whispered in one corner is perfectly audible in the opposite corner. In this way, the Carmelites could communicate without breaking their vow of silence, even if most of the time the topics were religious.

The same effect is found in the Ermita del Secreto of the former convent of Desierto de los Leones, as well as in the twin bell towers of the Metropolitan Cathedral. Both buildings are open to the public.

PHOTO OF 'EL INDIO' FERNÁNDEZ

The photo that inspired the Oscar statuette

Zaragoza 51
Colonia Santa Catarina
Inside the fortress home of Emilio 'El Indio' Fernández
Visits on reservation by phone or email, or during the Day of the Dead
(+52) 5658 9619
casadelindiofernandez@hotmail.com

Guided tours of the Coyoacán fortress that once belonged to Emilio 'El Indio' Fernández, a film director from the golden age of Mexican cinema, must be pre-booked. His bedroom has a photograph of him along with a replica of an award from the Academy of Motion Picture Arts and Sciences, better known as the Oscar. Interestingly, this very picture was the model for the famous statuette.

Towards the end of his life, Fernández used to say that he was the model for the Oscar – a story given little credence at the time. After his death in the United States in 1986, MGM began an exhaustive investigation into the company's history. When archives of the early days of the studio were found, a photo belonging to El Indio was among them.

In the 1920s, MGM's art director Cedric Gibbons was commissioned to design the Academy Award trophy. His research turned up the photo of Fernández ready to dive from La Quebrada cliffs at Acapulco. Inspired by the image and persuaded by his then wife, Mexican actress Dolores del Río, Gibbons called the film director in order to start work on the statuette.

Fernández, who was then working as an extra in Hollywood, initially refused to pose in the nude but finally agreed. So was born the coveted statuette, designed by Gibbons and sculpted by George Stanley.

Inside the house is a print from the same negative, together with a replica of the statuette sent from Hollywood.

Among the other strange souvenirs kept in the house are a piano dating from 1906, which Agustín Lara used to play at parties; an excerpt from the original screenplay of the film *María Candelaria* (1944, directed by Fernández and starring Dolores del Río); and some personal possessions, most with their own stories to tell. For example, the electric lamp hidden behind some Puebla Talavera pottery, because 'El Indio' didn't want to see *gringaderas* (pejorative reference to objects of Anglo-Saxon origin) in his house.

HOOP FROM A *PELOTA* GAME

Cosmic forces of the universe in the tiny courtyard of a cultural centre

Casa de la Cultura Jesús Reyes Heroles
Francisco Sosa 202
Colonia Santa Catarina
(+52) 5659 3937
Daily 8am–8pm
Admission free
Metro: Miguel Ángel de Quevedo

The hoop from a ball game, *pelota*, is displayed in a little courtyard inside the beautiful Jesús Reyes Heroles House of Culture. It's behind a grille through which you can see the front part, eroded by the passage of time. A plaque indicates that it was found in what is now Plaza Hidalgo in Coyoacán.

Pelota was more than a sport; it was an important ceremony in different parts of Mesoamerica. Each element and player represented a different cosmic force in the universe. Every time the ball went through the hoop, it signified the triumph of the Sun and the rebirth of a new day. The progress and ending of the game would reveal the forces of a celestial prediction.

In Coyoacán, *Xócotl Huetzi* or 'fall of the fruits' was also celebrated during the Day of the Dead festival in September. A tall tree trunk fixed in the centre of the plaza was decorated with *amate* bark paper, with a bird or bat made of amaranth at the top. After dancing, some indigenous people in disguise would attempt to climb the trunk and knock it over. The celebration closed with the distribution of food for a feast.

After the Spanish conquest, the status of the conquerors was symbolised by the *pelota* hoops with which they decorated the façades of their houses. Many years later, people began to make copies of these ornaments as hitching points for their horses. There are still many of these hoops in Coyoacán, although it's rare to find an original.

The entrance to the House of Culture has an atrium cross dating from the 17th century, when the site was a paper factory. In the garden stands a monument erected by the Italian community in Mexico and dedicated to the Italians who fell in the antifascist resistance movement.

Tears of the Virgin

Behind the House of Culture is Callejón del Aguacate, which is associated with various urban myths and horror stories. One of these tells of a little mosaic Virgin who cried at night because of the apparitions. You can still see the holes in her eyes made by people searching for the source of her tears.

THE FORMER CINE ESPERANZA

Maestro Agustín played here

Cerrada de Francisco Sosa, junction with Presidente Carranza 294
Colonia Santa Catarina
Coyoacán

Many of the visitors strolling through the old district of Coyoacán (along Presidente Carranza, just before Plaza Santa Catarina) will walk past a colourful building dating from the early 1970s without realising its significance. A mosaic above one of the windows features a lithograph of the former Esperanza Cinema – a venue (closed in 1966) dating from the era of silent movies.

Like many other large cinemas of the time, the Esperanza hired musicians who accompanied the films on piano, violin and other instruments. The audience could buy food and drink, such as sandwiches and agave juice, at the entrance.

In the early days, the cinema is said to have been frequented by a future legendary musician then living at his aunt's home nearby. This young man went on to play in saloon bars, at social gatherings and even in brothels. With the given name of Ángel Agustín María Carlos Fausto Mariano Alfonso del Sagrado Corazón de Jesús Lara Aguirre y del Pino, he's better known as Agustín Lara.

The decline of Mexican cinema led to this venue, like so many others, closing its doors. The mosaic shows the façade with a vintage car parked outside. The promotional material reads: 'Today's premiere: Douglas Fairbanks in *The Thief of Bagdad*'. This film dates from 1924. You can also see an announcement for a Charlie Chaplin film.

CASA DE OTELO

The house inspired by Verdi's Otello *is now a jazz school*

Fernández Leal 31 – Colonia Concepción – Coyoacán
Open only to students or during public concerts
escuelasuperiordemusica.bellasartes.gob.mx
Metro: General Anaya

The Escuela Superior de Música (ESM – Higher Academy of Music) has two locations: the first at the Centro Nacional de las Artes

(National Centre for the Arts) and the second in the Casa de Otelo, one of the beautiful early 20th-century Porfirian residences on Calle Fernández Leal in the heart of Coyoacán.

The story goes that the former owner – of whom only the surname, Velasco, is known – based the design of his house on the set of *Otello*, Verdi's opera inspired by Shakespeare's play. The opera was performed at the Teatro Nacional around 1900, and in 1902 a house in the background scenery caught Velasco's attention. No trace of the stage set remains today.

In the opera, Othello the Moor lives in Venice, which explains why the Venetian-style residence has elements of Arab architecture, such as the coffered ceiling in the lobby and the inscriptions on the walls. The library ceiling is decorated with cherubs. The third floor is even more richly decorated than the lobby. However, as the stage set showed only the front of the house, one of the sides had neither doors nor windows. When the real house was built, this problem was solved by the addition of majestic exterior plasterwork. One of the rooms has a mural entitled *El festín de los jazzeros* (The Jazzmen's Feast), painted in 1992 by contemporary artist Jazzmoart for the International Jazz Festival in Mexico City. At every ESM Jazz Festival, the six panels of the mural are displayed in the Angélica Morales Von Sauer concert hall next to the house.

It's worth checking the Lunes de Jazz (Jazz Mondays) programme and the festival dates. Once inside the house, if you see only the lobby, you won't be disappointed.

> A dinner was apparently held in 1919 at Casa de Otelo for Italian tenor Enrico Caruso, who was on tour in Mexico. In the middle of the dinner, when Caruso heard the story of the house, he sang an excerpt from *Otello* right there on the terrace.

> Caruso was guest of honour at the Teatro Iris before he left the country. When soprano María Conesa pointed a prop gun at him, he let out a strangled cry that triggered laughter and applause from the audience.

NEARBY
The first newsstand

The city's first newsstand appeared in 1908. It still exists: a small blue kiosk at the junction of Higuera and Caballocalco. The vendor will gladly tell you how his great-grandparents, the original owners of the kiosk, lived through the Mexican Revolution in Coyoacán and the 1934 *Cristiada* (Cristero War; see p. 193), some of whose bloody scenes occurred in the plaza opposite. Most passers-by and customers of this quaint little kiosk are completely unaware of this.

PARQUE MASAYOSHI ŌHIRA

A Japanese-style park

Calle Country Club junction with Calle de los Ciclistas
Colonia Country Club
Metro: General Anaya

n the grounds of the luxurious Colonia Country Club, the Masayoshi Ōhira Park – originally Parque Pagoda – a rather faded Japanese garden, is worth a trip if only for its curious decorations.

The garden, surrounded by small artificial hills, was opened in 1942 by the then governor, Javier Rojo Gómez.

At first the garden had a pond with lotus flowers and ducks, grassy slopes where exotic animals grazed, and a huge pagoda. The nearby Country Club golf links were already established, and in 1945 the Churubusco film studios opened a few blocks away. In subsequent years, the district was home to some of the great artists of the time and the pagoda was used as a real estate office. Visitors to the park could enjoy their games and the maze until, in 1970, the pagoda was completely destroyed by arsonists.

In May 1980, the Japanese Prime Minister Masayoshi Ōhira visited Mexico for the establishment (later cancelled) of the Pacific Economic Cooperation Council. Ōhira died in June that year from a heart attack: a plaque was installed in the park in his memory on 30 July 1981, and it was renamed Parque Masayoshi Ōhira.

Today, over 30 years after its last restoration, the pond is used as a skatepark and a parkour trail. The concrete base of the pagoda can still be seen from the street. Many of the original decorative elements remain, such as the *torii* (a Japanese gateway to mark the difference between the profane and the sacred) and a brightly painted lighthouse.

If you happen to be there at the weekend, you'll see the park used as a set for cosplay photo shoots.

ESCALERA AL CIELO MONUMENT ㉕

The controversial mask that caused popular indignation

Central reservation of Avenida Aztecas, between Rey Topiltzin and Rey
Ixtlixóchitl
Coyoacán
Metro: Universidad; Tren ligero: Nezahualpilli

Escalera al cielo (Stairway to Heaven), a statue on the central reservation of Avenida Aztecas, shows three children standing on one another's shoulders like in a circus performance. The monument caused great controversy when first erected on this site, which lies under high-voltage cables and in a children's playground, because one of the characters is wearing a mask resembling a well-known Mexican ex-president.

In the 1990s, the country was in turmoil. President Carlos Salinas de Gortari (1988–94), overwhelmed by a grave economic crisis, government corruption and the emergence of the political and military movement known as EZLN (Ejército Zapatista de Liberación Nacional / Zapatista Army for National Liberation), bore the brunt of public anger. The appearance of a series of masks representing Mexican and international politicians, among which Salinas often cropped up, was proof of this.

It was common at the time to see urchins performing acrobatics at street crossings: they would climb up and over one another until the one at the top, wearing a mask, did a dance with obscene gestures. The unveiling of this statue by sculptor Sixto Sánchez at Coyoacán in November 2005 brought back memories of those hard times and a general feeling of disgust swept the neighbourhood.

Although the artist's and the delegates' intention had been to ridicule the former president, people failed to comprehend how they could erect a statue depicting someone who had left them in poverty for so long.

The 'anti-monument monument', as some called it, generated such controversy that a 24-hour police guard was put in place. A group of neighbours campaigned to have the statue removed and a referendum was held, but it's still there.

MUSEO DE ANATOMÍA Y PATOLOGÍA ANIMAL

Cabinet of horrors, animal version

Universidad Nacional Autónoma de México (UNAM)
Circuito Escolar, Facultad de Medicina, Veterinaria y Zootecnia (FMVZ)
Dr Manuel H. Sarvide research building
Monday to Friday 8am–4pm, times may vary
Admission free
Pumabus: Routes 1, 5, 6, 12

Although the Museum of Animal Anatomy and Pathology is principally for FMVZ researchers and students, anyone can inspect the plastinated specimens in the display cases of this small university museum.

Along the narrow corridors, five gigantic double showcases preserve creatures affected by all sorts of pathologies: cysts, osteosarcomas, dislocations, and even organs infected with cysticercosis, one-eyed monsters, and a four-legged chicken – victim of a congenital anomaly.

This exhibition, although basically a study aid for students and their teachers, can give visitors the impression of a cabinet of horrors, largely because many of these pathologies also affect humans. The mere sight of canine liver cirrhosis is enough to make you give up drink.

The museum started this collection at the suggestion of Dr Manuel H. Sarvide (1903–78), who worked on some of the specimens himself. In 1971, the idea of turning them into a museum took root, backed by Dr Sarvide, a known educator. The museum's present location dates from 1991, following the opening of new postgraduate facilities. The plastination process started in the same year. This unique museum is the most comprehensive of its kind in Latin America.

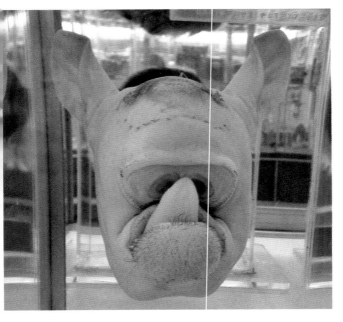

Jardín de los Perros

The park known as Jardín de los Perros (Garden of Dogs), in the grounds of the FMVZ, was baptised by the faculty and the Federación Canófila Mexicana (Mexican Dog-Breeders' Federation). Throughout the park there are statues of various breeds of dog, each with a plaque bearing a quotation appropriate to the breed. They include basset hound, German mastiff, English bulldog, German shepherd and two local breeds: chihuahua and xoloitzcuintle (Mexican hairless dog).

NEARBY
Lost Talavera tiles depicting Don Quixote

When a group of FMVZ students stayed at a farm in Zapotitlán, they discovered Turkish baths decorated with 600 original Talavera tiles telling Don Quixote's life story. The mosaic was relocated to the faculty entrance hall, where emeritus professor José Manuel Berruecos, assisted by his students, identified 36 different passages, several duplicates, and other pieces that didn't closely follow the plot. While doing so, they established that some of the tiles were inspired by the work of French engraver Gustave Doré.

INVERNADERO FAUSTINO MIRANDA

A rainforest in the city centre

Circuito Escolar, Universidad Nacional Autónoma de México (UNAM)
Between Torre de Ingeniería and Instituto de Investigaciones en Matemáticas
Aplicadas y en Sistemas (IIMAS)
(+52) 5622 9047 / 5622 9063
Guided tours on reservation
Monday to Friday 9am–3pm (only during academic term)
Admission free
Pumabus: Routes 6, 8, 9, 12

Behind the tower of the Institute for Research in Applied Mathematics and Systems (IIMAS) in University City, a metallic dome can be glimpsed between the trees. This is the Invernadero (hothouse) Faustino Miranda, which reproduces the hot and humid conditions of a rainforest several metres underground.

The volcanic rock on which the hothouse is built forms winding paths, some of which lead to small caves. Wherever you look, you'll see dense green foliage, sometimes palm trees, sometimes a lily pond.

Among this verdant abundance, it's easy to miss a guava, vanilla or coffee tree, which show how these fruits grow. Orchids hang at the entrance and the volcanic rocks are covered with ferns. A *ceiba* (Mayan sacred tree) and an elephant's foot (ponytail palm) are also to be seen.

The *chocho* tree is entirely covered with thorns and the *clavelina* (little bottle) has showy hair-like flowers (in pre-Hispanic days it was known as *xiloxóchitl*, or corn on the cob). The tree fern envelops visitors with its leaves and pretty spiralling branches.

This beautiful place is an extension of UNAM's botanical garden at the other end of the campus, which was established in 1959 by botanists Faustino Miranda and Manuel Ruíz Oronóz. The Spaniard Faustino Miranda, who had a particular interest in tropical plants, chose to build the hothouse on this volcanic formation. Scientists and students collected the species now growing inside the tropical enclosure.

The lesser-known heritage of the Central University City Campus

Although the tourists who visit the UNAM campus (a UNESCO World Heritage site) tend to concentrate on the Central Library's famous murals, the Olympic stadium or the sculpture collection, there is another type of heritage that is equally interesting but far less well known.

Of the 37 murals around the campus (two of them in the library), three are particularly interesting. In the panels of Mexican artist José Chávez Morado's *La ciencia y el trabajo* (Science and Work, 1952), a huge mural outside the Alfonso Caso Auditorium, metal tubes seem to emerge from the walls in a kind of optical illusion. *Abstracción integrada* (Integrated Abstraction, 1967), made in Talavera ceramics by Guatemalan muralist Carlos Mérida, was originally in a candle factory but is now at the entrance to the Circuito Cultural (Cultural Circuit). *Poema pictórico* (Pictorial Poem, 1987) is in the Faculty of Architecture's Lino Picaseño Library: here German-Mexican sculptor Mathias Goeritz encaptures a sculptural poem, pictorial and emotional. The small Rayos Cósmicos (Cosmic Rays, 1954) pavilion, now a storeroom, was one of Félix Candela's early architectural experiments, with walls just 1.5-centimetres-thick. Behind is the Faculty of Dentistry, whose library has faithful replicas of three dental surgeries, one from the 19th century and two from the 20th, complete with contemporary instruments and drugs.

The Faculty of Law's Jardín de los Eméritos is a rather eccentric garden planned in memory of its emeritus professors. In the courtyard of the Faculty of Engineering, a rail depot is used as a lecture hall.

In the sports area, architects Félix T. Nuncio, Ignacio Bancalari and Enrique Molinar designed a swimming pool that was used for the 1968 Olympic Games in Mexico City: seen from above, it's in the shape of the Mexican Republic. At the same time, Alberto T. Arai built eight open and two closed volcanic stone pediments reminiscent of pre-Hispanic pyramids.

Two of the sculptures are outstanding: Rodrigo Betancourt's *Prometeo Quetzalcóatl*, in the courtyard of the Faculty of Sciences; and sculptor Yvonne Domenge's representation of the AH1N1 (swine flu) virus, made during the 2010 epidemic, in the parking lot of the Biomedical Research Institute.

The trees around the campus rate a special mention, most of them introduced for research purposes. The strangest is the Cheirostem, or 'tree of hands' (opposite the Institute of Biology), whose flowers look like little hands. Although this tree is native to Mexico, there aren't many in the city. UNAM also runs an ecological reserve with nature trails. With a little luck, you'll spot butterflies and moths, bats, foxes, salamanders, snakes and owls.

Last but not least, on one side of the reserve is the Túnel del Tiempo (Tunnel of Time), a wooden construction that links the Hemeroteca (Newspaper Library) with the National Library. Inside the library is a superbly designed space, with restricted access, known as the Sala del Tesoro (Treasure Room) and filled with the country's most precious books. It can take a whole day to explore and unravel all the lesser-known aspects of Mexico's largest academic centre.

RUTA DE LA AMISTAD

The longest sculpture route in the world

mexico68.org
Trefoil 1: Periférico – Insurgentes Sur; Metrobus: Perisur
Trefoil 2: Periférico – Viaducto Tlalpan; Tren ligero: Xomali

The monumental sculptures that formed part of the 1968 Ruta de la Amistad (Route of Friendship) were relocated in 2012 to two interchanges of the Periférico – the city's outer ring road. You can walk or cycle along the route. In parallel with the 1968 Olympic Games held in Mexico City, a Cultural Olympiad was organised to celebrate art and culture as an integral part of the event. As well as film retrospectives, theatre and dance performances, art installations and even exhibitions of philately, nuclear energy and space, the Route of Friendship was created: a series of 22 huge concrete sculptures from various countries, installed with the help of Mexican-Polish sculptor Mathias Goeritz. The route was laid out along a 17-kilometre section of the ring road that passed in front of the Olympic Village and connected the various sports facilities in the south of the city. An association set up in 1994 to conserve the artworks created for the Cultural Olympiad was responsible for moving the sculptures to their new location.

Some of the best-known are *Señales* (Signals), by the Mexican Ángela Gurría, which recalls how African countries jointly demanded that the Olympic Committee exclude South Africa because of its policy of apartheid; *Sol* (Sun), by the Japanese Kiyoshi Takahashi, which when seen from a moving vehicle gives the impression of turning on its axis; *México* (Monument to Mexico), with a suggestive use of the name by Spanish artist José María Subirachs; and *Torre de los vientos* (Tower of the Winds), by the Uruguayan Gonzalo Fonseca, a geometric building now used as an experimental space for contemporary art.

NEARBY
Prehistoric pyramid

Close to Trefoil 1 of the Route of Friendship are the athletics tracks and the *Disco solar* (Solar Disk) by Belgian sculptor Jacques Moeschal, which has the most prestigious site along the route: on top of the oldest pyramid in Mesoamerica. This ancient pyramid was discovered in 1957 by archaeologist Robert Heizer along with ten other ruins. In 1968, seven of these were destroyed when the Olympic Village was built. Three were reconstructed, but only the one dating back to 1000 BC – made from compacted earth and preserved by the eruption of Xitle volcano (AD 245–315) – is still standing. Lava still covers the southern section, but the site can clearly be seen from the surrounding railings, next to the ensemble known as El Palacio (The Palace) in the northern part of the Olympic Village.

FAÇADE OF CASA DE LA CULTURA DE TLALPAN

The building that reminds the city of a water shortage

On Camino a Santa Teresa, s/n, junction with Zacatépetl
Colonia Parques del Pedregal
In Bosque de Tlalpan
Monday to Friday 9.30am–5pm, Saturday and Sunday 10am–1pm
Admission free
Metrobus: Corregidora

The façade of the Tlalpan House of Culture, designed in 1907 by Alberto J. Pani, used to stand 20 km from its present site. It was part of the Casa de Bombas de La Condesa (Countess's Pumphouse) on Xochimilco aqueduct, which in 1922 witnessed one of the most stressful weeks that the city ever lived through.

The pumping station used to distribute water throughout Mexico City. An explosion caused by human error completely flooded the building, the machinery failed and the city's 615,000 citizens were left without water. The problem was aggravated by an announcement that it would be three days before the clean-up operation began. On the third day, the washrooms of canteens, cinemas, theatres and restaurants were still flooded, and there were interminable queues at the city's wells. Having once been an enormous lake, the city was now dying of thirst.

The situation worsened as repairs were delayed yet another week. Some shops closed because of the lack of water, and the wells at San Rafael and Santa María began to sell water to passers-by, while those in Las Lomas de Chapultepec (on the other side of the city) distributed it free to anyone in need. People were so desperate that they began to dig for water around their homes.

Eight days of drought were enough to incite demonstrations in the main square. Most of those involved were trade unionists protesting against Alonzo Romero's municipal government. They were met with gunfire, but rather than panic they set fire to the town hall. During the night, an armed group attacked Romero's house. The demonstrations resulted in 21 deaths, 64 wounded, and the town hall in flames with no water to put it out.

The water shortage lasted 12 days until the machinery was repaired at last. New pumping systems were installed and the pumping station demolished – with the exception of the façade, which was dismantled stone by stone and dumped in the woods at Tlalpan. In 1986, a team working under the direction of Chilean architect Juana Paz Gutiérrez went in search of the lost stones and used them to build the House of Culture, designed by architect Pedro Ramírez Vázquez. Several fragments from the face of Neptune, centrepiece of the façade, were never found. They had disappeared, like the water, in 1922.

The ornamentation on the façade reflects its former association with water: turtles surrounded by irises, water lilies and gannets; marine monsters lapped by waves guarding the main vault; sea shells of different types at the top; intertwined swans, and so on.

VESTIGES OF TLALPAN FACTORIES

Signs of the industrial age in Tlalpan's alleyways

Piedra Durmiente: junction of La Fama and Félix Cuevas
Escuela Dietética: Callejón de San Fernando 12
Plaza Inbursa: Insurgentes Sur 3500
Metrobus: Corregidora

here are still some vestiges of the industrial age on the outskirts of
Tlalpan, including three factory buildings that played an important

part in the area's history

Although the architecture of La Fama Montañesa, a textile factory, is intact, access is restricted as it's now a warehouse. Local residents who wanted to open a museum on the site were given a millstone by the Morgado family. This stone, made for the Ostotome mill in 1561, is preserved in a little shelter on Calle La Fama. In 1831 it was in use at La Fama, turned by Fuentes Brotantes spring water.

The San Fernando yarn, fabric and cashmere factory now houses the Escuela de Dietética y Nutricion (School of Dietetics and Nutrition). The original 1845 building can still be seen from the rear entrance. One block away (32 San Pedro Apóstol) is the parish church of San Pedro Apóstol (St Peter the Apostle), for which the congregation of factory workers raised funds to build an extension in 1894. The chapel and confessional are worth a visit, as is the petroglyph of the hermitage that formerly stood on this site. A plaque in the garden marks the spot where Father Luis Barragán died when he fell on his head while pruning a tree.

The Fábrica de Papel Loreto y Peña Pobre, now a historical monument, is almost intact. Although the factory dates back to the time of Martín Cortés (son and heir of Hernán Cortés), it was making paper in 1846. Mechanisation was introduced in 1863. The chimneys were given the name Plaza Inbursa when the site was converted into a shopping centre. Some of the machinery is preserved as museum pieces, such as the Supercalandria, a machine for making China paper that's now in a bar. The workers' quarters are still outside, and the chapel is open to visitors.

The three factories had much in common. Between 1860 and 1870, the workers lived nearby – some of their houses can be seen in the San Fernando, Santa Úrsula and Niño Jesús neighbourhoods. In 1866, San Fernando and La Fama saw the country's first strikes: the factory bosses chose to hire women to produce the fabric and children to clean and maintain the machinery. The factories closed some years after the Mexican Revolution. Only Loreto carried on until the 1980s, when it went bankrupt.

An enchanted forest

Callejón Camisetas, to one side of La Fama, leads to the little wood of Fuentes Brotantes. This is a desolate place at night because many of the neighbours have spotted goblins, monsters and all kinds of ghouls there. In 1926, an exorcism was carried out but sadly that wasn't enough. So the locals have hung a sign in the alleyway that reads: '*Caminante Buen Vecino, Dios ilumina tu camino*' (Good Neighbour Wayfarer, God lights your way).

QUINTA CASANOVA PLAQUE

*An upside-down plaque, 14 kilometres from
the event it commemorates*

San Fernando 173
San Fernando Cuicuilco, Tlalpan
Metrobus: Ayuntamiento

A country house dating back to the mid 20th century, Quinta Casanova with its beautiful female figureheads has a little-known detail that can only be seen by carefully examining its adobe walls: a commemorative plaque dating from 1763 set upside down.

Even more curious is the inscription in old Spanish which mentions the construction of a water reservoir 14 kilometres from the current site of the plaque.

Researchers Delfina López Sarrelangue and Robert Hayward Barlow both state in their work on Tlatelolco that in the 1940s there was a plaque in what is now Calle Constancia in Colonia Morelos, which was similarly inscribed. It could well be the same one.

Legend has it that during the construction of the building, the owner asked for the plaque to be set in the wall here, but as the workmen were illiterate, they fixed it the wrong way up.

In the 1950s, it was common for houses to reuse old stones from demolished buildings. This is probably why this commemorative plaque was found here.

Dear Mr Barlow

On 4 January 1951, the press published an article on the death of an anthropologist following an overdose of barbiturates. A note written in Mayan was found beside his body, which read: 'Eduardo, I want to sleep, and to see no one else.' So died Robert H. Barlow, who committed suicide because of rumours about his homosexuality. Barlow studied archaeology in Mexico City and lived at Tlatelolco, where he published *Tlaltelolco, rival de Tenochtitlán* in 1948. He then moved to Azcapotzalco, where people remembered him strolling in the sunshine from his house at 37 Santander – a very different image to what might be expected of H.P. Lovecraft's youngest disciple. The American horror fiction author sent him letters that began 'Dear Mr Barlow' and were later signed 'Grandpa'. After Lovecraft's death, Barlow described him as follows: 'His acute knowledge of astronomy, history and literature ... made him a civiliser among barbarians, a closet Quetzacóatl, an imprisoned Akhenaton.'

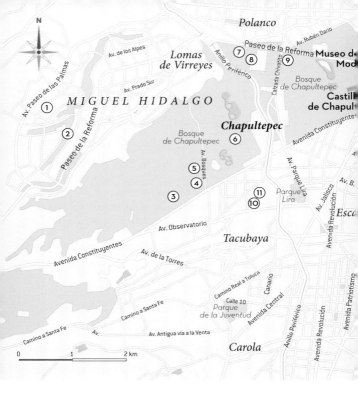

From Chapultepec to la Doctores

CASA HOLTZ

The world's largest Art Nouveau house, according to the Musée d'Orsay

Monte Ararat 5
No public access
Microbus: Route 2-17, get off at Paseo de las Palmas, junction with Monte Ararat
(Chapultepec metro station)

Towards the end of the 1960s, engineer Ignacio Holtz and his wife Beatriz Mendivil de Holtz came across an Art Nouveau vase in La Lagunilla market: this sparked off their interest in collecting objects in that style. They decided to build a house where they could install their collection. Since 1989 it has been known as Casa Holtz.

The house is an imposing mansion, whose quality of workmanship can be appreciated even from the street. The paving in front of the entrance is decorated with arabesques that seem to embrace the sidewalk. Two magnificent columns and a beautiful green gate mark the entrance; curved lines predominate throughout the house. The outdoor planters incorporate modernist metalwork, the garden railings too.

At the back of the house, three windows emerging from the foliage of a climbing plant seem to have a personality of their own. At the front, the majestic bay windows, with their semi-spherical eaves, look like huge concrete curtains, sweeping down gracefully. The mahogany windows, with their veneers, are an equally astonishing sight.

This residence seems to have come straight out of the 1900s, but was actually built 90 years later, long after the modernist style was outmoded. Such an enterprise proved difficult for the Holtzes, who carried out extensive trials with different metalworkers and carpenters.

The house had its own workshops for metalwork, carpentry, tapestry and resin. Overseen by the Holtzes from start to finish, it became a magnificent tribute to Art Nouveau architects Victor Horta and Hector Guimard.

If the house seems fairylike from the outside, from the inside it's straight out of a dream: a mahogany and bevelled-glass elevator, an interior garden with a stained-glass ceiling and, of course, the Holtzes' huge collection of Art Nouveau items, sourced mainly in Budapest, Lyon, Milan and Paris. Pieces by Louis Majorelle and Tiffany rub shoulders harmoniously. In fact, while Ignacio supervised the exterior work, it was Beatriz who took care of the interior decoration.

On completion, the four-storey, 2,300-square-metre house was designated by the Musée d'Orsay in Paris as the world's largest Art Nouveau house.

Admire the view from a balcony, on a bridge dating from the 1920s

1: Calle Monte Tabor
2: Sierra Aconcagua, junction with Monte Antuco
3: Monte Líbano, junction with Sierra Tezonco
4: Sierra Tarahumara, junction with Sierra Tezonco
5: Calle Lope Díaz de Armendáriz
Microbus: Route 2-36 destination Río Elba, Lomas km 13
Microbus: Route 2-11 towards Ahuehuetes
(Both depart from Chapultepec metro station)

ive huge, beautiful stone bridges built between 1921 and 1935 cross the hills and *barrancas* (ravines) of Chapultepec Heights. But you can't really get a good look at the bridges without leaving your car because of the vast number of trees and luxurious mansions that hide them from view. It's worth the walk ...

The bridge on Calle Monte Tabor is the only one to have been renovated in a completely modern style.

The neocolonial Sierra Aconcagua bridge, decorated with original Talavera ceramic tiles, has the best view of the watershed of Barranca de Barrilaco.

The Monte Líbano bridge is perhaps the finest of the five. Built using small pieces of *tezontle* (volcanic rock) in Art Deco style, it originally had balconies and a bench at the centre with a splendid view of the ravine. The concrete foundations still exist but a wrought-iron gate blocks off the balcony.

The Sierra Tarahumara bridge, built in '*neocolonial californiano*' style (Spanish colonial revival), on the other hand, still has its narrow balconies and some magnificent wrought-iron lamps. A narrow flight of steps leads to the base of its stone arches.

Finally, the brownish-red Lope Díaz de Armendáriz bridge, also in neocolonial style, has several semi-circular balconies. This is the lowest of the bridges, accessible from the Parque Público Cárpatos – entrance in Calle Montes Cárpatos (Barrilaco also has an athletics track, but it's closed after 7pm).

The residential area of Chapultepec Heights, designed by architect José Luis Cueva in the 1920s, was planned as a garden city. A large number of houses were built in the neocolonial style of the time, with stone carvings around windows and doors, and pitched roofs. As the residents were unhappy with the English-sounding name, President Obregón himself had it changed to Las Lomas de Chapultepec (The Hills of Chapultepec). This is still the most exclusive neighbourhood in the country.

TOMB OF TINA MODOTTI

A poem by Pablo Neruda dedicated to Tina Modott

Pantéon de Dolores: Section 18, Row 28, Tomb 26
Avenida Constituyentes, junction with Avenida Bosques
Delegación Miguel Hidalgo
Daily 7am–5pm
Admission free
Metro: Constituyentes

When celebrated Chilean poet Pablo Neruda came to Mexic as consul-general in 1940, he became friends with sever

intellectuals, among them Italian photographer Tina Modotti who had lived in Mexico since 1923. Modotti had portrayed the aesthetic side of Mexico as well as its misery – perhaps that was the reason she joined the Communist Party in 1927. But she also scandalised people as a woman who went outside after 8 o'clock at night, lived with a man who wasn't her brother or husband, and had a habit of taking a bath in the nude on the roof of her house when it rained.

Neruda cared little about the lifestyle of the photographer, who was unjustly accused of being an accomplice to the murder of her husband Julio Mella in 1929. In 1942, Neruda invited Modotti and her partner Vittorio Vidali to see in the New Year at his house. Five days later, the couple went to a party at the home of Bauhaus architect Hannes Meyer. On the way home that very night, Modotti died of heart failure.

When the press learned what had happened, a sensationalist campaign to discredit her was launched and all kinds of slander invented: they called her a communist spy, 'the mysterious Moscow woman', and even said that she'd been poisoned by Vidali himself. In the face of this scandal, Neruda composed the poem *Tina Modotti ha muerto* (Tina Modotti has died), an epitaph in which he evokes the spirit of his friend while castigating the press. Neruda sent the poem to all the newspapers and, to his surprise, they published it next day on the front page.

In his memoir *Confieso que he vivido* (I Confess that I Have Lived), Neruda describes the wake: 'To see the suffering of such a tough, brave man [Vidali] is not a pleasant sight. That lion was bleeding when his wound received the corrosive poison of the infamy that wanted to stain Tina Modotti once again, but she was already dead.'

It was impossible to raise enough money for the funeral, so Modotti was buried in the paupers' section of Dolores cemetery. Her grave was covered with the communist flag, engraver Leopoldo Méndez drew her profile on the granite and Neruda came to read her epitaph, part of which was later inscribed in the tomb.

Modotti still rests in the same place. Her grey tomb would pass unnoticed if it weren't for Neruda's poem and Méndez's portrait marking it out among the weeds.

There is another funerary monument to Tina Modotti in the Italian section of the cemetery, as a tribute to their compatriot.

TOMB OF FATHER PRO

Go down to the crypt and discover a shrine

Pantéon de Dolores
Constituyentes, junction with Bosques - Delegación Miguel Hidalgo
Daily 7am–5pm
Admission free
Metro: Constituyentes

Among the tombstones of the 9th section of Dolores cemetery is the old Jesuit plot where the remains of martyr Miguel Agustín Pro were laid to rest (see p. 193). The entrance gate to his tomb, covered with depictions of his miracles, is always open to give the faithful and the curious access to the crypt. Inside is a rather gloomy shrine decorated with flowers and a picture of Father Pro.

During the persecution of Catholics in the Cristero War and the struggle against the laws on religion, an attempt was made on the life of General Álvaro Obregón on 13 November 1927. Father Pro was accused of being implicated in the attack and sentenced to death, without trial or proof. He was shot on 23 November the same year.

A procession of around 500 cars and over 20,000 people is said to have lined the 8-kilometre-route from the place of execution to the crypt in Dolores cemetery, venting their anger at the government and singing the Cristeros hymn.

The entrance to the crypt and the medallion bearing Father Pro's portrait were made by his followers, who represented eternal glory by the crown of palms and the colourful decorations they added.

Just three months later, they began to receive favours and miracles on matters where they had asked Father Pro to intervene. Throughout the 1940s and 50s several plaques were erected to thank him. The first was from a woman who had asked him, while he was still alive, for help with her financial problems. On learning of his execution, she went to see the lawyer dealing with the case. He replied that Father Pro himself had come to sort out her situation just ten minutes earlier.

Since the beatification process began, at some point in the 1980s or 90s the martyr's remains were transferred to the Sagrada Familia parish, but this shrine is still visited by pilgrims, especially on the anniversary of his death, 23 November.

TOMB OF CONCHITA JURADO

'The great Don/Doña of spoofers'

Constituyentes, s/n
Panteón de Dolores
Tomb on Avenida Bosques, Gate 6 of cemetery
Daily (except public holidays) 7am–5pm, Gate 6 open 8am–5pm
Admission free
Metro: Constituyentes

Near Gate 6 of Dolores cemetery is the strange tomb of one of the most loved and most hated women to captivate Mexican society in the early 20th century.

The tomb of actress Conchita Jurado, better known as the tomb of Don Carlos Balmori, is covered with hand-painted tiles. Although some are missing, the tomb is still elaborately roguish.

In 1926, Spanish millionaire Carlos Balmori had just arrived in Mexico. He had the reputation of being extremely generous and well connected. He was a friend of Tsar Nicolas II and Alfonso XIII of Spain, owned iron foundries in Durango and coffee plantations in Brazil, as well as interests in Canadian forestry and whale oil fisheries.

Politicians, servicemen, businessmen, everyone down to the most humble, wanted to meet Don Carlos at a *balmoreada*, as they were called – social gatherings organised in his Coyoacán villa. All the covetous guests vied to become Don Carlos's friend, but his party piece was to threaten a new 'friend' with death or even propose marriage to someone's wife. When the joke reached its climax, Don Carlos would whip off his moustache, slouch hat and glasses to reveal a 60-year-old woman, merrily apologising for the hoax.

Conchita deceived countless people for five action-packed years, until she died on 27 November 1931. A year later, all her friends met in Dolores cemetery to build this tomb as a lasting reminder. Each tile illustrates one of her *balmoreadas*. The only picture of Conchita herself has disappeared, but a verse at the site recalls: 'Here ends the tale that entertained great and small, and that still rings with her cruel laughter.'

Her tomb is a picturesque vignette of early 20th-century society. The band of mourners even made a punning epitaph for her tomb: 'the great Don/Doña of spoofers', who still behaves mischievously at 'fiestas of unsurpassed fantasy'.

CÁMARA LAMBDOMA

A sound installation activated by light, air and water

Museo del Cárcamo de Chapultepec
Avenida Neri Vela, s/n
Second section of Bosque de Chapultepec
planverde.df.gob.mx/carcamodedolores/
Tuesday to Sunday 10am–5pm
Entrance ticket includes admission to Museo de Historia Natural

As you enter the little museum of Cárcamo de Chapultepec, dedicated to the work of Diego Rivera, metallic voices seem to emanate from the walls. The sound comes from copper and brass tubes inside the museum. Outside, past Rivera's mural, a strange metal tube overhangs a walkway. Inside the building is a black and gold case that resembles an Art Deco radio.

All these elements, often missed by visitors, make up the *Cámara Lambdoma* (Lambdoma Chamber), a sound installation designed by Mexican artist Ariel Guzik and activated by light, air and water.

The outside tube records the light intensity and the air speed, as well as the movement of the water from the Lerma river flowing beneath the building. It sends this information to the *Cámara Lambdoma*, which generates signals that control the sounds of the various instruments.

One organ reproduces harmonic sounds and another subharmonic sounds, in other words those that can be heard and those that can be felt. So close proximity to the subharmonic organ can affect your senses and state of mind.

Numbers on the machine and on the floor are accompanied by strange words that seem to be written in Arabic. In fact, they are the frequencies of the instruments in a notation invented by the artist, reflecting the natural elements – each coloured pebble in the *Cámara Lambdoma* signifies a particular element.

Rivera wanted water to be a fundamental part of the mural *El Agua, origen de la vida* (Water, Source of Life), so it was intended to be viewed alongside running water. Unfortunately the painting deteriorated and, in an effort to conserve it, the flow of water was stopped and the mural was no longer in harmony with nature. The *Cámara Lambdoma* was created to give it a voice again.

The security guards say that the best tunes are those played during electrical storms, on windy days, or at night.

MEMORIAL A LAS VÍCTIMAS DE LA VIOLENCIA

An imposing memorial

Paseo de la Reforma, junction with Anatole France
Admission free
Metro: Auditorio

The Memorial to the Victims of Violence, at one end of the first section of the Bosque de Chapultepec (Chapultepec Park), is a place of reflection that seeks to pay tribute to all those affected by the violence in Mexico City in recent decades.

The path begins in the far north of the park and follows a trail of horizontal steel plates bearing quotations on death, violence and peace. They lead to the centre of the memorial, where four pools of water mirror an imposing landscape of huge vertical plates and trees. Along the entrance path, visitors sometimes leave signs, graffiti or messages relating to their experience of violence, as a way of coming to terms with it.

A total of 64 steel plates have been inscribed with the names of victims of violence. One of them picks out the groups affected in different colours, such as the students massacred during 'El Halconazo' of 1971, the EZLN (Zapatista Army for National Liberation) militants who disappeared and were executed in 1994, the people tortured and executed in Atenco in 2006, the journalists murdered since 1973, the victims of femicide and the some 116,000 deaths recorded by INEGI (National Institute of Statistics and Geography) during the war on drug trafficking in 2005 and 2012. One by one, the names of all the victims are listed.

On a plaque by the entrance path, Comité 68 explains its background (it was set up in 1968 as the Committee for Democratic Liberties) and how information was collected for the memorial.

The installation was created with the support of the Colegio de Arquitectos de la Cuidad de México, which chose the Gaeta-Springall Arquitectos project following a competition in 2012. In order to make the memorial accessible to as many people as possible, Braille plates for the visually impaired are placed along the trail, which is also wheelchair accessible.

SCULPTURES IN PLAZA DEL SERVICIO A LA PATRIA

Decommissioned weapons made into sculptures

Paseo de la Reforma, junction with Auditorio Nacional
Plaza del Servicio a la Patria
Tuesday to Saturday 10am–6pm
Admission free
Metro: Auditorio

The Plaza del Servicio a la Patria, a garden in Campo Deportivo Militar Marte (venue for military and equestrian events), is a tribute to soldiers killed in the service of their homeland.

Each of the 32 marble sculptures spread around the garden represents one state of the Mexican Republic. Like a jigsaw puzzle, they fit perfectly with the central fountain.

The 32 sculptures made from arms confiscated from organised crime are, however, the most curious feature of this site. Each weapon has been carefully treated to prevent it ever being used again. Like the blocks of marble, the arms sculptures each represent a state: a scorpion for Durango, a deer for Nayarit, a wolf for Sonora and a whale for Baja California Sur.

Among the sculptures of cactus, macaws and horses, weapons such as rifles, pistols, revolvers and even shotguns, are clearly identifiable. The back end of the bison that represents the state of Chihuahua is a striking silver revolver with a fanciful design.

The most awe-inspiring is perhaps the head of the Mayan ruler Pakal, which represents the state of Chiapas. This sculpture is an optical illusion – seen from the front against background light, his face emerges among the weapons.

The most unusual sculpture relates to Mexico City: a bicycle with 10 saddles and weighing 800 kilos to represent the ecological culture and friendliness of the city.

From the iguana and the toucan to an Atlantean stone warrior from Tula and a *chinelo* (dancer's) mask, each sculpture has its own fact sheet with the exact weight, height, length and width, so that no details are missing.

The plaza also has its own cultural centre and a permanent guard of honour.

A sculpture on the Mexico–USA border

During the Mexican drug war, a controversial sculpture – also made from the decommissioned weapons of organised crime – was installed at the border crossing between Mexico and the United States. Unveiled by former president Felipe Calderón, it was a spectacular work 21-metres-high bearing the legend 'NO MORE WEAPONS!' This message was addressed to the US following the discovery of the huge volume of arms sales and trafficking across the border into Mexico. The sculpture was removed in 2015.

POEM AT PABELLÓN COREANO

Lamentations from exile

Jardín de Adultos Mayores
Avenida Chivatito, junction with Paseo de la Reforma
Park open only for the over-60s
Daily 9am–5pm
Admission free
Metro: Auditorio

As its name suggests, the Jardín de Adultos Mayores (Garden of the Elderly) in the city's Bosque de Chapultepec is only open to those over 60. So all the rest will just have to wait a while to discover the secrets of the beautiful Korean pagoda there.

This is a replica of a pagoda in Seoul's Tapgol Park, starting point of the South Korean Independence Protest in 1919. Construction began on 26 October 1967 and the pagoda was opened in 1968 on the occasion of the Mexico Olympic Games, symbolising the friendly relations between Korea and Mexico.

While the interior shows great artistic skill, the best-kept secret is inscribed around the walls – the poem *Sok Miin Gok* by Jeong Cheol, Korean Buddhist politician and poet. This was written in 1584 when Cheol was falsely accused and sent into exile on an island off the Korean peninsula. He describes the magnificent mountainous landscape around him and the feeling of nostalgia when living away from the empire. Although the poem has been interpreted as a widow in mourning, it's actually the servile lament of a woman before an emperor who ignores her.

The poem is particularly difficult to understand nowadays as the script is no longer in use. It was written in the 16th century, when the classical Korean alphabet was still competing with Hangul, the alphabet created by Yi dynasty monarch Sejong to eradicate illiteracy. Aristocrats, scholars and poets resisted the introduction of Hangul until 1894, when the new script was accepted, although it underwent considerable transformations under Japanese rule. Since 1945, when South Korea gained its independence, Hangul has been in general use and the classical alphabet can now only be deciphered by experts.

Under the Joseon dynasty (1392–1897), the Buddhist Temple in Seoul's Tapgol Park adopted the poem reproduced in the Chapultepec pagoda.
A curious coincidence, because Tapgol is now the main meeting place for Seoul elders, while the Mexican park is exclusively for over-60s. As if older people were the only ones who can understand the feelings of nostalgia and melancholy felt by the neglected woman of the poem.

MAPOTECA MANUEL OROZCO Y BERRA

The most extraordinary maps in the Mexican Republic

Avenida Observatorio 192, between General Platas and Ex Arzobispado
West wing of Servicio Meteorológico Nacional headquarters
(+52) 3871 8500 Ext. 48205 / 48206 – mapoteca.siap.gob.mx
Monday to Friday 9am–3pm and 4pm–6pm
Admission free
Metro: Tacubaya / Constituyentes

Despite the vast space, it's hard to believe that the Manuel Orozco y Berra Cartographic Library contains over 150,000 documents and topographic maps, most of which date from the 19th century (the library was established by the Cartographic Department in 1877).

Admission to the building usually includes a guided tour – it's more like visiting a museum with a friend than going through an archive. The shelves reveal early surveying instruments, such as the 20-metre chain used in the 17th century to measure land, and topographical machines from the early 20th century, so fragile that they have to be stored in a metal capsule inside a wooden box. The practice of topography was very complex in the 19th century, as borne out by the showcase full of objects whose use is unknown.

If you decide to look round on your own, don't miss the atlas commissioned by Porfirio Díaz to clarify the boundaries between Mexico and Guatemala – it's housed in huge boxes at the entrance.

Don't forget to ask to see the first panoramic photograph of Mexico City, and the map showing Cíbola and Quivira – two of the mythical cities of gold. On the 19th century maps, try to locate Bermeja, a phantom island in the Gulf of Mexico that delimits the country's maritime territory but has never been found.

Framed on the staircase is the most emblematic and curious document in the library: the Cuadro Sinóptico de Historia Natural (Synoptic Table of Natural History). Influenced by Mexican positivism (the guiding philosophy of the Porfirian era, which sought to bring order to society), it depicts the mineral, animal and plant kingdoms as the branches of a tree. Below, the development of the Earth, the formation of continents and volcanic eruptions are all covered. Note that the top of the tree represents what was once considered the peak of human evolution, the 'Caucasian caste'.

During the Mexican Revolution, it was probably women who carried out the topographical surveys. Two photos of young women displayed on the wall seem to confirm this.

Don Manuel's collection

When historian Manuel Orozco y Berra aspired to write a complete history of Mexico in 1860, he noticed that the national territory was not clearly defined. So he began to collect all kinds of maps of the country, even pre-Hispanic codices. When he couldn't acquire the originals, he copied them by hand. On his death in 1881, he donated his collection to the state, which named the Cartographic Library after him. All his maps, both copies and originals, are preserved here.

MUSEO DE GEOFÍSICA

Explore a seismological station dating from 1910

General Victoriano Zepeda 53
(+52) 5271 1068
Reservations and guided tours: museo@geofisica.unam.mx
Monday to Friday 10am–2pm
Admission free
Metro: Tacubaya

n 1910, the Estación Sismológica Central (Central Seismological Station) of Tacubaya was opened in three separate buildings. It was equipped with the most advanced measuring instruments of its day, including a 17-tonne seismograph. All these instruments are still on site, which is now open to the public.

The tour begins in the central building with a display of recordings of the 1985 earthquake and the famous 1911 earthquake known as the *temblor de Madero* (Madero tremor). In the basement are instruments such as astrolabes and gravimeters, for celestial and terrestrial measurements respectively. There's also a tide gauge that measures sea levels and recorded the tsunami that hit Acapulco in 1995.

The architecture of the other two buildings is very unusual. Each building houses different seismographs, but the three are connected in a way that's designed to maintain the stability of the instruments during an earthquake of any magnitude. In both buildings the instruments are sited as if the station was still operating.

The oldest instrument in the building on the right is known as the Bosch-Omori seismometer, in tribute to its inventors (although pioneer Fusakichi Omori, who arrived in Mexico in 1904 as the country's first seismologist, did most of the work). The conservation conditions are so good that the seismometer is still in working order.

The most recent device is a Güralp seismic sensor, donated to the museum in 2010, which can show movement in real time on a screen. Even someone jumping around the room will be recorded. There's also a seismometer with a vertical pendulum, which was the station's first instrument.

The building on the left holds the museum's star attractions: the Wiechert seismometer and the Grand Wiechert of 17 tonnes, whose pendulum can oscillate up to 2,000 times in order to measure the

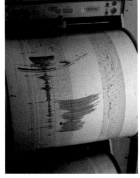

magnitude of an earthquake as accurately as possible. In addition to the age and historical importance of this instrument (German geo-physicist Emil Wiechert was a pioneer of the study of seismic waves), it's one of the few in the world still functioning.

The museum also features original instruments from the former Rayos Cósmicos pavilion (see p. 150), which can measure cosmic and solar radiation, and even has a complete station for analysing variations in the Earth's magnetic field.

CAPILLA ALFONSINA

Last refuge of Alfonso Reyes: a unique collection of lead soldiers

Benjamín Hill 122
(+52) 8647 5410 – capillaalfonsina.bellasartes.gob.mx
Monday to Friday 9am–3.30pm; visits can be booked outside opening hours
Admission free
Metro: Patriotismo

The library of Alfonso Reyes (1889–1959), one of the most distinguished Mexican men of letters of his time, was all he needed to complement his genius. That's why his friend, Spanish poet Enrique Díez-Canedo, baptised the sanctuary Capilla Alfonsina (Alfonso's Chapel).

Although construction only began in 1938, the building had long existed in Reyes' imagination. He was looking for something functional: two floors with a mezzanine and an office at the top, near the windows for natural light, and some little tables for reference works. The image he had in mind was so clear that it only took a single sketch for architect Carlos Rousseau to bring it to life.

Reyes was a small, corpulent man. He spent whole days in his 'chapel', sometimes down on the carpet with his son playing at soldiers, sometimes gazing at the scale models of Columbus's three ships or amusing himself dressed up to dance the *zarzuela*.

In public life, he was a diplomat serving as ambassador and sometimes minister, a life that allowed him to acquire some Brazilian modernist paintings. To his friends he was a writer who gave advice with humility

and who received with open arms anyone who asked for his help. To thank him for his generosity, the foundry in his home town of Monterrey presented him with the steel beams that support the chapel roof. He zealously guarded the portraits painted by his friends Rodríguez Lozano and Roberto Montenegro. He also possessed a Cubist canvas by Diego Rivera, a wonderful bust of Adolfo Ponzanelli, and watercolours by Angelina Beloff. Artists' muse Kiki de Montparnasse drew him with angel's wings and asked when he was next coming to Paris, while Argentine author Jorge Luis Borges considered him a close friend.

The library is preserved just as it was: the letters, the paintings, the little soldiers and even the sketch of the chapel. Only the books have been moved to Monterrey, but the collection of crime novels that were so close to his heart – and which he used to rate from 1 to 10 – is still there. When inside, you almost expect the man to appear any second on the threshold, come over and sit in his chair, read a book and smoke his pipe.

Despite Reyes' poor health, he continued to write poems, scripts and above all, folktales, while enjoying time spent in the company of fellow writers Carlos Pellicer, Salvador Novo, Rodolfo Usigli and Xavier Villaurrutia, not to mention fine wine. Sadly, his fifth heart attack killed him: two days after the Christmas dinner prepared by his wife Manuelita, Reyes died in his bed (which is still there), in the shelter of his chapel.

Reyes' collection of lead soldiers, dating from 1927 and unique of its kind, represents the protagonists of the 1521 conquest of Tenochtitlán.

HAND-CRANKED CAR

13

A life-size piece of nostalgia

Junction of Guadalajara and Veracruz
Colonia Condesa
Metro: Chapultepec

A car parked at the junction of Guadalajara and Veracruz, fitted with a huge key, looks like one of those old metal wind-up toys.

If you look through the window, you'll see that the driver and the car fittings are actually made from brass. The steering wheel is labelled *Chevrolet D.F. y Condesa*, indicating that the car belongs to the hotel of that name, on the same corner.

The 1949 Chevrolet is a work by Mexican visual artist Betsabeé Romero, who made it for the Hotel Condesa in 2005. At the time, Agustín Lara's song *Veracruz* rang out when the key was turned.

In 2009, when the car was shown at the *A Vuelta de Rueda* (At Snail's Pace) exhibition, it was nicknamed '*el carrito de cuerda*' ('the hand-cranked car') but unfortunately the song no longer played.

The exhibition involved the artistic transformation of various cars, each on a different theme: history, religion, migration, the environment, etc.

This *carrito* alludes to cars seen as playthings by humans, and recalls the time when they became fashionable in Colonia Condesa, in the 1940s. Romero took six months to complete his work, which he called *Memoria de hojalata* (Tin Memory), like a life-size piece of nostalgia.

NEARBY

Fideicomiso Archivos Plutarco Elías Calles y Fernando Torreblanca

(+52) 5286 8339 / 5211 4999
fapecft.org.mx
fapec@fapecft.org.mx

The magnificent and imposing residence at 104 Guadalajara is home to the Plutarco Elías Calles and Fernando Torreblanca Archives Trust. Built in 1922, it was the home of Hortensia Elías Calles (daughter of former President Plutarco Elías Calles: see p. 21) and her husband, Fernando Torreblanca. In 1986, Hortensia donated the archives that told the story of her controversial father, together with the house, as a valuable historical testament. Visitors are only received by appointment after writing to explain why they would like to visit.

CENTENARY TREE

14

His ashes lie scattered under the tree he planted to celebrate the centenary

Sonora, junction with Oaxaca
Parque España, Colonia Hipódromo Condesa
Metrobus: Sonora

A t the northern end of Parque España, between Oaxaca and Sonora, an *ahuehuete* (Mexican cypress) stands among the trees and shrubs. The marble plaque in front of it, dated 21 September 1921, bears the name 'Árbol del Centenario' (Centenary Tree).

Colonia Hipódromo Condesa began to take shape in the 1920s, coinciding with the 100th anniversary of Mexico's independence from Spain, which involved grand fiestas and commemorations.

The economic crisis that Mexico was going through at the time meant that not all planned public works could be completed. In the Hipódromo district, however, a decision was made to celebrate the centenary by planting the native tree of Mexico to inaugurate the park - causing quite a sensation around the city.

The park was designed by architect José Luis Caves. The mayor of Mexico City, Herminio Pérez Abreu, had chosen the site because, among other things, it was opposite his house. Pérez Abreu planted the tree as part of an elaborate ceremony in the presence of Spanish minister Saavedra de Magdalena, while the police band played the Spanish royal march.

When Pérez Abreu died, his daughter scattered his ashes around the tree, and some years later did the same on the death of her husband. The ritual became part of a family tradition, and the ashes of the academic and writer José María Pérez Gay (1944–2013, grandson of Pérez Abreu), also rest at the base of the tree.

Ironically, the tree dedicated to the centenary of Mexico's independence from Spain was planted in a park that was later to be called Parque España (Park of Spain).

The racecourse that was never used

The racecourse that was never used is the site of the main parks and avenues of Colonia Hipódromo Condesa.

The track is now Avenida Ámsterdam, which encircles Parque México, while nearby Parque España was to have been the main entrance to the racecourse.

AGUSTÍN LARA'S LITTLE LAMPPOST

An Art Deco lamppost that inspired Agustín Lara?

Central reservation of Avenida Ámsterdam, junction with Celaya
Metrobus: Sonora

n the late 1920s the central reservation of Avenida Ámsterdam was given a series of benches and lampposts in a blend of Art Deco and neocolonial styles, said to have inspired composer Agustín Lara's famous song *Farolito*.

He rented a studio one block away, in Edificio San Antonio (number 5 Celaya), a huge Art Deco building owned by a French woman named Pampin, in which he organised wild parties and gatherings. It was here that songs such as *Serpentina* and *Concha nácar* were written. In 1935, the Águila sisters sang *Farolito* for the first time. The writers Guadalupe Loaeza and Pável Granados claim that their performance was so extraordinary that Agustín didn't notice that they'd forgotten the tune.

Art Deco in Colonia Hipódromo

The sale of land in the Hipódromo neighbourhood took place in 1927, at the height of Art Deco's popularity, as in many other places in Mexico City (Colonia San Rafael and Villa de Cortés). This explains why it now has one of the largest open-air Art Deco displays to be seen anywhere. From the Centro Histórico to the Panteón Francés cemetery, shops, galleries, cultural centres and administrative buildings bring alive this architectural style found all over the world: Rio de Janeiro, New York, Paris, Brussels. The most beautiful examples are in the buildings around Parque San Martín, for example numbers 6, 33, 123 and 188 Avenida Mexico. Other splendid façades are Edificio Lux (Popocatépetl 36), Edificio Michoacán (Michoacán 54), numbers 408 and 418 Insurgentes, as well as 8 and 46 Chilpancingo, 235 and 241 Ámsterdam, and 11 Ozuluama.

In the neighbouring Colonia Roma, Edificio Río de Janeiro (Orizaba 56), which in fact dates from 1908, is an example of subsequent architectural modifications. Through the window at the entrance you can admire the interior, restored in the 1930s in Art Deco style by architect Francisco Serrano.

MUSEO DEL PADRE PRO

Hold a clandestine Mass in Chinese disguise, with a suitcase for an altar

Puebla 144
Colonia Roma
(+52) 5511 9035 Ext 21
padrepro.com.mx
padre.pro@hotmail.com
Tuesday to Sunday 10am–1pm
Donations welcome
Metro: Insurgentes

The Museum of Father Pro, next to Sagrada Familia church, holds the personal belongings of the Blessed Miguel Agustín Pro, a man falsely accused without proof and sentenced to death for supporting an attempt on the life of former president Álvaro Obregón on 13 November 1927. Father Pro was shot on 23 November, spreading his arms and proclaiming '*Viva Cristo Rey!*' (Long Live Christ the King!). This happened during the *Cristiada* (Cristero War), when the Roman Catholic bishops had suspended all public worship in protest against the Ley Calles (Calles Law) regulating religious freedoms. In addition to Father Pro's personal items, the clothes he was wearing at his execution and the act of beatification granted by Pope John Paul II are on display.

Newspapers, photographs and books retrace the context of his life and death. Among the most interesting are the objects he used to officiate at clandestine Masses. Although the celebration of Mass had been banned by the bishops and the government, the priests (among them Father Pro) and the people kept up their religious traditions, relying on their audacity and creativity to fight against repression. Among the equipment for the clandestine Masses was a suitcase that served as an altar. The vestments and liturgical objects were reversible: violet for worship and black for ceremonies relating to death.

Thanks to his many disguises, Father Pro escaped the attention of the authorities. In one of the photos he is disguised as a workman and in another as a Chinese mandarin, though he also used to dress as a farmer or a man about town. He sent balloons with religious propaganda flying round the city and heard confessions on a stone bench in Paseo de la Reforma. When addressed as Pbro. (*presbítero*: priest), he replied that there must be some confusion with his name, Pro.

It's said that while he was holding Mass in someone's house, the police came to arrest him. He greeted them cigar in hand, showed them round the house (which he wasn't familiar with)  and, pretending to be the owner, told them, 'Gentlemen, it's getting late, I'm planning to go out with my fiancée and don't have time to wait until you arrest this shameless priest who's making a fool of you ... '

Father Pro was convinced he'd be canonised one day. One of his sayings in the care of the museum bears this out: 'I want to be part of this class of saints: a saint who eats, sleeps, makes mischief and many miracles!'

Father Pro is buried in the baptistery of Sagrada Familia church.

REVOLVING STATUE OF CANTINFLAS

A Latin American icon

Álvaro Obregón 123, in front of Obregón Hospital, between Orizaba and Jalap
Colonia Roma
Metrobus: Álvaro Obregón

Anyone visiting Colonia Roma has to walk along Avenida Álvaro Obregón. Because of its strange location on the sidewalk near the Obregón Hospital, looking out over the ambulances, the statue of comic actor and screenwriter Mario Moreno (known professionally as Cantinflas) is easily missed.

There's something curious about the design of the monument. You'll see a disc at the base that can be pushed to turn the statue around. Whatever position the statue is in, thanks to the general subsidence in Mexico City (aggravated by the construction of the hospital, which was only built in 1995), the principle of inertia always returns it to its original position. Don't be afraid to spin the statue around to fully appreciate it – if it falls on someone, first aid is always at hand.

It would be interesting to know why a statue of Cantinflas was erected here: perhaps because he was a local personality, living at number 11 Bajío. But this is strange as he owned a number of houses all around Mexico.

When the statue was ready, the administrative formalities to install it on the central reservation of Álvaro Obregón began, but authorisation was refused on the grounds that it would spoil the character of the avenue. The Galería Nonita gave permission for the statue to be installed on the sidewalk in front of their premises, thus leaving the central reservation intact.

ARCHIVO GENERAL DE SUEÑOS Y UTOPÍAS

'Please don't leave nightmares'

Chihuahua 129, Colonia Roma
(+52) 5584 5613
tallertlamaxcalli.wordpress.com

A plaque on the wall of a building in Huasteca Chilanga reads 'Archivo General de Sueños y Utopías' (General Archive of Dreams and Utopias). Below is a little transparent box, the 'mailbox of dreams', in which anyone is invited to leave a note telling of their dreams – with a warning not to leave any nightmares.

This mailbox is the property of craftworkers Álvaro Santillán and Jazmín Juárez, who archive all kinds of dreams and turn them into stories to entertain people. They have collected dreams of love and romance, as well as sad dreams and mournful stories.

Next door is the Tlamaxcalli workshop, where Álvaro and Jazmín make cardboard *alebrijes* (fantastic animal sculptures from the popular art of the Mexican state of Oaxaca), based on the notes they've received. They also create and sell curious, popular Mexican toys, which are becoming increasingly hard to find. In addition to readings of stories and legends, they organise workshops to make masks, puppets, devils and of course, *alebrijes*.

Alebrijes

The origins of *alebrijes* – colourful animals made from wood and cardboard, with a bird-shaped body, mammalian head and reptilian tail – are shrouded in mystery. Some say that they were invented by painter José Antonio Gómez Rosas, known as El Hotentote, others that they were popularised in 1927 by Oaxaca tailor Manuel Jiménez, but the generally accepted version is that of filmmaker Judith Bronowski, who made the 1975 documentary *Pedro Linares, artesano cartonero* (Pedro Linares, Artisan in Cardboard). In it, we get to meet the *alebrijes*, monstrous figures that, according to the story, Pedro Linares dreamed of when he was very ill. In his dream, the strange animals were shouting 'Alebrijes!', and when he awoke he made cardboard models of them. Such figures are now traditional Mexican crafts, and every year the Museo de Arte Popular organises a nocturnal parade of monumental *alebrijes*. Afterwards they are hidden in various cultural venues around the city.

MONUMENT TO ROCKDRIGO

The prickly pear prophet lost in Balderas metro station

Inside Balderas metro station, interchange between Line 3 (green) and Line ▪
(pink)
Metro: Balderas

I n the corridors of Balderas metro station, between Line 3 (green
and Line 1 (pink), the statue of a guitar player merges with the

hurrying crowd oblivious to his presence. A plaque bears the message: '*Gracias Rockdrigo, un homenaje de la vieja cuidad de hierro*' (Thank you Rockdrigo, a tribute from the old iron city).

The man with guitar is Rodrigo González, a musician who lived in an apartment in Colonia Juárez and played in a bar at Insurgentes junction. Better known as Rockdrigo, he was the promoter of the Mexican 'Rupestre' rock movement of the late 1980s. In his manifesto, Rockdrigo gives the following explanation:

'*Rupestres* are usually simple people, and unlike some artists they don't overdo it. They have so much to offer with their guitars and their rum-soaked voices; they are poets and lunatics, rockers and troubadours. Simple yet complicated, in love with fantasy, they insult everyday life; they play like Venusian carpenters and bellow like calves at a final conservatoire exam.'

One of Rockdrigo's best-known songs, accompanied simply by guitar and harmonica, *En la estación del metro Balderas* (In Balderas Metro Station), is the reason why the monument was erected here:

... It's been four years since I lost my love,
Among the crowds that are forming here.
I looked for her on the platforms and in the waiting rooms,
But she got lost in Balderas station.
In Balderas metro station, a human wave bore her away,
In Balderas metro station, my love, I've searched for you from train to train ...

Rockdrigo died on 19 September 1985, when an earthquake destroyed his home in Colonia Juárez. Also known as 'the prickly pear prophet', on the anniversary of his death he is remembered with a pot of the cactus placed at the foot of his statue. As the song says, it too goes unnoticed among the crowds at Balderas metro station.

MUSEO DEL JUGUETE
ARTE-OBJETO FRIDA

Art treasures in the basement of a tram station

Claudio Bernard 111, Colonia Doctores
Basement of Estación Indianilla
(+52) 5761 9058
estacionindianilla.com.mx
Daily 9.30am–6pm
Admission free
Metro: Niños Héroes

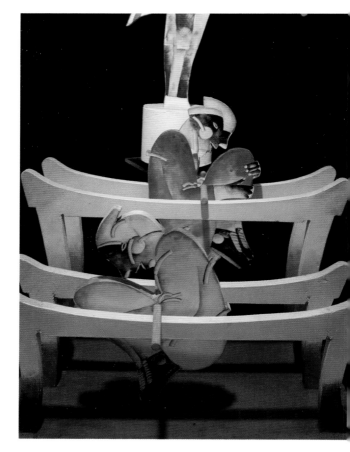

In the bowels of the Centro Cultural Estación Indianilla – a contemporary art gallery in the former Indianilla tram station – is an unusual museum devoted to art objects and toys.

The exhibits displayed in the ancient labyrinthine basement corridors, and which come from four Bienales Internacionales de Juguete Arte-Objeto (International Creative Toy Biennials), are among the city's art treasures.

The most eye-catching objects, reinterpreted by contemporary artists, are the incomparable faces of muralist José Luis Cuevas's wrestlers, Francisco Toledo's friendly carved wooden horses, Vicente Rojo's unusual building blocks and surrealist Leonora Carrington's bewitching silver cow.

To see all the exhibits you'll need to lose yourself in what was once the station repair shop, so don't be surprised to see the huge machinery still hanging from the roof. Jazzamoart, Raúl Anguiano, Gabriel Macotela, Manuel Felguérez, Olga Dondé and Joy Laville are among the well-known artists exhibiting puzzles, dolls, trains, model horses and a puppet theatre, all reinterpreted in their own way.

El Calacóptero and *El Calacarro* by Fermín Vissuet are two unusual vehicles made from chicken heads and feet. But it's a shame you can't watch Brian Nissen's acrobats perform, nor play with *Mujer sensual* (Sensual Woman), a rag doll with the suggestive apples that are typical of Martha Chapa's work.

The museum is named after Frida Masri Dabbah, Isaac Masri's sister, killed when the truck she was travelling in fell into a ravine. Isaac decided to set up a museum in her memory. At the entrance to the exhibition, visual artist Yani Pecanins uses everyday objects to pay tribute to Frida.

In addition to the museum, the Cultural Centre has a workshop for lithography, engraving and binding, as well as a cafeteria and bookstore.

Isaac Masri is a dentist who opened a practice in Las Lomas de Chapultepec. In 1974, one of his first patients was José Luis Cuevas and the two men became firm friends. Soon afterwards he was enjoying the company of Leonora Carrington, Alberto Blanco and Gunther Gerzo. Later he met other intellectuals, cultural experts, gallery owners and politicians. On the advice of museum expert Fernando Gamboa, Masri became a patron of the arts. He has curated exhibitions on the Reform laws and the construction of Indianilla station. Known as 'the last of the patrons', he boasts of knowing Mexican culture inside out.

INSTITUTO DE CIENCIAS FORENSES STAINED-GLASS WINDOWS

The city's tragedies in spectacular stained glass

Avenida Niños Héroes 130
Colonia Doctores
Metro: Niños Héroes

Although the Dr Guillermo Soberón Acevedo Institute of Forensic Sciences is off-limits to the public, you can still admire its spectacular stained-glass windows that illustrate the great tragedies the city has known. The images can be seen from the street, especially when the inside lights are on.

In the window that represents Day, an angel weaves a DNA chain that the god of the afterlife leads towards a mound of skulls, then into the world of shadows. In the lower corner, a body is being examined by several doctors on a dissection table imprinted with a large question mark. The window at the entrance embodies Night, and in the centre two doctors are consoling a woman dressed in white. The metaphorical disasters are instantly recognisable to any resident of Mexico City: the clock that stopped at the beginning of the 1985 earthquake; the two trains that collided at Viaducto metro station in 1975; the plane that crashed at Mexico City international airport in 1979; a helicopter falling from the sky; and a pack of wolves in one of the city's urban parks.

In other horizontal windows on the first floor, forensic scientists are shown at their graduation through to their presence in court, as well as in the fingerprint, dissection and ballistic laboratories. The highest window on the third floor is an allegory of life and death, where an indigenous Mexican is shown bidding farewell to his family before journeying to the Aztec underworld, Mictlán.

A little further north, on the wall of the medical forensics building, is a stone diptych called *La vida y la muerte* (Life and Death). Opposite is a replica of the mother earth goddess Coatlicue. A plaque explains the carving: on the left, the female deity Omecihuatl exhales life (represented by a foetus) while the Sun god Tonatiuh warms the new life. He is surrounded by a frame created by Quetzacóatl, who gave the world fire. On the right a *tzompantli* (wall of skulls) shelters Coyolxauhqui, goddess of the Moon, who watches over human existence. Above the scene, the male deity Ometecuhtli (counterpart of Omecihuatl) completes the cosmic duality of life and death.

MALVERDE'S STATUE

22

The only life-size statue of Jesús Malverde

Dr Liceaga, corner of Dr Vértiz
Colonia Doctores
Metro: Doctores

The Capilla de Malverde (Malverde chapel) is a shrine built in 2005 among the shops in one of the city's most infamous districts. Behind the barrier are various statues of the Santa Muerte (Holy Death). In a display window on the sidewalk nearby stand two life-size statues: one of Jesús Malverde and the other of the Santa Muerte. Neither figure is recognised by the Roman Catholic Church although some people have begun to revere them as saints.

Malverde, wearing his trademark shirt and boots, sombrero and moustache, has a noose hung around his neck as usual. Bottles of liquor, tequila and other alcoholic drinks are piled on shelves at the back of the window, as offerings in thanks for favours that the saint is said to have granted.

There's an urban legend that a 15-year-old boy named Marcos was involved in a dramatic car crash in this neighbourhood. Hovering between life and death, he entrusted his fate to Malverde, whom he knew through his mother. He miraculously survived, and promised to dedicate an altar in Malverde's honour: he kept his promise with this life-size statue. There's nothing like it in any other Mexican chapel – the Malverde cult is usually found in the north of the country rather than here in the central region.

Jesús Malverde, patron saint of drug traffickers

The story goes that Malverde, a bandit born in the late 19th century in the Mexican state of Sinaloa, stole from ranchers to redistribute their wealth to the poor. During a police chase, an officer shot him in the leg. The wound became infected and gangrenous, so Malverde asked one of his comrades to hand him over to the police for the ransom, then distribute the money to the poor

Malverde was hanged on 3 May 1909 in Culiacán. His body was left outside, exposed to the elements, but the local residents covered it over with stones and decorated the makeshift grave with flowers and candles. When their wishes and prayers were answered, they considered him a saint.

No portraits or photos of Malverde survive, but it's said that in the 1940s a grateful taxi driver ordered a bust of him with the features of Mexican film stars Pedro Infante and Jorge Negrete – the image that we know today. Yet his most devout followers are of dubious morality because he's now known as the patron saint of drug traffickers and illegal immigrants.

POSADA DEL SOL

A lugubrious abandoned hotel, source of urban myths

Niños Héroes 139
Colonia Doctores
No public access
Metro: Niños Héroes

The imposing Posada del Sol (Sun Hotel), abandoned since the 1940s and frequently used as a set for horror films, has inspired a number of urban myths.

The hotel, designed by engineer Fernando Saldaña Galván as an artists' lodge and cultural centre, opened in 1945 and was highly praised by Diego Rivera, Raul Basurto and Salvador Echegaray.

Eight months later, following Galván's death, the municipality took over the building. It became a primary school, then an institute of indigenous affairs and subsequently the attorney-general's office. Nowadays, the Desarrollo Integral de la Familia (DIF – Integral Development of the Family) uses it as a venue for photographic and cinematographic sessions.

Posado del Sol, with 650 rooms over half a block, is a pastiche of modernist and neocolonial architecture. The main entrance, a seven-storied building in volcanic rock, is at the junction of Niños Héroes and José Navarro. From outside you can see the semicircular tower that held the administrative offices, bar and tea rooms. There was also a hair salon, a dining room and a conference room named after Sor Juana Inés (see p. 49), where the seats still have their original ashtrays.

At the rear of the building are the main hall and the music room, its wooden rails engraved with guitars, harps and trumpets. The coffered wooden ceiling has carved Greek deities associated with the Bellas Artes movement. The monumental brick and stone fireplace in the main dining / ballroom is inscribed with a poem dedicated to fire and eternity.

In the main courtyard, endemic plants run wild in a tangle that covers Olmec and Aztec pre-Hispanic sculptures, not to mention a wishing well. The corridors are decorated with 15 murals by Mexican painter and sculptor Francisco Montoya. The main corridor, leading to the courtyard shows the signing of the Constitution of Apatzingán (1814, during the War of Independence) in the foreground, and in the background Galván consulting the hotel plans. At the back of the building is the 'meditation chapel' protected by a statue of St Francis and the Wolf.

The mysterious atmosphere that fuelled the urban myths stems from symbols of unknown origin scattered throughout the hotel: signs of the zodiac in the chapel, a stone fawn in the dining room, five-pointed stars in the patios, a mural depicting two suns in the basement, the seven-storied building, and the lugubrious marble inscriptions that tell of the profligate and problematic construction work.

Some people see these symbols as merely whimsical, whereas others see them as the vestiges of an artists' lodge inspired by Freemasonry but never completed.

MONUMENTO A LA COSTURERA

One of the most distressing episodes of the 1985 earthquake

San Antonio 151
Colonia Obrera
Metro: San Antonio Abad

n a small courtyard behind vast yellowish apartment blocks, the *Monumento a la costurera* (Monument to the Seamstress) depicts a woman with a sewing machine, stitching a Mexican flag. The monument was erected here because this was the site of one of the most distressing episodes of the 19 September 1985 earthquake.

Seconds after the quake, neighbours realised that the textile factory where a number of seamstresses worked had collapsed on them. A few managed to escape by throwing rolls of cloth into the street and sliding out on them. People began to clear the rubble to try and help, but despite their efforts more than 600 workers died. Following the disaster, around 11,000 were left without a job.

On 24 September the factory owners tried to salvage the machinery, but were prevented by the neighbours until all the bodies were recovered, fearing that there were insufficient assets to pay compensation.

The story was reported by the media, but details were omitted because of collusion with the employers. Very few of the media reported that a construction permit had been granted without prior inspection, the seamstresses had been denied union protection, they worked more than eight hours a day, and their wages were below the legal minimum.

The leader of the Confederation of Mexican Workers (CTM) dissociated himself from the case, alleging that the work was clandestine and that the only seamstress he knew was the one who sewed on his buttons! In response, the workers set up their own union, the 'Sindicato Nacional de Trabajadores de la Industria de la Costura, Confección, Vestido, Similares y Conexos 19 de Septiembre'.

The statue, by sculptor Patricia Mejía, was funded by workers of the *delegación* in 2003 as a permanent reminder of the time when union and government corruption made light of the consequences of an earthquake.

A commemorative bell

A bell in Hospital Juárez rings every 19 September at 7.19am.
The old hospital, 19 storeys high, collapsed in the 1985 earthquake.
Wall plaques list the names of the staff who died that day.
An urn in front of the bell contains the first stone to be laid for the new Hospital Juárez. Tourists are not allowed inside the hospital.

PASEO DEL ROCK MEXICANO

The 50 most representative Mexican rock songs

Avenida Cuauhtémoc, junction with Huatabampo
Northern end of Jardín Ramón López Velarde
Metro: Centro Médico

At the northern end of the Ramón López Velarde gardens, the huge black guitar plastered with fan stickers marks the site of the Mexican Rock Walk.

Next to the guitar are 50 concrete columns, each with three pillars like organ pipes, forming a kind of sound wave. This monument claimed to record the 50 most representative titles of Mexican rock, but as some purists disagreed with the list, a decision was made to remove all the song titles. The selection ranged from *onda chicana* (Chicano Soul) to rock, not to mention punk and ska.

It's worth salvaging the titles:
1960 – Locos del Ritmo, *Yo no soy rebelde*
1960 – Teen Tops, *Pensaba en ti*

1960 – Blue Caps, *Vuelve primavera*
1968 – Javier Bátiz, *Comin' home*
1970 – La Revolución de Emiliano Zapata, *Nasty Sex*
1971 – Love Army, *Caminata cerebral*
1971 – Peace and Love, *Latin Feeling*
1971 – Dug Dugs, *La gente*
1971 – Enigma, *Bajo el signo de acuario*
1975 – Three Souls in my Mind / El Tri, *ADO*
1981 – Kenny y los Eléctricos, *No huyas de mí*
1984 – Rockdrigo González, *En la estación del metro Balderas*
1984 – Botellita de Jeréz, *Charrock and Roll*
1985 – Jaime López, *1ª calle de la soledad*
1986 – Mama-Z, *M'amor (no me dejes solo)*
1986 – Luzbel, *Pasaporte al infierno*
1987 – Real de Catorce, *Azul*
1987 – Trolebús, *Barata y descontón*
1987 – Banda Bostik, *Abran esa puerta*
1987 – Cecilia Toussaint, *La viuda negra*
1988 – Dangerous Rhythm / Ritmo Peligroso, *Déjala tranquila*
1988 – El personal, *No me hallo*
1988 – Caifanes / Jaguares, *Viento*
1989 – Tex Tex, *Un toque mágico*
1989 – Rostros Ocultos, *El final*
1989 – Rebel D'Punk, *San Felipe Punk*
1990 – Víctimas del Dr. Cerebro, *El esqueleto*
1990 – Los Amantes de Lola, *Mamá*
1990 – Haragán & Cía., *No estoy muerto*
1991 – Maldita Vecindad y los Hijos del Quinto Patio, *Pachuco*
1992 – La Castañeda, *Noches de tu piel*
1992 – Santa Sabina, *Azul casi morado*
1992 – La Lupita, *La paquita disco*
1992 – La Cuca, *El son del dolor*
1992 – Tijuana No, *Pobre de ti*
1992 – Café Tacvba, *La chica banda*
1996 – Control Machete, *Comprendes Méndes*
1997 – Julieta Venegas, *De mis pasos*
1997 – La Barranca, *Día negro*
1998 – Plastilina Mosh, *Mr. P Mosh*
1998 – Los Esquizitos, *Santo y Lunave*
1998 – Los de Abajo, *Pepepez*
1999 – El Gran Silencio, *Dormir soñando*
1999 – Moenia, *Manto estelar*
2001 – Ispector, *Amnesia*
2001 – Zoé, *Miel*
2001 – Kinky, *Ejercicio #16*
2002 – Panteón Rococó, *La dosis perfecta*
2002 – Ultrasónicas, *Qué grosero*
2003 – Molotov, *Frijolero*

HERBARIO MEDICINAL DEL IMSS

Remedies for diarrhoea, coughs, epilepsy, alcoholism and the evil eye …

Avenida Cuauhtémoc 330
Centro Medico National Siglo XXI, Unidad de Congresos basement
(+52) 5588 5607
Monday to Friday 10am–2pm; times may vary
Admission free
Metro: Centro Médico

n the labyrinthine basement corridors of the 21st Century National Medical Centre, the Medicinal Herbarium of the Instituto Mexicano el Seguro Social (IMSS – Mexican Social Security Institute) houses a :tle-known collection of over 15,000 medicinal plants.

The herbarium was founded in 1981 by Prof. Abigail Aguilar ontreras, a specialist in medicinal plants. Many of the plants were ollected at that time, when native wildlife was being revalued around le world. A selection is presented in the permanent exhibition.

In addition to a data sheet giving the scientific name, family, ommon name, usage and harvesting details, the herbs are presented tea caddies or packets of powder, just as they can be found at the arket or in shops.

The instructions are important. They describe, for example, how lava leaves should be boiled in water to relieve diarrhoea ('*pasamiento*'); ow to infuse leaves of epazote in milk to use as a vermifuge ('*arrojar s lombrices*'); and a home remedy for coughs involving boiled fig leaves ixed with honey and brown sugar.

Although most of the medicinal herbs are used for common ailments ich as coughs, flu or stomach pains, others are effective for more rious diseases: Chiranthodendron (devil's hand tree) flowers to treat ilepsy, Damiana leaves to lift depression (and libido ...) and peanut ots for alcohol abuse. Other plants are claimed to prevent hair loss, in allergies, menstrual pain, etc.

The studies carried out at the herbarium also reveal the mystical and agical uses of plants. Fumigation with Vera Cruz pepper conquers ar. Remember that *chaneques* are small ythological creatures that transmit seases to people. The rue herb is lpful for breathing difficulties ('*mal aire*') in childbirth, and baccharis roundsel tree) and aromatic pepper anches treat anxiety and the evil eye.

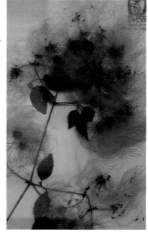

While the medicinal study of plants s allowed chemical components be synthesised as drugs, the plants emselves are still used in Mexico. though the effectiveness of most them has been proven, the active gredients could aggravate someone's ndition in case of uncontrolled lf-medication.

PANTEÓN FRANCÉS

A melancholy open-air museum of architecture

Avenida Cuauhtémoc, junction with Miguel Alemán
Open only on the Day of the Dead
Metro: Centro Médico

The Panteón Francés de la Piedad (French Cemetery of La Pieta), founded at the time of Maximilian's Empire in 1865 and inspired by the famous Père-Lachaise Cemetery in Paris, is open to the public once a year on the Day of the Dead. Although the cemetery was available to everyone, its architectural riches are explained by the high cost of burial there. It is now private.

The entrance is a wide avenue lined with the most prestigious mausoleums. In the centre of the cemetery stands an architectural gem, a now disused neo-Gothic church.

Wandering along each of the avenues is like losing yourself in a sea of funereal sculptures ranging from neocolonial to modernist, although the majority are Art Nouveau. Among them is a group of mourning women leaning over the grave of actor Vicente Miranda. Another shows the baby of the Creel family lying in a marble bed protected by a cherub. A little girl called Pina, seated on a bed of flowers, looks out at visitors on the other side of the cemetery. The Chambon family tomb seems to have sprung from the imagination of Egyptian pharaohs, while that of the Laporte family still has its woven floral wreaths, as was the custom in 1900.

The cemetery is believed to contain 9,298 monuments of great artistic merit, many of which were designed by sculptors such as Rivas Mercado, Adolfo Ponzanelli, or César and Norville Navari.

Two well-known monuments are the vast mausoleum dedicated to the French soldiers who died in 1865 while saving victims from a burning building, and another commemorating the Franco-Mexicans killed in the First World War.

All this sculptural and architectural beauty may be impressive, but so are the cemetery's incumbents.

Well-known names on epitaphs include actor Mauricio Garcés, impressionist painter Joaquín Clausell, serviceman Benjamín Hill, MP Serapio Rendón, poet Otilio González, activist José Revueltas, pianist Ricardo Castro, businessman Torres Adalid and Czechoslovakian-born actress Miroslava – all important figures from early 20th-century Mexico, most of whom died in strange circumstances.

CORREDOR DE CACHARROS

Sculptures locally made from auto parts

Dr Vertiz, between Eje 3 Sur, Dr Morones Prieto and Viaducto
Colonia Buenos Aires
Metro: Centro Médico / Lázaro Cárdenas

At the centre of the narrow thoroughfare of Dr Vertiz, on the short stretch that runs from Eje 3 Sur to Viaducto, is a series of 11 sculptures made from auto spares and other mechanical bits and pieces.

At the start of this curious walk, a white horse welcomes you with its hind legs in the air. Among the artworks are turtles, ants, caterpillars, as well as humorous creations such as a figure wearing a sign that reads 'Hombre supercargardo' (Overloaded Man). They were installed here in 2001, as part of a scheme designed by sculptor Yvonne Domenge Gaudry.

The idea behind the project was for Colonia Buenos Aires residents to reuse unwanted car parts to create a sculpture of their choice, supervised and helped by Gaudry. The exhibition was planned to last for five months, but it has never been dismantled.

Several sculptures, such as flamingos made from pipes, have deteriorated over time; but fortunately some of the neighbours have decided to restore the artworks and even make new ones.

The site, officially called Paseo Escultórico Buenos Aires (the Buenos Aires Sculpture Walk), is colloquially known as Corredor de Cacharros (Jalopy Corridor) or Paseo de la Chatarra (Scrap Metal Walk). Springs, spark plugs and gear wheels now compete with the curiosities on the other side of the central reservation, where businesses have started to make decorative objects and furniture in the same style, in addition to selling spare parts.

IGLESIA DE NUESTRA SEÑORA DE LA PIEDAD MURAL

The 32-metre Apocalypse

Calle Obrero Mundial 320
Monday to Friday 8am–1pm and 5pm–9pm, Saturday 9am–2pm
Metro: Centro Médico

Behind the altar, a huge mural standing 32-metres-high will surprise visitors to the vast, austere church of Our Lady of Mercy, which was built between 1945 and 1957 on the site of a demolished colonial convent.

The mural, by Mexican architect and artist Pedro Medina Guzmán (1915–2000, better known as 'El Charro' – The Cowboy), reinterprets a scene from the Apocalypse. On approaching, you'll see traces of the church rafters blending with the figures to create an optical illusion.

Details of the acrylic painting are given in a brochure by the priest Manuel Santamarina, available from the church offices. He explains, for example, the significance of the four hands of God: the top pair illustrate His serenity and immensity, the bottom pair the diffusion of His works throughout Creation.

Below the hands, Lucifer is shown engulfed in flames that represent St Michael in spirit form, tormenting the 'rebel angel'.

The white horse in the centre represents Christ and the Church being born in the form of a circle of the chosen.

On the right of the mural you'll also find a red horse alluding to the persecutions of pagan Rome, a brown horse to the persecutions of the Muslims, and a black horse with the image of the atomic bomb emerging from one of its legs – symbolising rebellion within the Church and the modern scientific inventions that bring about Evil.

The blue background symbolises God in Heaven and the golden colour that floods much of the mural is the all-enveloping Apocalyptic vision of God (as Santamarina says).

MADONNA OF MERCY

An acheiropoietic image that calmed a storm at sea

Church of Nuestra Señora de la Piedad
Obrero Mundial 320
Monday to Friday 8am–1pm and 5pm–9pm, Saturday 9am–2pm
Metro: Centro Médico

The modern church of Our Lady of Mercy, built on the ruins of a colonial church consecrated on 2 February 1652, has a painting venerated for its miraculous origins.

When the church first opened, this image was accompanied by descriptive verses written by a poetry-loving priest. The text inspired impresario Manuel Rivera Cambas and writer Artemio de Valle-Arizpe, who many years later elaborated on the legend in a history of viceregal Mexico (first published 1936).

During a visit to the Vatican to settle some church affairs, a Dominican friar came across so many beautiful paintings of virgins and saints that he decided to take a painting of the Madonna back to New Spain. It took him a whole day to find the right artist, who suggested an original instead of the copy the friar had asked for. When the time came to collect the painting, imagine his surprise to see that the artist had barely finished the preliminary sketch. Despite his annoyance he took the canvas away with him, as his ship was about to sail.

During the voyage, a dreadful storm arose and to a man the crew members were convinced that their time had come. Only the friar was confident they'd be saved, and he and another passenger prayed for mercy. When all was calm again, they managed to land at Veracruz and tell their story, but when they removed the cloth protecting the painting they were amazed to discover that the image had been miraculously completed. Hence the term acheiropoietic – 'not made by the hand of man'. Since the demolition of the colonial church, this miraculous image has been displayed in the new building.

For more on acheiropoietic images, see the following double-page spread.

Acheiropoietic works of art

In the Christian tradition, the term *acheiropoieton* refers to works of art 'not made by the hand of man'. Thus it relates to images created either by transposition from direct contact (as with the Shroud of Turin and the Veil of Veronica) or by divine intervention.

This term was apparently coined by St Paul himself in a particular context: during a stay at Ephesus, he rose up against pagan idolatry and especially against the numerous many-breasted statues of Artemis, mother of the gods.

He declared that the 'gods made by the hand of man are not gods'. With the use of this term *acheiropoieton* he showed respect for the Judaic prohibition of images, attacked pagan idols by setting the actual body of Christ against them, and limited eventual abuse by also claiming that this body of Christ was exclusively in the form it took after the transfiguration, in other words after an event that followed the Resurrection.

Besides the celebrated Shroud of Turin and the Veil of Veronica (see *Secret Rome* in this series of guides), tradition holds that a few other rare *acheiropoietic* images still exist today.

One example is to be found at Mount Athos in Greece: this theocratic monarchy, isolated on a peninsula in north-eastern Greece since the 11th century and out of bounds to women, children and female animals, is home to two *acheiropoietic* icons. One is in the monastery of the Great Lavra and the other in the monastery of Iviron.

In France, there is also an *acheiropoieton* in the church of Notre-Dame-des-Miracles at Saint-Maur near Paris.

Similarly, the Holy Visage of Edessa, now in the Bartholomite Church of Genoa (Liguria, Italy), is said to have been painted by Christ himself.

The painting of Christ in the Santa Sanctorum of the Lateran in Rome is said to have been drawn by St Luke and then completed by angels, and the famous sculpture of the Holy Visage in Lucca (Tuscany) is said to have been started by Nicodemus (who, together with Joseph of Arimathea, was present at Christ's crucifixion), but then completed by angels (see *Secret Tuscany*).

LA PIEDAD BATHTUB

How to prevent sinful thoughts

Avenida Cuauhtémoc 494, junction with Obrero Mundial
Inside Fundación de Arte Down
+52 55 5690 3133
culturajuan.club
Admission free
Metrobus: Obrero Mundial

When strolling along Avenida Cuauhtémoc, look to your left or you'll miss one of the city's most recent archaeological discoveries. Through a window, part of the Dominican convent of Nuestra Señora de la Piedad (Our Lady of Mercy) can be seen in the subsoil.

Although not all the details of the find are documented, one half of the vestiges is probably the convent entrance and the other half is part of a bathroom. This section is the most interesting: it is recognisable because it contains a colonial-era bathtub. Although the tub is damaged, its shape can easily be imagined and could be taken for a 17th-century jacuzzi. But it wasn't as pleasant as that.

Dominican rules forbade nuns from bathing too frequently in case their own nakedness aroused carnal desires. So they were washed by servants or other nuns to avoid contact with their own bodies, which is why the bathtub is so small and has a kind of step to sit on.

In this convent, baths could only be prescribed by a doctor, and this didn't happen very often in order to prevent sinful thoughts. Illness was thought to be a trial sent by God, so the nuns had little use for the doctor and tended to turn to their confessor instead. Even when sick, they avoided showing their bodies to the doctors, who in any case had to be authorised by the bishops and archbishops. A doctor also had to be accompanied by a nun who would watch out for any bad behaviour.

The site is now run by the Juan González y García Centre for Social and Cultural Co-investment, a cultural organisation. Unfortunately a car park has been built over the archaeological remains, despite a number of objections.

If you think Dominican hygiene measures were harsh, you've heard nothing yet. At the time, the rules were so strict that all nuns had to have short hair to avoid pride and feminine vanity. The Augustines were only allowed to wash their hair seven times a year. The main thing was always to wear clean clothes and keep the convent tidy, not for hygienic reasons but to please God. Washing, ironing and repairs were tasks reserved for servants or lay nuns.

EL AMANECER TAPATÍO RESTAURANT WALL

Last traces of a mariachi restaurant in a parking lot

Obrero Mundial 583
Junction of Eje Central Lázaro Cárdenas, Obrero Mundial and Alfonso XII
Metro: Lázaro Cárdenas

I n the mid-20th century, part of the Álamos neighbourhood had a vibrant nightlife thanks to its many saloons and restaurants. At the junction of Eje Central and Alfonso XII, at the back of a parking lot, is a wall covered with mosaics. Each element of this mural has a link with Mexican mariachi culture: the typical sombrero of a *charro* (cowboy), a guitar, tequila, a violin, cockfights, piano keys, and at one end a pre-Hispanic warrior performing a fire ritual.

This is one of the walls from the famous El Amanecer Tapatió restaurant, which closed in the early 1990s to make way for a parking lot.

In the 1960s, the restaurant's five rooms offered a wide repertoire of Mexican *ranchera* (folk and country) music. The owners, Eduardo Kensaku Endo and María de Jesús Chavarrín (locally known as 'La Chuy'), had arranged the space in such a way that the wall we see today was the backdrop.

Vicente Fernández, the 'king of *ranchera* music', and the Mariachi Aguilar band, led at the time by Felipe Arriaga, had their debuts here; and it was where the Los Panchos trio discovered Jorge Valente, a singer who was to reach the height of his popularity in the 60s.

A couple of decades later, the restaurant saw the first World Mariachi Day, launched by jazz musician Chucho López and introducing singer and actress Amalia Mendoza, nicknamed 'La Tariácuri'.

Despite the closure and demolition of the restaurant, it was decided to preserve the mural on the back wall, as well as part of the floor that had been trodden by such well-known exponents of *ranchera* music as Lola Beltrán, Lucha Villa and Javier Solís, and many others who filled the nights with their bittersweet tunes.

MUSEO DE ARTE EN AZÚCAR MÉXICO

And it's really all sugar?

Avenida Cuauhtémoc 950
Colonia Narvarte
Guided tours on reservation
(+52) 5523 7493 / 5523 8434
artemexicanodelazucar@gmail.com
Metro: Eugenia

A small building in Colonia Narvarte houses the Instituto del Arte Mexicano del Azúcar (Institute of Mexican Sugar Art) museum, as well as a workshop and living quarters. It has a magnificent exhibition of work by Marithé de Alvarado dating from the second half of the 20th century. Visits by appointment only.

The guided tour, sometimes led by family members or friends, is like a journey back to the 1950s, the time when the institute was founded here. Little dioramas of life in the 19th century, elegant muses from Greek mythology, ballet dancers and even Baroque churches, all made from sugar, are displayed in the museum's five rooms.

As the building is De Alvarado's home, you can also see her workshop and dining room, which has some amusing anecdotes associated with it. For example, it was in the dining room that she challenged one of her students to make sugar hands – unsuccessfully. Also on display are the countless awards she has received, both national and international, from Spain, France, Argentina and the United States (don't miss the photo on the staircase of legendary Mexican singer Pedro Vargas with cake, alongside actress María Victoria).

Marithé de Alvarado has published six books in which she tells the story of each of her 2,000 creations, such as the Eiffel Tower she built in 1937, early in her career, a replica of which is in the museum. Made entirely of spun sugar, with no supporting structure, and visitors always ask: 'And it's really all sugar?'

MUSEO CASA
DE BENITA GALEANA

*Communist Mexico through the eyes of 'the girl
with the plaited hair'*

Cerrada de Zutano 11
Colonia Segunda del Periodista
(+52) 5609 1687
Monday to Friday 9am–5pm, Saturday and Sunday 9am–3pm
Admission free
Metro: Nativitas

The little house-museum of Benita Galeana (1904–95) opened in 2000 as a tribute to this writer and defender of social rights. In the 1920s, Benita had joined the then underground Communist Party, where her comrades nicknamed her 'the girl with the plaited hair'. She took part in a number of strikes and demonstrations and was jailed no fewer than 54 times.

There are many memories in the collections of this unpretentious museum: photos of Benita on the run from the police for selling the newspaper *El Machete*, a watercolour showing her walking around the city centre, showcases filled with her books, her *huipiles* (traditional clothing) and other personal effects. While it's a pity there isn't more information about her life, the curators are always ready to answer questions from the public.

Benita was fiercely opposed to the Yankees and an admirer of Fidel Castro. She owned a necklace with a portrait of Lenin and supported Panamanian general Manuel Noriego, whom she met during the economic boycott of his country. There's a reminder of that visit in the living room.

Benita Galeana and Trotsky

Leon Trotsky's visit to Mexico in 1937 is said to have worried Communist Party members, including activist José Revuelta … an anxiety not shared by Benita, who considered the Trotskyists to be old comrades.

On her marriage to journalist Mario Gil, she rented part of her home in the Centro Histórico to party members such as artists Luis Arenal and Isabel Chavarría. Isabel was involved in the first attempt on Trotsky's life in Mexico City, in which artist David Alfaro Siqueiros took part. When the police turned up at Benita's house, she found machine-guns hidden in a box of brushes in the room her friend shared with her husband, Andrés Salgado.

Benita's collection of books on social conflict and the writings of Mario Gil can be seen in the library.

NIÑO EN EL VIENTRE DE CONCRETO

The raw representation of an iconic picture of Mexican poverty

Galería de la Fundación María y Héctor García
Cumbres de Maltrata 581
Colonia Segunda del Periodista
(+52) 5539 5393
fundacionarchivohectorgarcia.net
Monday to Friday 10am–6pm, Saturday 10am–1pm
Metro: Nativitas

On one side of the María and Héctor García Foundation Gallery is a niche containing a bronze statue of a child by Alberto Carbot. Curled into a foetal position, head down, feet sticking out of the small space. The sculpture is based on a legendary photograph by Héctor García.

Taken in 1943 in Garibaldi, near the Follies Theatre, the photo is of a street urchin sleeping inside an iron crawl hole in the wall, his pants torn and his feet dangling.

Ten years later, the photo was included in an exhibition entitled *Una fiesta de muertos mexicana* (A Festival of Mexican Dead) in Paris. The French Minister of Culture, André Malraux, is said to have called it *Niño en el vientre de concreto* (Child in the Concrete Womb), declaring it to be one of the cruellest images of our time.

Héctor García became a celebrated photojournalist and many of his pictures of the 'soul of Mexico' are iconic. He worked for the *Excelsior* and *Siempre!* newspapers, and with the help of journalist Horacio Quiñones launched *Ojo* (Eye) magazine, despite the media censorship of the late 1950s.

Following the 1985 earthquake, Héctor García's Foto Press studio moved to Cumbres de Maltrata, the gallery's current location. It was opened in 2008 to display the collection of García and his wife and colleague, María Sánchez. Empathising with the child in his photo, García commented: 'It's a screwed-up guy that tells us what we already know: he's the child of a city that's a very bad mother, one that gives his childhood no chance. I speak of myself, and of the city itself.'

When García died in 2012, a minute of flashbulbs popping was requested at his wake. The identity of the child he snapped that night in 1943 was never discovered.

When the Italian neorealist screenwriter Cesare Zavattini came across the photo, after seeing Luis Buñuel's *Los Olvidados* (*The Forgotten Ones*, English title *The Young and the Damned,* 1950), he called it 'the icon of an unforgettable forgotten'.

As well as hosting the permanent exhibition, the gallery organises temporary shows and photography workshops.

From Tacuba to Peñón de los Baños

MUSEO DE LA CABALLERÍA MODELS

5,000 lead soldiers hand-painted by Lorenzo de la Hidalga

Avenida México Tacuba, junction with F.C. de Cuernavaca
Inside Campo Militar 1-B
ID required at the entrance
Tuesday to Saturday 10am–6pm, Sunday 10am–4pm
Admission free
Metro: Colegio Militar

The Cavalry Museum, still little known to the public, is home to a treasure even more impressive than the Asian carved crossbow or the Persian and Hindu pottery of the 17th century. It's not the revolver bearing the inscription 'To my friend Don Plutarco Elías Calles' presented by Carranza to the former president, nor the competition medals and trophies won by the one-eyed horse Arete. It's not even the wall dedicated to the women who took part in Mexican wars, such as Mother Cuca, a nun who joined the army in 1915 as a military nurse, lady colonel Alanis, cavalry captain Rosa Padilla, and Amelia Robles who dressed as a man to join the Zapatista army and died a colonel.

The proudly guarded treasure consists of six 19th-century dioramas with over 5,000 pieces, designed by the architect Lorenzo de la Hidalga.

The buildings designed by De la Hidalga have largely disappeared. Among them, the Gran Teatro Nacional was demolished, the Plaza del Volador burned down, Tampico Cathedral collapsed and the Monumento a la Independencia was never completed. So all these models that the architect made and hand-painted in his free time have become precious relics.

Three of the dioramas represent the Napoleonic wars: the French campaign in Egypt where Napoleon routed the English near the pyramids (spot the Sphinx), the famous battle of Waterloo, and the battle of Baylen (Bailén in southern Spain) – the first defeat of Napoleon's troops in the open field.

Another diorama illustrates the battle of Sedan, when Napoleon III surrendered to the Prussian army: the French fields are swarming with troops and a house has been completely destroyed.

The battle of Tsushima shows the Japanese army ruthlessly attacking Russian ships during the Russo-Japanese war. Finally, there's a 19th-century military camp with wounded soldiers, nurses, military tents and training grounds.

These dioramas are of far-reaching significance for the museum: they are reminders of the days when horses were of vital importance in battle as well as a means of transport. The traditional configurations and equestrian skills could determine the outcome of a battle in the days long before tanks and motorised vehicles.

MEMORIES OF EL HALCONAZO

Blood shed for the new dawn

Calzada México–Tacuba, junction with Avenida de los Maestros
Metro: Normal

T he work by Mexican monumental sculptor Sebastián, *10 de jur*
no se olvida (10 June Is Not Forgotten), at Normal metro statio

exit, is composed of a fallen cross from which emerges a column of five flowers. Each flower symbolises Nahui-Ollin day (see box) in the Aztec, Mayan, Toltec, Teotihuacan and Huastec traditions.

The fallen cross recalls the sacrifice of mankind and the red of the sculpture represents the blood of those who died on this site. Inside the station there is also a commemorative plaque installed in 2001 and photos along the platform, to remind people of what happened that day.

On 10 June 1971, the Thursday of Corpus Christi, a demonstration (mainly students) was held on the Mexico City to Tacuba road, demanding the end of trade-union corruption and the release of prisoners detained during the 1968 movement (Sebastián among them, held in military zone 1). According to the information in the metro, during this peaceful march, the paramilitary group Los Halcones (The Falcons), whose members passed themselves off as students, was brought to this crossroads. On the orders of city governor Alfonso Martínez Domínguez, Los Halcones suppressed the demonstration – first exploding a grenade in Normal station.

The next day, the press claimed that the clashes had been incited by radical students and that there were only four victims. However, a plaque at the foot of the sculpture cites 38 names, adding that there were 'many other anonymous victims'.

This brutally suppressed march is known as 'El Halconazo' (The Hawk Strike). Disgracefully, neither those who gave the orders (reputedly the then president Luis Echeverría among them) nor the Halcones were ever called to account.

Nahui Ollin – The Legend of the Fifth Sun

In pre-Hispanic understanding, humanity has been destroyed four times. The Aztec calendar specifies that on the day of Nahui Atl (Four Waters, in the Nahuatl language), a great deluge came upon the world and turned men into fish. On the day of Nahui Ocelotl (Four Jaguars), the Sun stopped shining and the world was immersed in an eternal night. On the day of Nahui Quiahuitl (Four Rains), fire fell from the sky and there were terrible volcanic eruptions. On the day of Nahui Ehecatl (Four Winds), the Earth was subjected to violent hurricanes. So began the world as we know it today, but the pre-Hispanics predicted that Nahui Ollin (Four Movements) would come soon, the day when massive earthquakes would put an end to humanity in order for it to regenerate for the fifth time. They call it 'blood shed for the dawn to rise', the cycle of life, which from death sees the emergence of new life.

ALTARS IN SANTA JULIA

Kitsch altars against crime

Barrio de Santa Julia, Colonia Tlaxpana
The most striking altars can be seen from Calles Quetzalcóatl to Atzcayán
(parallel streets) and from Calzada México–Tacuba to Marina Nacional, in
Colonia Tlaxpana
Some altars also in Colonia Anáhuac
Best to visit after 12 December
Metro: Normal

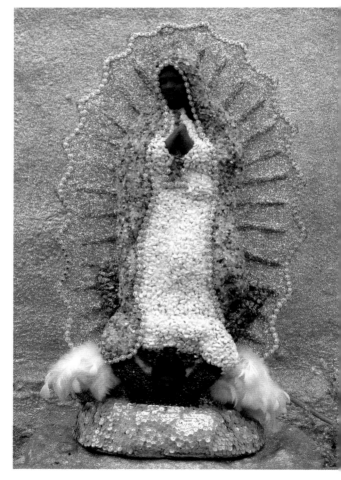

O f all the altars to be seen around the Roman Catholic Mexico City, the kitsch examples in the Santa Julia district of Colonia Tlaxpana take some beating. The best time to see them is after 12 December (Day of Our Lady of Guadalupe).

It all started in the 1940s, in a cellar at the corner of Quetzalcóatl and Xólotl where a certain Miguel Cortés lived. Cortés had a statue of the Virgin at home and every 12 December he used to set it on an altar at the street corner. The neighbours then adopted the tradition, erecting altars that stood there for days.

Although over the years this became a popular celebration, the security of the district started to experience high crime rates. With no response from the authorities, the neighbours sought divine intervention and decided to make the altars more striking.

Nowadays, during the December holiday, no street is without them. Their designers invest time and money to make theirs the most attractive possible, taking over sidewalks and streets, and building concrete fountains and little houses destined to disappear in a few months.

You can see glittering walls, heart-shaped basins, little neo-Baroque chapels in pastels or vibrant colours, and hand-painted plastic angels hanging on the walls. There are altars made out of PVC tubes, visual effects where it seems that the Virgin is floating, and even neon-lit tanks of artificial fish. Graffiti in fluorescent colours on the walls evoke the Virgin.

Year after year the altars change, are destroyed or remodelled. In recent years more have appeared in surrounding districts, although most are within the Santa Julia boundary. Even though some are permanent fixtures, most are knocked down to make way for the following year's efforts.

It's worth mentioning that the crime rates fall considerably while the altars are there!

'WONDER ROOM' AT MUSEO ÍDOLOS DEL ESTO

A fragment from the Berlin Wall, a Uruguayan officer's baton, a gold and jade crown …

Guillermo Prieto 7, junction with Serapio Rendón
Colonia San Rafael
Organización Editorial Mexicana building
Thursday to Tuesday 9am–6pm
Metro: San Cosme

BERLINER MAUER
1961 – 1989

This cabinet of curiosities is one of three sections in the Ídolos Museum run by ESTO, a daily paper specialising in celebrity articles and Mexican sport. It has a collection of gifts presented to newspaper magnate Mario Vázquez Raña by various personalities.

In the display cases, a Uruguayan officer's baton sits alongside an Arab-made sword, some African sculptures, two vases made entirely from seashells, and even a fragment of the Berlin Wall. There's also a replica of the crown of the Silla dynasty of ancient Korea, in gold and jade.

Other notable curiosities are the Olympic Orders of gold, silver and bronze awarded to Mario Vázquez by the International Olympic Committee to mark his distinguished contribution to the Olympic movement: he was an IOC member between 2000 and 2012 and president of the Mexican Olympic Committee from 1974 to 2001.

Objects displayed in the other rooms of the museum range from outfits worn by cabaret artist Tongolele and actress María Victoria, to a collection of photos of the life of movie star Pedro Infante, not to mention a soccer ball from 1930, a rice-paper sculpture of Olympic trophies, and various items that used to belong to famous boxers, wrestlers, footballers, bullfighters and racing drivers.

NEARBY
Grave of Pedro Infante

In the courtyard of the *ESTO* building, visitors might be surprised to hear the voice of Pedro Infante indicating the site of his new funerary monument.

The grave of Mexico's idol in the Panteón Jardín had so many visitors that a decision was made to organise a sale at the Luis C. Morton art auction house and use the funds to build a new tomb. The following year, the anonymous buyer donated the tombstone to the *ESTO* museum, together with the funerary plaques included in the sale. Only a few blocks from the place where his funeral procession set off over 50 years ago (one of the best-attended the country had ever seen) is the original grave of the man who personified the last days of the golden age of Mexican cinema: Pedro Infante.

RETRATO DE LA BURGUESÍA MURAL

The worst side of capitalism

Calle Maestro Antonio Caso 45
Premises of Sindicato Mexicano de Electricistas (SME)
sme.org.mx
Monday to Friday 8am–6pm
Admission free
Metrobus: Reforma

Although there are no staff on duty at the entrance, if you're asked the reason for your visit to the premises of the Mexican Electricians' Union (SME), just mention the mural and members will happily take you to see it.

The mural, at the head of the stairwell on the left, is much smaller than those usually found in Mexico, but packed with more detail than any of them.

Retrato de la burguesía (Portrait of the Bourgeoisie) was painted by Mexican muralists Luis Arenal, José Renau, Miguel Prieto, Antonio Pujol and David Alfaro Siqueiros. Completed in 1940, it contains numerous allegories of capitalism from the communist point of view: the bourgeoisie, wearing gas masks to demonstrate the buying power that protects them in the face of war; the Nazi army marching behind Fascist Blackshirts led by a demagogue, represented by a parrot, a combination of Hitler and Mussolini; on the centre wall two raptors embody American imperialism, one of them gripping in its beak a hanged black man as a sign of US racism. All the soldiers wear bloodied medals to show that they won them by killing; while the proletariat, the bedrock of society, emerges from cracks in the ground only to be trampled by the bourgeoisie.

The mural is dizzying in its multiple meanings: each fragment, according to its creators, illustrates the death of capitalism. But not all the painting you see is original: the SME asked Spanish artist Josep Renau (José's son, in exile in Mexico in the 1940s) to tone down the most violent scenes, because after the attempt on Trotsky's life in Coyoacán (see p. 231) the Stalinist ideas of Siqueiros were considered too radical. Some of the massacred children were hidden (perhaps symbolically) behind coins showing the economic impact of any war, and dismembered corpses were obscured by octopus tentacles at the bottom of the painting, but bodies thrown from the German Parliament and bursting into flames can still be seen. In front of the parliament, the motto 'Liberty, Equality, Fraternity' is masked by a stock exchange.

The upper section of the mural is the union's pride and joy: the scene is crowned with electricity pylons that point the way to change and light. The tallest pylon is topped by a red flag and the emblem of the SME, one of the few unions in the area that still retains the idea of social struggle at the root of its existence.

CASA DE MARÍA ANTONIA

The house where Fidel Castro and Che Guevara met

José de Emparán 49
Colonia Tabacalera
Metrobus: Museo San Carlos

Although the story goes that Fidel Castro and Che Guevara got to know one another in Café La Habana on Avenida Bucareli, both of them swore that they first met at number 49 José de Emparán in the Tabacalera district. At the entrance to the house, a plaque bearing their portraits reads: 'At this place of Cuauhtémoc there occurred, in the month of July 1955, the first meeting between the Cuban lawyer, militant, politician and statesman Fidel Castro Ruiz, and the Argentine doctor, politician and ideologist Ernesto Guevara de la Serna.'

The house belonged to María Antonia González, a Cuban woman whose brother had died under torture by supporters of Cuban President Fulgencio Batista. She offered shelter to political exiles, and Fidel Castro and his brother Raúl took meals there. In *Guerrillero del tiempo* (The Age of the Guerrilla), Fidel acknowledges that he used to prepare food with her and mentions the difficulties of cooking rice in the high-altitude city.

Raúl was the first to meet Che, who had a room in an adobe house on Diagonale San Antonio y Anaxágoras, in the Narvarte district. He introduced him to Fidel. The men formed a strong bond and began to plan the Cuban Revolution. Their usual meeting place was María Antonia's house, although guerrillas gathered in other parts of the city, such as the safe houses in the State of Mexico where weapons were stored ready for the revolution.

On 20 June 1956 the Federal Police arrested Fidel, followed by Che. Despite their ideological differences, only the intervention of former president Lázaro Cárdenas secured their release. Once freed, they went back into hiding to prepare their departure for Cuba and the beginning of the revolution.

'41, understand? 41'

A clandestine party at a house on Calle Ezequiel Montes was the site of the legendary 'Dance of the 41': a police raid was launched on 18 November 1901, ostensibly because men were dancing dressed as women. The story goes that when the police informed President Porfirio Díaz that his son-in-law Ignacio de la Torre was among the 42 men detained for immoral behaviour, Díaz replied: '41, understand? 41.' Since that day, '41' has been used as a pejorative reference to gay men. It was, however, well known that member 42 was the owner of the house and rumours were spread about Ignacio's sexuality. As a result of this story, a plaque demanding respect for the LGBTTTI (lesbian, gay, bisexual, transsexual, transgender, transvestite, intersexual) community has now been hung on the wall of the Centro Cultural José Martí (junction Dr Mora 1 and Hidalgo).

MEDALLIONS AT THE CASA DE LA CULTURA DE SANTA MARÍA

The face of a forgotten intellectual

Jaime Torres Bodet 160
Colonia Santa María la Ribera
Casa de la Cultura de Santa María la Ribera
Metro: Buenavista

The House of Culture of Santa María la Ribera is a modern building that has retained the side wall of a villa built in 1906. At that time, it was customary to install medallions depicting residents' faces: the two medallions on the windows represent the illustrious María Enriqueta Camarillo.

Already known in literary circles as an eminent writer, Enriqueta married historian Carlos Pereyra in 1898. The couple arrived at Alameda de Santa María in 1906 but only lived in the villa for four years. The Mexican Revolution and the diplomatic career of Don Carlos obliged them to travel to various countries.

The face on the medallions shows Enriqueta when she was 34 years old and contributing to the poetry revue *La mujer mexicana* (The Mexican Woman), one of the latest and most modern feminist magazines in Mexico. Her work was published in the *Revista azul* (Blue Review) and in *El mundo ilustrado* (The Illustrated World). She wrote collections of poetry (years earlier, she'd had to use the pseudonym Iván Maszkowski in *El Universal* to avoid being refused as a woman writer). She was a concert pianist and also illustrated her own books. Even when abroad, she carried on with her intellectual pursuits.

The villa in Santa María stood empty for 38 years until Enriqueta returned to Mexico at the age of 76. Received with honours in 1948 and awarded a house in her home town of Veracruz, she decided to see out her life there, although she still visited the Santa María villa. She died in 1968 in straitened circumstances, her name forgotten, and denied access to the new academies.

MUSEO FERROCARRILERO VÍCTOR FLORES

A bag of sand from the place where the 'Hero of Nacozari' died

Avenida Ricardo Flores Magón 206
Colonia Guerrero
Premises of the Sindicato de Trabajadores Ferrocarrileros de la República Mexicana (STFRM)
Monday to Saturday 10am–3pm
Admission free
Metro: Buenavista; Metrobus: Manuel González

To the side of the STFRM (Union of Railroad Workers) premises is the little-known Víctor Flores Museum, which tells the story of the railroad.

After the entrance (done up like a guard's van), the first room is a mock-up of the railroad's administrative and telegraph offices, while the next gives a brief overview of the history of the railroad in Mexico. Other rooms explain the different operations, and the visit ends with an account of the creation of the STFRM and the life of union leader Víctor Flores.

Patience is needed to browse through the museum – the space is so cramped that the exhibits are stacked one above another, and some deserve particular attention. Note a little bag of sand picked up from the site where railroad brakeman Jesús García died. He was dubbed the 'Hero of Nacozari' for preventing a train with a cargo of dynamite from exploding and wiping out the village of Nacozari in 1907.

Other gems are the miniature paintings by engine driver Alfredo Galicia dating from 1965, a flask of *bismadona* powder from the former railway medical department of Hospital Colonia, a golden nail used at railroad track opening ceremonies, an STFRM coat of arms made from real feathers, and a complete set of Pullman dinnerware dating from the mid-70s.

On the shelves where the railworkers' equipment is displayed, several of the pieces were specially made for the exhibition by artisans faithfully copying sections of track, tools and keys in light materials. The most unusual is the points switch made entirely from wood.

On the way out, don't miss the steam engine *La Mochita* (The Mongrel) in the parking lot. In 1905 the engine had to be recalibrated to match international track dimensions, and was reduced in width by 3 feet – hence the nickname.

CARRILLÓN TLATELOLCO

The world's largest carillon, housed in an iconic building

Avenida Insurgente Norte 423, Unidad Nonoalco Tlatelolco
Top of Torre Independencia (former Banobras building)
Closed to the public
Metro: Manuel González

Although everybody knows Banobras tower, few people are aware that it houses the world's largest set of bells.

As access to the tower is restricted, the only way to see the 47 bronze bells – now silent – is through binoculars.

The bells used to be rung constantly, whether electronically, automatically or manually, until lack of maintenance silenced them in 1993. They are rarely heard nowadays.

Following the 1985 earthquake the building was abandoned, and the Mexican bell-ringer Yolanda Fernández only came to ring the bells three times a week. Although they can be rung manually, 'concerts' are only held very occasionally: the last was to celebrate the 50th anniversary of the Unidad Tlatelolco apartment block in 2014, and before that a short session was held in 2006.

The bells, designed in Luxembourg, were donated by Belgium in 1963. When the first four were installed, they were engraved with the names Morelos, Hidalgo, Cuauhtémoc and Madero. The fifth was named after the then president, López Mateos, and the sixth after Elisabeth Lacroix, the Belgian ambassador who had sponsored the carillon.

Note that when the bells were installed in Banobras tower (the second-tallest building in Mexico in the 1960s), nobody foresaw that the sound would travel upwards and make them difficult to hear.

Although the top floor of the tower has been used as a viewpoint and concert venue in the past, it's currently off-limits to the public.

Mural abstracto

Torre Insignia, renamed Banobras and then Independencia, was designed by architect Mario Pani. The two main façades are covered with glass, while the others are concrete: here the artist Carlos Mérida created a monumental work entitled *Mural abstracto* (Abstract Mural) in which he sought to combine geometry with Toltec images. There are two windows in the centre from which the sound of the bells emerged. Some of the concrete sections of the mural have disappeared.

SALA DE HOLOGRAMAS

Exhibition of holograms in the metro corridors

Túnel de la Ciencia, inside La Raza metro interchange
Monday to Friday 10am–5pm
Metro: La Raza

When, in 1988, it was realised that the interchange of La Raza metro has some of the longest corridors in the world (just over 00 metres), a plan was developed to refurbish them and, at the same me, help to popularise science. Thus, in consultation with engineer osé de la Herrán, the idea of a Túnel de la Ciencia (Science Tunnel) as born.

One of the permanent exhibitions is the Sala de Hologramas (Hall f Holograms), a small gallery that displays two- and three-dimensional mages.

The framed subjects come in a variety of sizes, ranging from a molecule to the control room of a life-size airport, little stickers and two-dimensional 'pylons' used as labels. The exhibition begins with presentation of the holograms, explaining how they are created by ser beam and the effect of white light on the frame. Some images are yperrealistic, others have impressive details, such as the tiny Tudor-yle house or the miniature villa (we challenge you to find the hidden icycle).

The Science Tunnel, which opened on 30 November 1988, is onsidered to be the world's first science museum in a metro station. s well as the Hall of Holograms, there is an exhibition space with Mexican muralist Ariosto Otero's *Monstruos de fin de milenio* (End-f-Millennium Monsters), a work that originally stood in a shopping entre.

The latest developments allow metro users to read the information anels on their way through the interchange without needing to stop. Iowever, many people linger in the Astronomy section of the tunnel, hich since 1988 has had a Bóveda Celeste (Celestial Vault) – a map of e heavens with signs of the zodiac.

PUENTE DE TOLNAHUAC

*The bridge that connected Mexico City to the Royal
Road north*

*Calzada Vallejo, junction with Juventino Rosas
Colonia San Simón Tolnahuac
Metro: Tlatelolco / Metrobus: Tolnahuac*

The two derelict walls roughly protected by a metal barrier on Calzada Vallejo are the remains of the old Tolnahuac bridge, which connected Mexico City to the Camino Real de Tierra Adentro (Royal Inland Road). The bridge, spanning a river that once fed into Texcoco lake, dates from the second half of the 17th century.

The wall on the left side of the road bears a cross and a sculpture of the Apostle St James, patron saint of Spain. On the other side is a plaque paying tribute to the Viceroy of New Spain, the Count of Galve, for his work during severe food shortages, as the bridge was built to transport supplies during the Gran Hambruna (Great Famine, 1691–92).

The walls also commemorate the reconstruction of Calzada Tenayuca, which connected the city to the north of the country.

Thanks to the new-found abundance of the 18th century, when vast deposits of silver were discovered in New Spain, the bridge became part of the Ruta de Plata (Silver Route). This was travelled by the convoys carrying silver to pay the *quinto real* (royal fifth) tax to the Spanish Crown in Mexico City.

The Great Famine

In July 1691, such torrential rain fell on Mexico City that the maize crop was destroyed. As all roads and causeways in the north of the city were flooded, the cost of imports rose dramatically. Only a month later, a total solar eclipse further depressed the citizens' spirits and coincided with a plague of flea-like *chiahuiztli* that in turn devastated the wheat crop.

In September, people in the south of the city began to feel the pinch. Until the month of January, the northern cities and Toluca had been sending adequate supplies, but the cold killed the cattle, so lack of meat aggravated the food shortages. One solution was to repair Calzada de Tenayuca for convoys transporting corn from the north, and the Tolnahuac bridge was built around this time. Although the shortages had eased by 1692, rumours spread about the lack of corn. On 6 July a mob surrounded the Viceroy's Palace and set fire to it.

The scientist Don Carlos de Singüenza y Góngora is remembered for saving historic documents from the flames, as is the Count of Galve, who escaped the riot disguised as a peasant while hurling insults at himself in order to avoid suspicion.

TLATELOLCO WATER DEPOSIT

The city's first neo-Hispanic mural: a puzzle showing indigenous resistance

Museo de la Caja de Agua
Inside old convent of Santiago de Tlatelolco
Eje Central Lázaro Cárdenas, junction with Ricardo Flores Magón
Advance booking required
(+54) 5583 0295 / 5782 7290 / 5782 2240
tlatelolco.inah.gob.mx
Monday to Friday 8am–1.30pm
Admission free
Metro: Tlatelolco

After a storm in 2002, thousands of stone and plaster fragments from ceremonial offerings were discovered in a pool of water in the archaeological zone of Tlatelolco. The site of this discovery is now the Water Deposit Museum, and the pieces of plaster form part of the city's first neo-Hispanic mural.

The colours have faded since its discovery in 2002, so the site museum only opens by appointment. Admission includes a guided tour during which the visual puzzle is explained.

The museum also houses a huge water tank installed by the Franciscan friars to bring drinking water to the Republic of Indians of Santiago Tlatelolco. Indigenous labour was used to build the tank and *tlacuilos* (Aztec artists) decorated the side walls. The base section is displayed in the subsoil where it was found, with fragments of the mural (destroyed by the friars) reconstituted on screens at the sides.

At first glance, these look like plain white walls, but with the help of the guide's explanations animal forms such as a jaguar, herons, a parrotfish and a rattlesnake can be made out. There's also a man setting a heron trap and others catching frogs with a rod and fishing with a net. The scene is dominated by the Christian Cross at the centre.

The *tlacuilos* had cleverly concealed pre-Hispanic symbols from the friars in what seems like an innocent tableau, such as the eagle poised over the jaguar (representing Mexican domination over Tlatelolco) and a fisherman with two right feet (symbolising the importance of fishing). The most curious creature, next to the Cross, resembles a dog. This is the *ahuizotl*, an Aztec aquatic monster said to have plucked out the eyes and nails of those who failed to ask permission to fish.

Also shown are ducks, lilies, shells and fish whose meaning is still unknown, but the artists' subterfuge was probably the reason why the Franciscans ordered the destruction of the images. The archaeological explorations have revealed that the tank was hidden in such a way that all sections would remain intact until rediscovered.

The minute pieces of the puzzle – some no bigger than a fingernail – are still being assembled, so only the completed sections are displayed near the tank. This site is a unique visual testimony to the indigenous refusal to be conquered.

Apparently the first sighting of the tank wasn't in 2002 – it had already been identified in 1966 while laying the paving around the Unidad Tlatelolco apartment block (see p. 253), only 8 cm from the mural. So the modern era has concealed its secrets, as did neo-Hispanic Mexico. The tank was covered over for the second time in the name of 'progress' by architect Mario Pani.

MONUMENTOS DE LOS MISTERIOS

A route designed for praying while you walk

Calzada de los Misterios (section of Paseo de la Reforma at Calle Zumárraga)
The old arch stands at the junction of Misterios and Leóncavallo
Metro: La Villa / Misterios

Since the Calzada de Guadalupe pedestrian walkway was built to allow thousands of pilgrims to reach Villa de Guadalupe, the

d Calzada de los Misterios has been forgotten. Along the route are 15 monuments representing events in the life of Jesus Christ and Mary – the Joyful, Sorrowful and Glorious Mysteries of the Catholic osary. The time it takes to walk between each monument is enough to recite the appropriate prayer and tell your beads.

Only eight of the Mysteries designed by Cristóbal de Medina in 1675 have survived. Each has three sections: the first is a base with no ornamentation; the second represents the mystery engraved in stone here were originally two saints in the lateral niches and the columns varied from one mystery to another); and the third features the Virgin of Guadalupe surrounded by Baroque ornaments, with a saint above her.

From south to north, the Mysteries are: (Joyful) the Annunciation, the Visitation, the Nativity, the Presentation, the Finding in the Temple; (Sorrowful) the Agony in the Garden, the Scourging at the Pillar, the Crowning of Thorns, the Carrying of the Cross, the Crucifixion; (Glorious) the Resurrection, the Ascension, the Descent of the Holy Spirit, the Assumption, and the Crowning of the Blessed Virgin.

From north to south, the saints are identifiable as St Michael the Archangel, St John the Apostle, St Thomas the Apostle, St Bartholomew, St Jude the Apostle / Judas Thaddaeus, St Sebastian, St Peter and St Roch.

The part of the route from the Crown of Thorns to the Assumption of the Virgin Mary was rebuilt in 1999 in different artistic styles that attribute a personality to each mystery. In the same year, the Baroque Mysteries were painted in yellow, blue and white. There used to be a monumental arch with a statue of the King of Spain between the Agony in the Garden and the Scourging, but it was demolished to allow vehicles through, leaving only the pillars at the sides of the road.

NEARBY

Biblioteca Teológica Lorenzo Boturini

Plaza de las Américas 1, Colonia Villa de Guadalupe
5th floor, Nueva Basílica de Guadalupe, administrative building
Monday to Friday 9am–6pm
Admission free

On the fifth of the eight floors of the New Basilica of Our Lady of Guadalupe, the Lorenzo Boturini Theological Library houses a collection of 22,000 books, sermons and facsimiles relating to the *Guadalupano* phenomenon'. There are also rarities such as the *Nican Mopohua* translated from Nahuatl to Chinese, as well as a Braille Bible and a book dating from 1814 entitled *El duelo de la Inquisición* (The Mourning of the Inquisition), commiserating with the Spaniards 'for the disappearance of the so holy and so useful tribunal'.

MAMMOTH AT TALISMÁN METRO STATION

The mammoth talisman with uplifted trunk

East entrance to Talismán station
Monday to Friday 5am to 12am
Saturday from 6am
Sunday and public holidays from 7am
Admission free
Metro: Talismán

Facing the window of the east entrance to Talismán station, a gla case displays some ribs, feet and tusks on a bed of sand – the remair of one of the 13 mammoths discovered during excavations when th metro was constructed in 1978.

According to archaeologists Francisco Ortuño and Luis Alber López Wario, who discovered the skeletons, this mammoth live 12,000 years ago and was fully grown when it died.

In addition to the mammoths, other specimens of Pleistocene fauna were discovered during the excavations: crane eggs between Pantitlán and Hangares, a fish at La Raza, a camel between San Joaquín and Polanco, and two bison at Tacubaya and Oceanía stations.

The station logo created in 1982 for the opening of Line 4 by American graphic designer Lance Wyman, who had worked on metro iconography from 1969, was inspired by the mammoth discovery. He chose to use a mammoth with uplifted trunk (in China and India, an elephant in this position is thought to bring good luck), in reference to the nearby Calle Talismán, which gave its name to the metro station.

Statistics reveal Line 4 of the metro to be the least used, and Talismán the second-least used station of the line. Perhaps the mammoth talisman is watching over users' peace and quiet …

TEMPLO MORMÓN

A Mormon temple directly inspired by the Mayans

Avenida 510, No. 90
Colonia San Juan de Aragón
No entry in temple
Visitor Centre: admission free 9am–9pm daily (except public holidays)
Metro: Deportivo Oceanía

O f all the temples belonging to the Church of Jesus Christ of Latter-day Saints (better known as the Mormons), that of Mexico City is the only one inspired by indigenous architecture. The Mormon

Temple, designed by architect Emil Baer Fetzer between 1979 and 1983, is decorated with grid patterns and ornaments found in Mayan palaces: they don't refer to any particular deity. The American sculptor Avard Fairbanks' angel Moroni (1974; see box) stands on top of the temple.

On one side of the temple is the Visitors' Centre, which sets out the basic Mormon beliefs. The main hall has a replica of *Christus*, the marble statue of the resurrected Christ by Danish neoclassical sculptor Bertel Thorvaldsen. A reproduction of this sculpture, adopted by the Mormons in the 1950s, was placed in all their temples. Another room displays the history of the first Mexican believers and the arrival of the Mormon Church in Mexico, and has a model of Jerusalem at the time of Christ. There's also an interactive room for children. Look for the fresco of Christ arriving in a pre-Hispanic Mayan city where Indians come to kneel before him.

Church of Jesus Christ of Latter-day Saints

Also known as the Mormon Church, the Church of Jesus Christ of Latter-day Saints is a Christian movement with its headquarters in Salt Lake City, Utah (USA).

With more than 15 million members worldwide (1.3 million in Mexico – the country with the second largest Mormon community after the United States, with 6 million), the Church owes its existence to the appearance of various biblical characters to Joseph Smith: God the Father and Jesus Christ (the First Vision) in 1820, as well as several apostles and prophets. Joseph Smith, the first president of the Mormon Church, and his successors are considered to be modern prophets appointed by God, as in biblical times. In 1823, the angel Moroni is said to have appeared to Smith and revealed the burial site (Mount Cumorah in New York) of the texts on which the *Book of Mormon* is based. This is a compilation of religious and historical texts of the prophet Mormon, who is said to have lived AD 311–85 on the American continent. The *Book of Mormon* is presented as complementary to the Bible in telling the story of the ancient inhabitants of America and their covenant with Jesus Christ.

In Mormon temples, the Christian Cross isn't used as a symbol because Mormons believe in the risen and living Christ, which for them is actual fact. So the usual symbol is the angel Moroni, son of Mormon, proclaiming the Gospel.

MUSEO INDÍGENA

Harvest amulet, seaweed doll, mantilla of silver threads ...

Paseo de la Reforma Norte 707
Colonia Morelos
(+52) 5529 4699
cdi.gob.mx
Daily 10am–6pm
Admission free
Metro: Tlatelolco

The Indigenous Museum, housed in the Antigua Aduana del Pulque de Peralvillo, holds 115 masterpieces from the collection of the Comisión Nacional para el Desarrollo de los Pueblos Indígenas (National Commission for the Development of Indigenous Peoples). The aim is to demonstrate the current world view of the country's 68 indigenous communities.

The objects on display include a Nahua mask dating from 1907, made from wax with human hair and used to mock the Spanish. There is also a *nahual* (mythical protective being) that bears a strong resemblance to a bearded owl; a *tenábaris* (foot rattle) made from butterfly cocoons; a seaweed doll in Seri costume, dating back to 1950; and necklaces of ancient coins, little flowers or precious stones.

Although the workmanship is admirable, the most interesting thing about these artefacts is that each has significance in the indigenous world view. One example is the *huipil*, an indigenous garment woven on a loom. A copy in red fabric is kept for the day of death. As well as a reference to blood, the lozenge pattern on the garment represents the universe and the woman wearing it as the centre of the cosmos. There is also an 18th-century mantilla made at Querétaro by the Otomí people using cotton, dyed silk and silver threads.

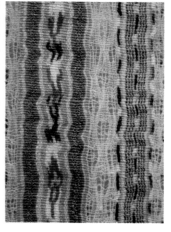

The *gigantón* is a Zoque object to be carried on the back, consisting of a wooden head with crocodile teeth that represents the plumed serpent Quetzalcóatl. It is used in ritual dances to bless the earth and its crops.

Other objects on show are clay dolls to be buried in the ground as an antidote to the evil eye, an Otomí book in *amate* bark paper with prayers to mestizo gods, a Nahua amulet in the shape of a tiny person to bring successful harvests, and an ornamental Maya table made from resin.

In Mexico, the survival of 20 out of 68 regional ethnic groups of the Aztec civilisation, such as the Lacandon and the Tlahuica, is threatened by widespread discrimination, exclusion and appropriation of their lands.

MONUMENTO
A LAS 7 CABRONAS

Monument that speaks for those who won't be silenced

Calle Rivero, junction with Toltecas
In the parking lot of La Fortaleza tenements
Metro: Tepito

Next to the parking lot at new Fortaleza (Fortress), in the north of the Tepito neighbourhood, an empty pedestal might surprise the keen-eyed visitor. There's no statue or artwork, just a plaque that reads: '*A las 7 cabronas e invisibles de Tepito. Las de antes y todas las que vendrán. Tepito, Julio 2009*' (To the 7 bitches and the unseen of Tepito. Those of yesterday and all those of tomorrow. Tepito, July 2009).

Over three Tuesdays in July 2009, Catalan artist Mireia Sallarès met the seven '*cabronas*' (meaning female dogs – in this case, an admiring epithet for tough matriarchs). The interviews she conducted with these women, in the presence of their neighbours, resulted in this monument.

Erected for these 'seven admirable women who look like pious little virgins, but who are really fierce little bitches who work, have kids, bring them up and support their families', it was billed as 'the monument that speaks for those who won't be silenced'.

Only their voices ring out from speakers, talking about the state of the neighbourhood. They speak, for example, 'of police operations, very impressive ... but just showing off'. They speak of their childhood: 'either you go to school or your brothers eat; of course, I had no childhood – playing with dolls doesn't mean anything to me, since my dolls, they were real!' And their private life: 'Nobody ever got one over on me, huh! Never! ... me, I always had a knife ready, and I told him, if you beat me up, I'll do you in, you son of a bitch. I was banged up for four years for not being a proper wife ... It's a great crime to be poor, to be a woman, to be a peasant. That hurts.'

Years later, the faces of the seven bitches were painted on the wall opposite the monument. Doña Queta, Lourdes Ruiz, Doña Chelo, Mayra, Véronica, Marina and Amelia are well known in the neighbourhood, but it takes an expert to recognise their portraits: the guardian of the shrine of Santa Muerte (Holy Death), the queen of dirty wordplay, or the defender of human rights who was attacked at UNAM. Some of their typical sayings are also on the mural.

Sallarès explains: 'A bitch isn't a woman that's never been fucked up. She's a woman who, despite all the blows that life throws at her, and when she's down or gets things wrong, always gets up and puts them right.'

LOS AUSENTES MULARAL

In memory of drug-trafficking victims

Junction of Mineros and Carpintería, Colonia Morelos
Guided tour recommended (see box opposite)
Metro: Tepito

F or over 20 years, a shrine known locally as the *Mural de los ausentes* (Mural of the Absent Ones) has stood at the junction of Mineros and Carpintería. The painting, marked by the passing of time, shows an elegantly dressed procession heading towards Cerro del Cubilete (a hill with a statue of Christ the King). These are well-known faces locally: street dealers, traffickers, drug addicts and innocent people who have died in a hail of bullets. All of them have been direct or indirect victims of the narcotics trade here in the city's worst trouble spot.

This mural was painted in memory of the humanity of these people, beyond the police reports in the newspapers and the violent incidents in which they died, all killed in painful circumstances linked to drug trafficking. The mural shows some of them smiling, others not. Both women and men are kneeling before Christ.

To one side is an altar and a huge wooden cross engraved with the nicknames of the fallen (many more than shown in the mural). The religious icons in glass cases represent families who have left someone's nickname on the cross.

On the other side of the street, pairs of trainers hung on the electricity cables represent the expression '*Ya colgó los tenis*' (He hung up his trainers), used to refer to someone's death. The deceased's footwear is tied together by the laces and thrown over the cables, as a reminder of those with no other way out.

Safari Cultural por Tepito

abcdetepito@hotmail.com or cronistasdf@hotmail.com
For more information: Galería José María Velasco, Peralvillo 55
Tepito is one of the most dangerous neighbourhoods in Mexico City, which is why few visitors venture there. But Alfonso Hernández, a local chronicler, organises 'Cultural Safaris'. This is the best way to get to know the streets, from the famous Shrine of Holy Death to the children's murals telling the mythical story of the nearby Casa Blanca.
Los ausentes and *Monumento a las 7 cabronas* murals are included in the tour. From its pre-Hispanic origins to its most celebrated affairs, this is without a doubt the best way to discover tough Tepito.

SOR JUANA'S CAMEO BROOCH

A coveted relic that belonged to the 'Phoenix of America'

Congreso de la Unión 66 - Museo Legislativo Los Sentimientos de la Nación
Monday to Friday 10am–6pm
Admission free (ID required)
(+52) 5628 1477
Metro: Candelaria

The Feelings of the Nation museum gives an overview of the history of Mexican legislation, but one exhibit has nothing to do with that theme: a 17th-century tortoiseshell cameo brooch, whose opaque surface reveals a wealth of meticulous Baroque detail. Juana Inés de Asbaje y Ramírez (also known as Sor Juana Inés de la Cruz), born around 1651, was the greatest intellectual of the Baroque era, described in such terms as the 'Tenth Muse' and the 'Phoenix of America'. Although celebrated for her poems, Christmas carols, songs of praise, prose writings and plays, her pursuits were not confined to literature. She also wrote recipes, composed music, and is even supposed to have made a self-portrait set in a ring.

In a Baroque world where learning was restricted in scope, Sor Juana prospered both intellectually and socially after she entered the convent of San Jerónimo in Mexico City. But, gradually overtaken by intrigue and the jealousy of her contemporaries, she fell ill and died on 17 April 1695 during an outbreak of the plague. She was buried within the convent, dressed in typical nun's attire with rosary and tortoiseshell cameo.

In 1978, an archaeological dig found the San Jerónimo burial site on land belonging to the president's sister, Margarita López Portillo. Based on a portrait made several years after Sor Juana's death, the anthropologist and archaeologist Arturo Romano Pacheco claimed to have found the nun's bones alongside the cameo brooch. Despite some doubts as to the veracity

of his claim, Pacheco took the brooch and gave it to Portillo – nobody could refuse someone in her position, after all. Then, in November 1995, the name of Sor Juana was inscribed in gilded letters in the Legislative Palace of San Lázaro and the cameo reclaimed. Three hundred years after the nun's death, it was reluctantly handed over for public display. Since then the brooch can be seen in its miniature showcase, even though there's still no proof that it belonged to Sor Juana. An odd ending for an unusual relic that has little to do with the seat of Mexican legislative power.

NEARBY

Garita de San Lázaro

Eje 2 Ote, Congreso de la Unión, junction with Emiliano Zapata

The San Lázaro *garita* (guardhouse) has a barely legible sign that says it was inaugurated by Viceroy Juan Ruiz de Apodaca, Count of Venadito, in 1820. Spanish playwright José Zorrilla (author of *Don Juan Tenorio*, a play about the life of Don Juan traditionally performed on All Saints' Day) took refuge there in 1855 when fleeing from his wife. The guardhouse also marks the beginning of the Porfirian canal system.

Hospital of San Lázaro

When the gates at the junction of Alarcón and Ferrocarril de Cintura are open, the church of the former lepers' hospital of San Lázaro, founded in 1572 by Dr Pedro López, can be seen in the background. The general air of abandonment led the Rolling Stones to use the site (which is closed to the public) for a video clip of their 1995 single, 'I Go Wild'.

VAULT OF PARROQUIA DEL PERPETUO SOCORRO

A colourful replica of Michelangelo's Sistine Chapel

Plaza de la Aviación 74
Colonia Moctezuma
Monday, Tuesday, Thursday and Friday 10am–1pm and 4pm–7pm, Saturday 10am–1pm
Metro: Moctezuma

he Perpetuo Socorro (Perpetual Help) parish church has an extraordinary replica (still unfinished) of Michelangelo's ceiling in the Sistine Chapel. The painter is Miguel Francisco Macías.

Although the paintings are identical to the original, as the artist is trying to be as faithful as possible, the replica is even more colourfully 'Mexicanised'.

This eccentric idea occurred to Don Miguel after he visited the Sistine Chapel in 1999. On his return from Rome, he asked for permission to make a copy in the vault of the parish church, and was allowed to start work on the 14 canvases that can be seen today. There's only an 85-centimetre difference in the dimensions of the Sistine and Perpetuo Socorro roofs.

The paintings are hung as and when they are completed: the first, *The Creation of Adam*, was blessed by Cardinal Norberto Ribera on 16 July 2006 at its unveiling ceremony. Since then, the comments have come thick and fast, both positive and negative, and some critics have even suggested adding Mexican ornamental elements – a proposal ignored by Don Miguel.

Although the artist is now retired, thanks to donations from the congregation he is still working on his project in order to realise his dream. It's definitely worth coming to see this great work in progress.

When visiting the church, don't miss the beautiful window in the choir, depicting Our Lady of Perpetual Help.

BAÑOS MEDICINALES DEL PEÑÓN ㉑

A mirror from the Empress Carlota in appreciation of Peñón spa

Puerto Aéreo 465
Peñón de los Baños
Open to visitors daily 6am–8pm
Metro: Oceanía / Terminal Aérea

The medicinal waters of Peñón de los Baños, on the ground floor of a group of anonymous buildings dating from 1975, are a well-kept secret. These waters, naturally saturated with carbon dioxide, sodium, calcium, magnesium, lithium, potassium, aluminium, chromium and even a certain amount of radioactivity, are good for you. According to a client's poem hanging at the entrance: *Dejará de sufrir / de los males que lo aquejan / porque a los enfermos dejan / con deseos de vivir* (He will no longer suffer / from the ailments that afflict him / because they leave the sick / with the desire to live).

Nowadays, sick people from the neighbourhood tend to go there to ease their pain by taking a dip in the private pools; a room with bath can be booked. The waters are piped from the depths of the mountain to the intimacy of the rooms. Massage services are also on offer.

In addition to the spa, the establishment has an interesting collection of souvenirs displayed in the entrance hall and corridors: the gold medal awarded at the Universal Exposition of St Louis (USA) in 1904; first prize at the International Hygiene Exhibition of 1907 in Madrid; a diploma from the International Association of Fairs in San Antonio, Texas. There's also a comprehensive study of the thermal waters carried out by the UNAM Institute of Geology in 2003, and a plan of Monte Peñón drawn up by the Mexican Geological Survey.

The most interesting piece of memorabilia is perhaps the mirror donated by Empress Carlota during her visit to the spa with Maximilian – it's still used by visitors today.

At the end of the 19th century, Don Manuel Romero Rubio set up a bottling plant to commercialise the spa waters and opened a hotel, which was abandoned following the Revolution. The only reminders of this project are four carved wooden chairs where visitors can still take rest.

The spa waters are said to have spouted from the heart of Cópil, who was captured and killed by the Aztecs and his heart thrown into the lake. His mother, the sorceress Malinalxóchitl, had been abandoned by him during their founding pilgrimage from the north.

Inside the spa complex is an 18th-century chapel with little carved faces on the walls. It is believed that these represent the flowers carved by indigenous people to bless the chapel, and that the columns allude to the two streams of drinking water that flowed alongside the spa waters.

STATUE IN PARQUE DEL NIÑO QUEMADO

The boy who braved a burning bus to save two little girls

Junction of Río Consulado and Quetzalcóatl
Colonia Peñón de los Baños
Metro: Terminal Aérea

arque del Niño José Luis Ordaz López, in the Peñón de los Baños district, is commonly known as Parque del Niño Quemado (Park f the Burned Child) in reference to the moving but little-known statue f the child José Luis saving two younger girls from the flames.

In 1959, in a spectacular accident at this spot, a bus overturned and ught fire. José Luis, who was barely 10 years old, ran inside to rescue vo little girls trapped inside. Then, as he was trying to save a third erson, the fuel tank exploded and killed him.

In 1964, local residents had is monument erected on the te.

The Secretary of Education at e time, Jaime Torres Bordet, tended the unveiling ceremony. he president of the D.F. Parents' ederation, *Licenciado* Morales ménez, said in his speech: 'To e so that others can live is one f the most sublime forms of eroism.' José Luis was hailed as a ipreme hero, and later that year newly built nursery school in the ort of Veracruz was named after m.

EARBY
he oldest human remains in Latin America

few blocks north of Parque del Niño José Luis Ordaz López, at e junction of Emiliano Zapata and Bolivares, the fossilised human mains of a woman were coincidentally discovered while a well was eing drilled in 1959. Carbon 14 testing revealed that this woman had ved about 12,700 years ago, making these the oldest known remains Latin America. Unfortunately there's no record of the find at the site, hich is a residential area.

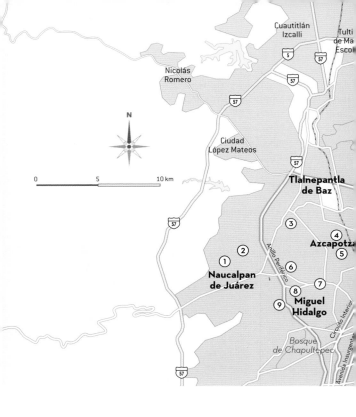

To the North

SENOSIAIN'S ORGANIC HOUSES

Unique multicoloured residences on the heights of Naucalpan

All these houses are in Vista del Valle and Paseos del Bosque, Naucalpan, State of Mexico
El Kiss: Morelia aqueduct
Ballena Mexicana: Tenantongo aqueduct
Nautillus: end of Calle Villa de los Encinos
El nido de Quetzalcóatl: between Villa de los Encinos and Villa de los Pirules / Villa de los Naranjos impasse
Private houses, not open to the public

Extraordinary forms emerge on the Naucalpan skyline like some gigantic multicoloured snake or a huge seashell – these are the stunning houses designed by architect Javier Senosiain, his version of what is known as organic architecture.

It's difficult to reach the residential area where the houses are situated without a car: Senosiain's creations are scattered around private land. But you can still get near enough to admire the façades and entrances (depending on the mood of the security guard on duty).

The first stop is a gatehouse built in 1999 and named *El Kiss*, after a well-known chocolate. The barrier that lets vehicles through is joined to the gatehouse like a medieval spear. Unfortunately, the owners have added a much less aesthetic barrier in front of it.

Built in 1992, the huge cetacean-like house is called *Ballena Mexicana* (Mexican Whale). Although you won't be able to see the house itself in all its splendour, the high outer wall is decorated with little triangular mosaics and huge planters, forming interesting geometric figures.

The last two properties, dating from 2007, are part of the Paseos del Bosque development. *Nautillus* is a snail-shaped house with a huge stained-glass window in the living room: you can see the character of the place, as well as its original entrance, from the street.

El nido de Quetzalcóatl (Quetzalcóatl's Nest) is the most impressive work of all: a large and cavernous gully that Senosiain has transformed into a fascinating snake-shaped residence, in reference to the Aztec legend of Quetzalcóatl. Initially, it wasn't meant to take the form of a snake, but Senosiain came up with the idea of adding not only a rattlesnake's head, but also a tail with multicoloured doughnut-shaped scales. You can see all this from the outside.

The gatehouse, like a sloughed snakeskin, can also be seen from the street. The outside wall and the main entrance gate a block away are beautiful creations that coexist in perfect harmony with the magnificent panorama of Naucalpan.

MONOLITH OF ACATLÁN

A volcanic rock with a mural about nuclear war

Avenida Jardines de San Mateo, junction with Yaquis
Facultad de Estudios Superiores (FES) Acatlán grounds
Restricted access
Buses to FES Acatlán depart from exit J of Cuatro Caminos metro station

The spectacular monolith of Acatlán, weighing 67 tonnes and measuring 6 metres high, stands in one of the courtyards of FES Acatlán. The stone is believed to have been ejected during the eruption of Xitle (3rd century AD) and come to rest on Monte Judío, from where it was moved to its present site in 1984. The mural is by the artist Roberto Roque y Manrique.

The stone is set on top of a mound of petrified lava on a bed of *tezontle*, emulating the volcanic eruption. The mural, entitled *La humanidad hoy* (Humanity Today), reflects on the dangers that humanity inflicts on itself.

On the surfaces of the rock we see the danger of a holocaust with weeping figures embracing, the threat of a nuclear and biological war with people wearing gas masks, the pollution of vast cities, and other contemporary threats.

One face of the mural also attempts to recreate empathy between man and nature, showing a human being observing a strange fish in the sea. On another face, shrouded in sun and wind, a woman views the cosmos through a telescope. The mural expresses the two sides of humanity today: the destructive and the creative.

The monolith was moved at no charge by the ICA company, using a crane travelling along the ring road. A misunderstanding about misappropriation of funds provoked a student demonstration against the move, which began at 11pm and was completed by 4am. In order not to damage the mural, the authorities had to prevent students from clambering all over it. This gave rise to the popular legend that the academic career of anyone who touches the monolith will come to an abrupt and permanent end.

The monolith was not supposed to be in this courtyard – the crane couldn't get between the buildings to reach the designated site, so set it down here instead.

HISTORY TRAIL IN PARQUE TEZOZÓMOC

A huge scale model of the vanished Texcoco lake

Entrance on De las Armas, Hacienda del Rosario, Hacienda Sotelo Zempoaltecas
Colonia Prados del Rosario
(+52) 5382 7209
Tuesday to Sunday 6am–6pm
Metro: El Rosario

The huge earth mounds of Parque Tezozómoc, contrasting with the surrounding Azcapotzalco plain, are not natural – they replicate the topography of the valley of Mexico as it was in the 15th century.

The model was the idea of landscape designer Mario Schjetnan who, when the park was planned in 1982 during the construction of metro line 6 (from El Rosario to Martín Carrera), suggested that the earth from the underground excavations should be used to represent the mountains and volcanoes around the city, as well as the former lake of Texcoco.

So a huge scale model was built, covering 28 hectares – this has recently been integrated with the history trail, consisting of a series of obelisks and a path linking them. Each obelisk marks the site of a pre-Hispanic settlement and illustrates its history.

Remember that Mexico City was built over what was once the huge lake of Texcoco, represented in the park by a miniature lake where you can take out a rowing boat and feed the ducks. In the centre of the lake, an islet marks the site of the great city of Tenochtitlán, capital of the Aztec empire. Sculptures of Mexican myths about the foundation of the city, such as the eagle perched on a prickly pear and devouring a snake, complete the picture.

Thirty years after it opened, the park had fallen into disuse and was looking extremely neglected until a restoration campaign was launched. In addition to the obelisks, photos of the construction history are now on display attached to lamp-posts.

Ancestors of the Tepanec people planted trees at Azcapotzalco

Tree 1: Plaza de los Ahuehuetes, Calle Lerdo de Tejada, Barrio Tezozómoc
Metro: Aquiles Serdán
Tree 2: Calle Central, junction with Tlatelco, Barrio de San Andrés
Metro: Ferrería

Two *ahuehuetes* (Mexican cypresses) rooted in pre-Hispanic myth survive in the Azcapotzalco municipality of north-west Mexico City. The first, on the border between the Tezozómoc district and San Juan Tlihuaca, is protected by a small fountain and gazebo but is half dead. The second, still flourishing in a plaza off Calle Central, offers shade to the residents of San Andrés.

Before Azcapotzalco developed into an industrial zone, its large plots separated by these huge cypress trees were popular with city landowners and put to various uses. Only after several archaeological surveys was it discovered that the trees were not there by chance but had been strategically planted by the pre-Hispanic Tepanec people, who arrived in the valley in the 11th century.

Since leaving Michoacán and heading east, the *teomamas* (tribal priests) had been carrying seven cypresses that represented their ancestors, which is why the Tepanec are said to be descended from trees. When they arrived at Azcapotzalco, they planted the seven trees to mark out the settlement, and the others have grown over time.

Most of the trees that delimited their property have not survived.

According to some historians, the Tepanec settled here in 1012, establishing one of the first colonies in the valley of Mexico. It appears that these two cypresses were among the seven original trees, and the fact that at least one is still alive would make the Tepanec proud.

Doubts about the history of the *ahuehuetes* have given rise to countless local legends. Many believe that the Aztec emperor Moctezuma hid his treasure from the conquistador Cortés among the tree roots. More recently, a woman who was attacked and murdered near the San Andrés tree is said to appear on the first Friday of each month to scare innocent passers-by on their nightly stroll.

ANT ON THE BELL TOWER
OF LOS SANTOS APÓSTOLES

The ant of the Apocalypse

Parish and convent of Santos Apóstoles Felipe y Santiago el menor
Avenida Azcapotzalco, s/n, opposite Jardín Hidalgo
Monday to Saturday 10am–8pm
Metro: Camarones

Azcapotzalco, a word derived from the Nahuatl language, means 'in the anthill', and the ant features in local iconography – public places and tourist sites usually have sculptures or images of ants. Even the metro station logo has a friendly cartoon insect.

There's a red ant crawling up the bell tower of the church of the Holy Apostles Philip and James the Less – some people take it for a spider. According to the older members of the community, the ant predicts the day that the world will end.

The enslaved indigenous peoples, who were 'asked nicely' to help build the church, are said to have put a curse on the conquistadors by setting the ant at the base of the tower. Since the 16th century, its little feet have been creeping up the wall from the original spot. Apparently, when the ant reaches the top, this will signify the coming of the Apocalypse.

Those who know about the legend are frequently unaware of its origins – the texts are confusing, with writers from different eras all describing the tower and the ant. When seen from the ground, each author judged the ant to be at a different height, and so the popular catastrophe theory was born. The truth is that the ant was simply placed there in the name of the feudal estate of Azcapotzalco, but the legend clings on, like the ant on the wall.

NEARBY

The parish church of the Holy Apostles has kept its original mural and some beautiful colonial wood-panelling inside the convent. An ancient arch at one end of the atrium led to the cemetery (the inscription can still be seen). Some of those who fought at the battle of Azcapotzalco are buried there. The last battle of the Mexican War of Independence is commemorated by a statuette in the main aisle of the atrium and a plaque on the outside wall.

TOMB OF CAROLINA TRONCOSO ⑥

The dead woman who works miracles

Calzada San Bartolo Naucalpan, junction with Calzada Ingenieros Militares
Panteón Español (Section G)
Tuesday to Sunday 8am–4pm
Restricted access
Metro: Panteones

n the huge Spanish Cemetery, it's easy to miss the tomb of Carolina Troncoso: a marble sepulchre surmounted with a statue of Christ. But close look at the white walls reveals written messages and petitions ddressed to the deceased.

It's said that Carolina Troncoso, who died in 1920, was a small, unchbacked woman who lived in the town of Tacuba. She had hoped ɔ be a nun, but abandoned her dream in order to look after her parents. he used to give advice to her friends and neighbours, who considered er saintly for being so charitable. A heart attack finally carried her off, ut two years later, when her sisters and friends had the sepulchre built, he whole town was surprised to learn that her body had not decayed.

When she was reburied in 1922, people began to visit her grave ɔ ask for miracles, a tradition that continues to this day. The only ondition is that you must leave a gift and pencil your petition on the ɔmb. For the miracle to happen, you must touch the stone as you write nd speak your request out loud.

In the 1950s, many supplicants were young people wanting to pass heir exams, so Carolina became known as the students' saint. But she believed to grant anybody's request. The messages often describe life xperiences. Some are thank-you letters and others are requests: begging ɔr a husband to return, a cancer patient to be cured, a family to be rotected, or to help someone find a job or give up alcohol, or even for usiness advice.

People greet her, treat her like a friend, leave her their credentials, weets, toys and flowers, draw hearts for her and ask for her compassion.

Among all the messages, only one is addressed to visitors. It was ngraved in the marble in 1922: '*Fue un alma grande; corazón de niño; n amarme cifró todo su anhelo; consagradle un recuerdo de cariño, pero no lloréis, está en el cielo*' (She was a great soul with the heart of a child; he was devoted to me; remember her fondly but do not weep for her, he is in heaven).

'If she doesn't want to be found, you'll never find her'

There is a legend that if Carolina Troncoso doesn't want to be found, her grave is impossible to reach: only true believers know exactly how to get there.

AZCAPOTZALCO'S 'CHALETS'

19th-century middle-class residences

Along Azcapotzalco, from Estío / Clavería as far as Pinitos
Metro: Refinería

When the imperious publisher of *El imparcial*, Rafael Reyes Spíndola, decided to establish a district named after his newspaper, he could never have imagined it would leave such a curious architectural memorial to the Porfirian middle class.

The district was soon filled with 'chalet-style' residences, with a narrow route linking the town of Azcapotzalco to the expanding city of Mexico. This is now Avenida Azcapotzalco, along which several of the residences still stand – some are neglected while others still look splendid.

There are only a few examples of this type of architecture in Mexico City. Ranging in style from Dutch colonial to English residential, the chalets were home to personalities such as actress and film director Patricia Reyes Spíndola, government secretary Ángel Zimbrón, editor-in-chief of *El imparcial* Carlos Díaz Dufoo, and member of parliament Aquiles Elórduy.

Some of these chalets can be seen at numbers 182 (now a restaurant), 196, 197 (this one looks like the set of a horror movie), 226, 229, 236, 254, 308 (a complex of several chalets now used by the Technological University of Mexico), 313, 318, 339 and 347. Numbers 84, 167 and 172, before the junction of Azcapotzalco and Clavería, are also worth a look. There are others, but unfortunately with garden walls that block the view.

It's worth mentioning that Reyes Spíndola, whose paper supported Díaz's government, made more from real estate than he ever did from publishing.

SAN JOAQUÍN WATER TANK

*In the middle of a cemetery, the remains of
a colonial water tank guarded by a lion*

*Calzada Legaria 449
Colonia Deportiva Pensil
Inside Panteón Francés de San Joaquín
Metro: Panteones*

The ruined structure at the end of the main pathway in the Panteón
Francés (French Cemetery) is the last vestige of an 18th-century
tank, still strangely beautiful despite its state of neglect. To reach it, first
climb a set of steps and then pass through an archway of the same era
into a side passage.

The basin is currently dry, but in colonial days it was fed by the
Remedios river and supplied San Joaquín convent. The tank and
cemetery belonged to the convent (which has kept its original medieval
style, thanks to the latest restoration), and they were run like the
Carmelite Order's kitchen gardens.

The construction, which forms a viewpoint with its ancient arcade
of enormous arches covered by barrel vaulting, is accessible from the
passages at the side of the tank. The site is guarded by the colonial statue
of a lion, which served as a kind of fountain.

It's believed that the tank was built during the second priorship of
Father Alejo de San Joaquín, between 1741 and 1744. There are still
some traces of murals inside the arcade, as well as a large stone bench
which the monks used for rest and contemplation. After the site was
deconsecrated, it was used as a recreational space by local people, who
even swam in the pool.

BAOBAB TREE
ON THE PERIFÉRICO

An African tree sprouting from a skyscraper window

Boulevard Manuel Ávila Camacho 184
Building not open to the public
Microbus: Line 2–32 (connection from Chapultepec and Polanco metro stations)

A baobab leans reflectively against the glass surface of a skyscraper among the concrete arteries of the second level of the Periférico (ring road). The tree is actually growing out of a planter on the ninth floor, right next to the window.

The planter, 2 metres across, stands in a rest area inside the building and contains a tonne of earth to keep the tree upright, as it's been trained to grow crookedly out through the window. Watering is automatic when needed, and the tree even has its own gardener.

The baobab is an African tree with a characteristic broad trunk and yellow flowers that bloom in summer. To prevent it growing too big and damaging the infrastructure, the branches are pruned regularly.

The idea of installing this tree is generally attributed to architect Víctor de la Lama, who apparently wanted to create a contrast between the natural and the built environment.

MONUMENT TO DRAINAGE PIPES

Commemorating the hydro engineers

Junction of Avenida Luis Espinoza with Benito Juárez
Colonia Solidaridad, Delegación Gustavo A. Madero
RTP bus: route 103; Metro: La Raza – Ampliación Malacates

To the north of the city, on land between the Tenayo and Chiquihuite mountains owned by the Centro de Estudios Tecnológicos Industrial y de Servicios (Centre for Technical, Industrial and Service Studies / CETIS), strange concrete towers support large metal plates gleaming against the sky. Although the site is off-limits to visitors, the towers can be seen in the distance.

When CETIS opened in 1998, the towers – the highest 30 metres and the lowest 13 metres – were already known as La Lumbrera (The Drainage Pipe). Before CETIS, the site was an outpost of the Deep Drainage System (see box), used for repairing water tankers. The employees founded a museum with descriptions and photographs of Mexico's hydro-engineering system. Sculptor Ángeles Gurría won a competition to design a commemorative monument, which was built between 1974 and 1975. The museum closed in 1997 and the building was handed over to CETIS, which has kept the monument.

What are 'lumbreras'?

Lumbreras are a series of gigantic water pipes built around Mexico City, designed to drain away and recover rainwater to prevent flooding. They can lower the water level by as much as 45 metres. One of these pipes is just across the street.

MUSEO DE GEOLOGÍA Y PALEONTOLOGÍA

Some of the Earth's surprising geological formations

Avenida Ticomán 600
Premises of the Escuela Superior de Ingeniería y Arquitectura Ticomán
(+52) 5729 6000 Ext. 56043
Monday to Friday 9am–6pm
Admission free
RTP bus: route 102

A group of low shelves in the entrance hall to the Museum of Geology and Palaeontology has a collection of 300 fossils, 308 rocks and 600 different minerals. You'll need to bend down to see the details of all these geological formations.

The museum is divided into three parts. The first (Palaeontology) has fossils such as a horse's skull, mammoth bones and cephalopods (marine mammals)/ molluscs) from the Cretaceous period.

The Mineralogy section is the most comprehensive: each stone and mineral has great aesthetic value. Understandably, the gemstones showcase is the most attractive of all: it contains wulfenite, tiger eye, agate, jasper, pyrite and quartz, all donated by the engineer Julio Eduardo Morales. Don't miss the opalised (iridescent) ammonite – in reality, a snail fossil.

Another showcase has calcites and malachites, but the most impressive of all contains a demonstration of the Mohs scale: this measures the hardness of minerals from 1 to 10, 1 corresponding to talc and 10 to diamond. The museum vault has a diamond that's only brought out for student group visits, although a replica is on permanent display.

The most intriguing stone is pyrite, the notorious 'fool's gold' that emits sparks when struck: because of its colour, people once thought it was gold. Some showcases hold sulphides, a mixture of sulphur and other chemical elements and magmatic rocks that forms when magma cools and crystallises.

Finally, in the Petrography (study of rocks) section, oil-extraction methods are described with the help of maquettes. It might seem less appealing but the tour continues on the campus patios, including a steam engine dating from the 19th century and another from 1924, as well as the extraction tower that dominates the exhibition.

The museum is particularly oriented towards students. Book a guided tour to benefit from the educational activities that give an insight into the geological sciences.

WATER TANK OF THE ACUEDUCTO DE GUADALUPE ⑫

Water tank of one of the city's last aqueducts

Cantera, junction with Misterios
Metro: La Villa

At the southern end of Parque del Mestizaje (Mestizo Park), on Calle Morelos, is a little building that seems to have been left to its sad fate. However, a plaque on the wall records its ostentatious inauguration in the 18th century. The building at the back of La Villa was actually the water tank for the Guadalupe aqueduct.

The tank's Baroque façade is built of stone quarried from the hills of Guadalupe. The rear wall has deteriorated over the years, although some restoration was carried out in 1970.

According to the records, an underground pipe fed water from the tank to La Villa esplanade. A huge fountain stood there, 10 metres in diameter, with a column representing the four parts of the colonial world: Asia, Africa, Europe and America. After eight years of work, water began to flow in July 1751 to great celebration.

Driving along, it's impossible to miss the 2,287 remaining arches that stretch for 7 kilometres (originally 10 kilometres), as they are such a feature of the urban landscape. The last 100 metres now form the southeast boundary of the park, but following the aqueduct from beginning to end you'll notice that one section is underground, another at a height of 3 metres and another at ground level.

The aqueduct was built so that pilgrims who came to worship Our Lady of Guadalupe had clean water to drink, as the water in both Texcoco lake and Guadalupe river was contaminated. Farms along the route could also irrigate their wheat and corn crops. A series of rest areas with statues of saints, some of which are still there, is a reminder of the aqueduct's religious connections.

Under the Porfirian government's slogan of 'order and progress', the aqueduct was replaced by an iron pipe. The huge fountain at La Villa disappeared, but the water tank and the aqueduct were preserved for their ornamental value.

In December 1815, the committee charged with taking José María Morelos to Ecatepec to be executed (see p. 313) stopped at the aqueduct to allow the insurgent hero a last drink. The nearby Calle Morelos is named after him.

MUSEO DE FIGURAS DE CERA

Harsh scenes of daily life immortalised in wax

Calzada de los Misterios 880
Daily 9.30am–7pm
Metro: La Villa

A lady of the night welcoming visitors with a strange grimace is the
only clue to the location of the Wax Museum, in an old mansion
on Calzada de los Misterios.

Although it isn't a big museum, it has a series of huge displays of historical and popular scenes featuring the most interesting characters from Mexican daily life. You're as likely to come across a prostitute or a drunk as a beggar or social outcast. Other showcases have fantastic scenes and real historical events such as the self-flagellation of Martín de Porres (patron saint of mixed-race people) or a soldier from the French intervention in Mexico of the 1860s.

The displays all have a short description to help visitors understand the context, such as biographical details, a verse or a quotation. The most shocking among them are a terminally ill tuberculosis patient and an artist attacked by his own creation.

Regular visitors will notice that some of the displays are changed every few months, because the museum only has space for a small part of the vast collection of the Neira Castillo family. They opened the exhibition in 1949 at a different venue – the present location has been open since 1957.

The prostitute at the entrance was immortalised in 1969, when Mexican photographer Graciela Iturbide discovered the waxwork in the museum. Her photo became one of Iturbide's most memorable images.

Some of the waxworks starred in the 1963 B movie, *Santo en el Museo de Cera* (Santo in the Wax Museum – featuring masked wrestler El Santo). The museum in the movie is actually the home of film director Emilio 'El Indio' Fernández (see p. 132).

MODEL OF LA VILLA

⑭

Monte Tepeyac in miniature, as it was in 1949

Plaza de las Américas 1
Ofrenda de las Flores shopping centre
Villa de Guadalupe
Daily 9am–6pm
Metro: La Villa

To the right of the sculptural group *La Ofrenda* in Villa de Guadalupe, at the end, is an arcaded shopping centre. At the rear of one of the shops is a door with a sign inviting you to come in and see *la maqueta* (the model).

Inside, you're confronted with a spectacular model that faithfully reproduces Monte Tepeyac and its surroundings as they were in 1949.

A plaque explains that the model was designed by engineer Manuel Calderón Leonardo Lemus in 1949, hence the innumerable contemporary details. Comparing the model to the present day, some changes are obvious: a public park on the site of today's Basilica of Our Lady of Guadalupe; a neocolonial market in the plaza where the Carrillón Guadalupano (the huge stone cross with bells that ring every hour) stands today; houses and entire neighbourhoods built on the steps leading to the shrine, and so on. You can also see the market stalls near the old basilica and the fountains and sculptures that were demolished to make way for Plaza de las Américas.

The model is so detailed that each individual tombstone in La Villa cemetery is shown at the top of the hill. Tiny trucks run through the streets that are now reserved for pilgrims on foot. The little houses that used to stand around Capilla del Pocito can now only be seen in the model.

Alongside this delightful miniature world are glass cases containing popular reproductions of the *Virgen Morena* (Brown Virgin, in her darker-skinned Mexican incarnation) made from seashells, wax, wood, carved stone, paper, seeds, palm leaves, and even a hologram.

Although the history of *la maqueta* is unknown, it was fortunately completed just three years before the Plaza de las Américas was built, when the hill and its surroundings became a shrine and lost its village atmosphere.

The shopping centre where the model is located was built in 1984 by the Tepeyac Trust. Past presidents and historical figures are depicted on the columns, along with anecdotes about their connection with Our Lady of Guadalupe. These include the moment when Agustín de Iturbide (Augustine of Mexico) passed the baton of the Imperial Order of Guadalupe to the Virgin, the official pilgrimage of President Ignacio Comonfort, and the day when President Ruiz Cortines gave a crown to the Virgin.

GUADALUPE'S FIRST HERMITAGE ⑮

Archaeological relics where the Guadalupano cult began

Plaza de las Américas 1
Colonia Villa de Guadalupe
Inside Capilla de Indios
Daily 8am–6pm (visits during Mass not advisable)
Admission free
Metro: La Villa

Visitors are generally discouraged from entering the presbytery of a Catholic church out of respect, but in this case it's the only way to reach the archaeological relics of a former hermitage.

The theatrically lit foundations mark the site where the first hermitage dedicated to the Virgin of Guadalupe was built in 1531, soon after her apparition. This is the place where the miraculous *tilma* (Indian cloak) of St Juan Diego was laid down. He lived there for 17 years until his death, and may have been buried there.

Because of the saint's indigenous origins, the hermitage was called the Capilla de Indios (Chapel of the Indians). This is the most modern chapel in the La Villa complex, having been renovated in 1556, 1622, 1649 and 1998.

According to legend, the Virgin of Guadalupe herself had asked for this hermitage to be built for her veneration. However, the growth of the *Guadalupano* cult led to a frenzy of church, hermitage, temple and chapel building, and the new Basilica of Our Lady of Guadalupe became the final home of the miraculous image.

After the insurgents' defeat at Aculco in 1810 (see p. 323), colonial soldier Manuel Perfecto found on the battlefield the mythical banner of Guadalupe that Hidalgo had raised at the beginning of the independence movement. Viceroy Apodaca ordered that the banner should be kept in the Parroquia de Indios (Parish of the Indians), where it remained until 1853.

There is a story that Juan Diego, his wife María Lucía and his uncle Juan Bernardino were buried in the Parish of the Indians. Diego's canonisation triggered a fruitless search for his remains, sparking controversy over whether he had really existed or was invented to help convert the indigenous people to Christianity. Those who believe in his existence claim that the remains were moved during the Cristero War when a bomb was planted to destroy the *tilma*. A glass case in the basilica contains a twisted metal crucifix that survived the blast. As for Juan Diego, a museum has been created in the conurbation of Cuautitlán where people believe the saint lived.

MUSEO DE LA PLUMA

The pen that writes under water, on greasy paper, in zero gravity and at any angle

Avenida Tecnológico, Colonia Valle de Anáhuac
Tecnológico de Estudios Superiores de Ecatepec, entrance 2
Monday to Friday 9am–6pm
Admission free
Metro: Ecatepec

The Pen Museum, housed in one of the rooms of Ecatepec Higher Education Technical College (TESE), traces the history of pens from the time of cave-dwellers, when ink was made from blood, to the modern digital age, when pens still survive.

To illustrate these developments, the collection includes pens of various shapes and sizes, ink-making equipment, Chinese brushes, and holders for different types of nib.

But the most curious part of the story dates from the development of the 'atomic pen' in the 1950s. As well as a recording pen of 1990, there's a pen with a mini-camera from 1956, pens with multiplication tables, craft pens with a blade, perfumed pens, and a collection of erotic pens that show nude images in the handle when moved.

The strangest example from this period is perhaps the Zero Gravity pen, which writes under water, on greasy paper, at any temperature or angle, and even in weightless conditions. It was made specifically for NASA astronauts.

Other curiosities are a pot-shaped pen used for writing in gold, and a 1905 pen 21-millimetres-long, only a hundred of which were made.

The collection also has pens belonging to celebrities such as actress Sara García, architect Pedro Ramírez Vázquez, writer Carlos Monsiváis, composer Manuel M. Ponce, and even a case holding two pens that belonged to Salvador Dalí. You'll also find the pens of members of the Congreso de la Unión (Federal Government), such as the one President Lázaro Cárdenas used to sign the Mexican oil expropriation of 1938, nationalising all petroleum reserves and facilities.

The collection belongs to engineer Humberto Rodríguez Lozada, who sourced the pieces in antique markets and set up the museum in 1998.

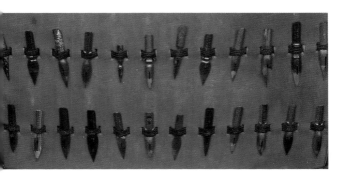

CENTRO CULTURAL PUENTE DEL ARTE

A museum inside a bridge, perhaps built by Gustave Eiffel

Vía Morelos, junction with 1 de Mayo – Colonia San Juan Alcahuacán
puentedelarte.blogspot.mx
Tuesday to Sunday 11am–5pm
Admission free
Mexibus: Puente de Fierro

Covered with aluminium sheeting to conceal the interior from passers-by, two twin bridges make up the old Puente de Fierro

(Iron Bridge), now the Arts Bridge Cultural Centre. One of the bridges is the home and studio of painter Manuel Bueno. The other is the result of his efforts to create a space open to the public as a museum and leading gallery in the municipality. Various arts workshops and frequently changing exhibitions are held in this space: the only permanent work is a mural on the history of Ecatepec by Manuel Bueno. The mural was inaugurated in 1993 at the Palacio Municipal de Ecatepec, but in 2000 it was moved to the bridge so that the public could see it. The artist is sometimes there to comment on details of his work, such as the face of María Félix playing a rural schoolteacher in the film *Río escondido* (*Hidden River*, 1948) filmed at Tulpetlac in 1936. Line B of the metro, the execution of independentist general José María Morelos by firing squad, apparitions of the Virgin, and various monuments and historical events from Ecatepec can also be seen in the painting.

The bridge, which was brought over to Mexico from Europe in 1879, still crosses the Gran Canal del Desagüe. In 1941, it was restored and connected to the México–Pachuca route as Puente Ing. Ernesto Uriegas. However, once a new highway was opened, the bridge was used less and less and eventually it was abandoned. It was converted into the Arts Bridge Cultural Centre in 1997.

Was Gustave Eiffel responsible for the plans?

The plans for the bridge are said to have been drawn up by Gustave Eiffel, although there's no real evidence for this.

But maybe it's not so far-fetched, given the design and date of construction. The story goes that Eiffel made the plans in France and the sections arrived in Mexico to be assembled by local engineers.

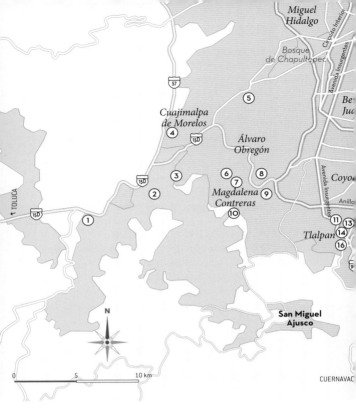

To the South

TOLSÁ'S OBELISK

An obelisk built 15 years before the event it commemorates

Parque Nacional Insurgente Miguel Hidalgo / La Marquesa
Inside the park, between highway and trunk road
Carretera México–Toluca, km 56
Route 76 destination La Marquesa (departure Chapultepec metro station)

a Marquesa is a huge expanse of land between Mexico City and Toluca made up of several parks. Its official name, Parque Nacional Insurgente Miguel Hidalgo, refers to Father Miguel Hidalgo, who led the insurgents at the battle of Mont de las Cruces on 30 October 1810.

Near the park entrance, between the highway and the trunk road, stands an obelisk commemorating this battle. It was erected in 1795, 5 years earlier. In 1791 Viceroy Vicente de Güemes ordered military engineer Manuel Agustín Mascaró to rebuild the road leading to Toluca. Mascaró's project included this obelisk designed by renowned neoclassical architect Manuel Tolsá.

Mascaró began work with two teams, one in Toluca and the other in Mexico City. When they met halfway, the monument was erected on a monolith placed on what was then the highest section of the route. Although there's no proof that Tolsá was responsible for the obelisk, it's based on a signed drawing that included a sundial on all four sides.

In 1852 the obelisk was recycled in the nationalist cause: the sundial was removed and plaques were added commemorating Father Hidalgo's 1810 battle.

Nowadays the park has facilities for hiking, horseriding and fishing.

The road leading to the Insurgent Miguel Hidalgo National Park was the old Mexico City–Toluca highway. Near the obelisk are an ancient stone bridge and a neocolonial arch dating from 1942, marking the beginning of the Mexico City–Toluca road from the borders of the State of Mexico. Its twin stands in the city of Toluca, along the Lerma river.

Tolsá erected a fountain in 1793 at the junction of Serapio Rendón and Gómez Farías, Tacubaya district, marking the beginning of Mascaró's road.

PASEO DE LAS ERMITAS (HERMITAGES WALK)

Discover hidden hermitages in the depths of the fores.

Parque Nacional Desierto de los Leones
Carretera México–Toluca; Autopista Constituyentes–La Venta, or Avenid.
Desierto de los Leones San Ángel–Santa Rosa
Best to ask for directions at the small gatehouse at the entrance to the 'Ex convento del Desierto de los Leones'
Tuesday to Sunday 6am–5pm

n accordance with the Council of Trent (ecumenical council of the Roman Catholic Church that took place in 1545–63), the Order of Discalced Carmelites decreed that the path of spirituality was to live as a hermit while creating holy 'deserts': vast lands far from urban centres, with a temperate climate, lush trees and abundant water. Carmelite monks found this land in the province of San Alberto that has since been known as the Desierto de los Leones (Desert of the Lions).

Eight hermitages (monastic retreats) still lie in the depths of the forest, hidden by the local fog, along two paths leading to the former convent. The wide path that starts to the right of the convent leads to five of them, while the others are accessible by the path at the end of the central car park.

The 'desert' was surrounded by the so-called wall of excommunication, which still exists. Inside were ten hermitages in addition to the former convent, which is now a museum. The surviving hermitages have the architectural features required by the Carmelites: they consist of a cell, small kitchen, private chapel, bell tower, kitchen garden and enclosure.

You can visit the interior of some of the hermitages, and even climb the steps that lead to the bell tower. Each one is different: at the entrance, generally on the portal, a carved stone indicates the name and the date of construction. This is how we know that eight of the hermitages are called Soledad, Trinidad, Getsemaní, Magdalena, San Juan, San Elías, San José and El Portón. Alongside the pathways are canals that supplied the hermitages with water. Built in 1618 under the priorship of Friar Juan de Jesús María, they are good landmarks for finding your way through the park. By the early 1800s the Carmelites had abandoned the site, and in 1876 the area was classified as a forest reserve. At the end of the Mexican Revolution, in 1917, President Venustiano Carranza declared it a National Park.

PROCESSIONAL CARPET
AT SANTA ROSA XOCHIAC

Bringing in the New Year with a pop culture carpet

From Calle del Carmen, follow Rafael Checa and Juárez along Real de Guadalupe
Entrance to gardens alongside Ojo de Agua chapel, Calle Vista Hermosa
31 December, 6.30am–10pm
RTP bus: route 118; Tacubaya metro exit

Every 31 December, the residents of Santa Rosa Xochiac, a community surrounded by mountains, create a *Tapete de Xochiac* (Xochiac Carpet) for a procession of religious images to pass along. Unlike other places in Mexico that also lay carpets in honour of the Virgin, the one in Xochiac has elements of pop culture.

Everything starts very early in the day, when the street is covered with a strip of white sand running from Santa Rosa church to Ojo de Agua chapel. People living along the route then divide it into sections to decorate with figures made from coffee beans, soap powder, seeds and (mainly) coloured sawdust. While the images are sometimes drawn from religion, most represent characters from TV series, cartoons and online celebrities. The route is then used for the procession that leaves the church at 8pm to head for the chapel.

Strung between houses along the route are origami figures, paintings, little toys, balloons, woven tablecloths and sometimes even crockery, all placed there by the local families.

This tradition was started in 1971, apparently by a man called Ignacio Morelos, who came up with the idea of laying a carpet for the Virgin Mary (a tradition he knew about from Huamantla, a city that holds its own annual homage to the Virgin). The locals adopted the idea and made a traditional family festival of it, but it was the children and young people who gave it the popular, 'globalised' character it enjoys today.

The carpet and the hanging decorations are usually ready to be admired from around 4pm onwards. Everything ends with fireworks and a concert, to see the New Year in together with the Virgin Mary.

The gardens alongside Ojo de Agua chapel used to be part of the woodland on the mountain slopes. Inside flows a crystal-clear spring that the residents protect by restricting entry. The gardens are only open once a year, on 31 December. They are divided into small areas decorated by the local gardeners with their most beautiful work – waterfalls, flowers, cacti and hand-painted stones.

The procession originated at a time of drought. People brought the statue of the Virgin to the Ojo de Agua chapel and, to punish her, warned that she wouldn't be returned to the church until it rained. Of course, a few days later rain began to fall and the community, as a sign of gratitude, began to celebrate this annual festival.

DECORATED COLUMNS
OF EDIFICIO JUÁREZ

*Pancho Villa once delayed a battle until the
cameramen arrived ...*

Explanada Delegacional, entrance to Edificio Juárez
Avenida Juárez, junction with Avenida México Cuajimalpa
RTP bus: route 110 (departs from Tacubaya metro station, get off at Delegación
Cuajimalpa building)

Y ou'll recognise the revolutionary leaders Emiliano Zapata and Francisco Villa on the decorated columns of the Juárez building in Cuajimalpa *delegación*. But Zapata has a strip of negatives strapped to his chest instead of a rifle, while Villa is listening to the advice of a screenwriter and a film director.

The two sgraffito columns, by muralist Ariosto Otero, were part of an arts project called *Cantos del pueblo* (The People's Songs). In addition to representing the people's warlords, they illustrate some strange anecdotes relating to the Mexican Revolution.

One of them shows Pancho Villa signing an exclusive contract with the Mutual Film Corporation in 1914, which specified that Villa would fight his battles in daylight so the sequences could be included in a feature film by D.W. Griffith. For the purposes of the film, Villa postponed executions from 5 to 7 in the morning, as well as holding up a battle until the cameramen arrived.

As usual, Villa's jovial profile contrasts with Zapata's hard, cold solemnity. It's difficult to believe that Zapata was concerned about his image, but in 1913, after the legendary meal at the Palacio Nacional, he went straight to H.J. Gutiérrez, the most prestigious photographic studio in the city. Apparently Zapata's popularity was such that he posed for almost four hours of portraits in order to satisfy his admirers by creating the image of 'Zapata, brave macho man' that's still recognised today.

NEARBY
Museo Mesón de San Luisito

On one side of Explanada Delegacional (Avenida Juárez, s/n) a little door leads to the tiny Museo Mesón de San Luisito, which holds copies of documents relating to the history of Cuajimalpa. The museum was established because it was here that Miguel Hidalgo celebrated his victory at the battle of Monte de Las Cruces on 30 October 1810. This is also the site of the most inexplicable strategy in the history of the independence movement. Instead of entering Mexico City, the insurgents made their way to Aculco, in the north of the State of Mexico. This led to Hidalgo's betrayal and execution in 1811, delaying the cause of independence until 1821. What led him to retreat instead of entering the colonial capital remains a mystery.

SANTA FE DE LOS ALTOS PUEBLO ⑤

Village designed on the principles of Thomas More's Utopia

Parroquia Galeana 110
Obliterated plaque: Gregorio López 2
Springs: on one side of Vereda de la Ermita (restricted access)
Hermitage: at the foot of Vereda de la Ermita (restricted access)
RTP bus: route 118 (Tacubaya metro terminus)

On the island of Utopia, everyone was a farmer and a supporter of patriarchal government and freedom of religion. All activities were

pleasant and there was no such thing as private property. Divorce was allowed and euthanasia and hospitals were free. This was the perfect place with the ideal society. There was only one problem: it was an invention of Thomas More's imagination … until Vasco de Quiroga arrived in New Spain in 1530. In response to the injustices meted out to the neo-Hispanic peoples by Nuño de Guzmán, colonial administrator and president of the Real Audiencia (High Court), Don Vasco launched an ambitious project. Inspired by *Utopia* (published 15 years earlier), he founded a *pueblo hospitalario* (hospitable village) based on Roman Catholic principles, which he named Santa Fe. Here the indigenous peoples received an independent artistic and agrarian education and enjoyed a certain autonomy. At its height, the pueblo had a population of 30,000 people. However, it was later dismantled by the liberal government of Benito Juárez (1861–72), despite having its own regulations and laws.

Very little remains of Don Vasco's utopia: the church of La Asunción (The Assumption) with his portrait in the sacristy and his coat of arms on the neoclassical façade. To one side is a building with grand doors in the colonial style, one of which still has the viceregal plaque that supposedly tells the story of the pueblo's autonomy. When it was dissolved under La Reforma (Reform laws, 1854–76), the text on the plaque was obliterated, although part of it is still legible.

Graffiti in Calle Vereda shows the tortures inflicted on the indigenous people by the conquistadors. A little further along are the Acubaya springs and the river, which supplied water to Santa Fe and the centre of Mexico City. On the other side of the river you'll see a plaque dating from May 1789. It was installed in gratitude to Spanish King Charles IV and viceroy Manuel Antonio Flórez for reinforcing the barrier around the springs.

On the other side of the ravine is the pueblo's best-kept secret: hidden in the forest is a hermitage built for meditation in Don Vasco's day. Nowadays the only access to the hermitage is during events such as plays or exhibitions. Behind the building is a cross indicating the house that belonged to a certain Dr Losa in 1589, when botanist Gregorio López lived in the hermitage.

Apparently the most impressive feature of the pueblo was its hospital, demolished under the Reform laws. In 1966, following a community initiative, a stone sculpture of the awesome Vasco de Quiroga was erected where the main entrance once stood.

MAZATEPETL MAQUETTE

800-year-old scale models

Parque Eco-Arqueológico Mazatepetl
End of Calle Las Cruces, Colonia Ejido San Bernabé Ocotepec, Cerro del Judío
(+52) 1718 3137
Saturday 8am–6pm, Sunday 8am–2pm
Microbus: Line 42 departs from Viveros metro station (go down Las Cruces, then
climb the hill to reach the park entrance)

At first glance, the significance of a pile of huge rocks at the top of Cerro del Judío (Hill of the Jew), behind the Tepaneca pyramid (AD 1200) in Parque Ejidal and Mazatepetl Eco-Archaeological Centre, is not clear.

A closer look reveals small cavities and engravings that form canals and steps – the rocks are in fact an enormous mock-up of pre-Hispanic pyramids.

The rocks represent the nearby mountains, the steps a pyramidal structure, and the holes the nearby lakes, joined by narrow canals.

Seen from above, one of these rocky outcrops looks like a huge foot, which ties in with a local legend. The site, whose original name was Cerro del Venado (Hill of the Deer), was renamed Cerro el Judío after a Jewish neighbour, the owner of a textile factory, who is said to have left his footprint at the summit.

Little is known about the Tepaneca pyramid. But recent research shows that this was an important place of worship dedicated to Tlàloc, god of water, because of the many altars and images found in the area.

A wonderful place for ecotourism

In addition to the archaeological remains used for religious festivals in the village, the park has an ecological trail, a small museum and a viewpoint with a magnificent panorama over the south of the city, from the skyscrapers and fairground rides to the Xochimilco canals.

PETROGLYPH OF TLÁLOC

The mystery of Moctezuma's headdress solved?

Callejón Granada, at the end of Granada y Justo Montiel
Colonia Los Padres, Delegación Magdalena Contreras
Bus: route 42, destination San Bernabé, Tierra Unida or Tenango, departs fro
Viveros metro station

One of the enduring mysteries of Mexican archaeology concerns an artefact kept in Vienna's Museum of Ethnology – a huge headdress thought to have been presented by Moctezuma II, the Aztec emperor at the time of the Spanish conquest, to Hernán Cortés, who sent it to King Charles V. For reasons that are still unknown, the headdress ended up in Vienna. Repeated requests for its return to Mexico have been unsuccessful.

The original function of the piece, generally known as 'Moctezuma's headdress' because it was thought to be his property, is still debated. Some claim it was used during a funeral rite, others that it was specially made for Cortés. The answer to this mystery may lie in the petroglyph in the corner of a garden in Colonia Los Padres.

At the end of the steep Callejón Granada, which runs halfway up Cerro del Judío, is a huge vertical stone on which is engraved the face of Tláloc, god of water and rain, looking towards the west of the city. This stone marked the antechamber of an important 15th-century ceremonial site on this hill: Moctezuma himself ordered a path to be built to it from Coyoacán.

Tláloc was a major deity in pre-Hispanic Mexico because of the settlement near the vast Texcoco lake. The most important ceremonies were dedicated to the deity, in one of which the emperor would place a huge feathered headdress on top of the monolith.

When Cortés and the conquistadors were received by Moctezuma, they are said to have attended this famous ceremony. So if the headdress was the one later given by the emperor to Cortés, it would solve the mystery once and for all.

PLAZA LÍDICE

A plaza commemorating the destruction of a Czech village

Magnolia, s/n, junction with Callejón Corregidora
Colonia San Jerónimo Lídice
Microbus: Route 42, departs from Viveros metro station (stop in the next street, Luis Cabrera)

A sculpture entitled *La muerte del hombre por el hombre mismo* (The Death of Man by Man Himself) by Sergio Guerrero, and the mural *Campos de luz y muerte* (Fields of Light and Death) by Ariosto Otero, can both be seen in Plaza de la Delegación Magdalena Contreras. This plaza was renamed Plaza Lídice on 22 June 1975 to commemorate the destruction of the Czech village of Lidice during the Second World War.

The mural shows soldiers attacking the villagers, and the caption below notes: 'During the conflict, the populations of the villages of Lidice and Ležaky were massacred on 10 and 14 June 1942.'

The destruction of Lidice by the Nazi army was widely reported in the American press and caused such reverberations around the world that the town of Stern Park, Illinois (USA), took the name of Lidice, soon followed by other places in Venezuela, Panama, Brazil, and of course Mexico.

On 30 August 1942, a memorial ceremony was held at the Escuela Superior de Guerra (Higher Military College) in Mexico City. The Minister of the Interior at the time, Miguel Alemán, announced that the name Lídice would be added to that of the San Jerónimo district. Thirty years later, the Plaza Lídice Rosedal de la Paz was inaugurated (the word *rosedal*, which means 'rose garden', refers to the roses sent to Czechoslovakia from all over the world in memory of the victims).

As the annual anniversary of the massacre approaches, a ceremony is held in the plaza, attended by members of the Embassy of the Czech Republic in Mexico City and the Delegación Magdalena Contreras. Ironically, this plaza conceived as a tribute to peace is very near the Military College.

NEARBY

The change of name was not welcomed by all San Jerónimo residents because it meant losing the pre-Hispanic name of Aculco ('where the water twists and turns'). When Miguel Alemán changed the name, part of the district was called San Jerónimo Lídice and the other San Jerónimo Aculco. As there was still great dissatisfaction with this solution, a transparent and almost invisible plaque hung on a post reminds us that the official name of the park is San Jerónimo Aculco-Lídice.

PADIERNA'S OBELISK

Obelisk commemorating a fleeting victory over
a North American invasion

Junction of Oaxaca, Fortín and Sonora
Colonia Héroes de Padierna
Delegación Magdalena Contreras
RTP bus: route 123A (get off at Calle Oaxaca, Colonia Héroes de Padierna)

At the junction of Calles Oaxaca, Fortín and Sonora, in the Héroes de Padierna district, a small obelisk recalls a lost battle that could have led to victory against the United States invasion of 1847. That's why two plaques pay tribute to those who fell during that particular battle.

In expansionist mood, the United States began to invade Mexican territory in 1846. On 19 August 1847, the North American army arrived in what is now Mexico City. The first battle took place at Padierna ranch. General Santa Anna sent orders from another position to General Gabriel Valencia, who was stationed at Padierna. On the afternoon of 19 August, Valencia attacked the American troops and emerged victorious, while Santa Anna had ordered a retreat. As Valencia and Santa Anna weren't on good terms, Valencia ignored the order and called for reinforcements. On the night of the 19th, rain and lack of food weakened Valencia's troops; Santa Anna failed to send reinforcements because the terrain was inaccessible for their cannons, and retreated to San Ángel nearby.

On 20 August, a second attack routed the Valencia army in just 17 minutes. That day, Santa Anna watched the battle from the top of a house in San Ángel, and having failed to send reinforcements he was considered a traitor. Because of these disputes and the strategic failures of the Mexican army, the North Americans won skirmish after skirmish until they arrived at the Palacio Nacional on 15 September 1847. There they hoisted their flag on the very day commemorating the 37th anniversary of Mexican independence.

This obelisk commemorates the fleeting victory at Padierna. Behind is Héroes de Padierna school, built in 1939 under the socialist president Lázaro Cárdenas. On the other side of the street is a 2002 mural by Ariosto Otero. The mural is divided into two parts, the first a tribute to former Chilean President Salvador Allende in memory of his resistance to the US coup d'état in Chile. On his uniform is an extract from Chilean musician and activist Violeta Parra's song *Miren cómo sonríen* (Watch How They Smile). The second part recalls the North American invasion: a map shows General Winfield Scott with huge claws encircling the current states of Texas, New Mexico, Arizona, California, Nevada, Utah, Colorado and Wyoming, all taken from Mexico during the invasion. On Mexican territory, the phrase '*patria mutilado territorio*' ('homeland your mutilated territory') can be read, while at the top are the smiling faces of Superman, Batman, Mickey Mouse and Spider-Man.

FUERA MÁSCARAS MURAL

The Saint vs Batman

Benito Juárez, junction with Emilio Carranza
On the side of the road leading to Los Dinamos
Metro: Universidad
RTP bus: route 128, destination San Bernabé; get off at Calle Del Rosal, La Peri
(Universidad metro exit)

O n the arches of the bus depot at the Los Dinamos stop, Ariosto Otero's mural, *Fuera máscaras* (Masks Off), has been portraying surreal struggle since 2002. An angry group of sombrero-wearers, pre-Hispanic divinities and indigenous figures confronts several wrestlers, prominent among them El Enmascarado de Plata (The Man with the Silver Mask), who is about to reveal the identity of Batman.

As well as El Santo (The Saint), there are other characters from *lucha libre* (Mexican professional wrestling) such as Rayo de Jalisco (the Lightning Bolt from Jalisco, with a jagged white line down the middle of his black mask) and Blue Demon with an arm lock on a blonde wrestler, certainly representing a foreign superhero.

At the bottom of the mural, another group holds placards among which a quote from Mexican philosopher Raúl Cardiel Reyes stands out: 'The man who wears a mask transforms, even if only temporarily, his being.' This is why, among the crowd, you also find *chinelos* (dancers in traditional costume) with their huge masks, popular masks alluding to *nahuales* (spirits), and even the mask of former President Salinas de Gortari. Finally, on the two arches, rows of masks made from sgraffito stucco are all watching what could well be the fight of the century.

Opposite the mural, the small church of María Magdalena, dating from 1760, is remarkable for its curious mortared façade.

NEARBY
Los Dinamos

Calle Emilio Carranza leads directly to the four entrances to Parque Nacional Los Dinamos. Inside the park are the remains of windmills dating from the Porfirian regime that supplied energy to nearby textile factories thanks to small waterfalls on the Magdalena river. These 16th-century mills were converted in the 19th century to run on dynamos, hence their current name. Traders set up their stalls in some of the ruins and you can still see the old dynamos. As it's located within a glen, the park is ideal for mountaineering, hiking, trout fishing and bird watching.

MONUMENTO AL PERRO CALLEJERO

An appeal against animal abuse

Insurgentes Sur, junction with Moneda
Tlalpan
Metrobus: Fuentes Brotantes

The *Monumento al perro callejero* (Monument to the Street Dog) has stood at the junction of Calle Moneda and Avenida Insurgentes in Tlalpan since 2008.

Mexican sculptor Girasol Botello based the statue on Peluso, a dog rescued by Patricia España, founder of the Milagros Caninos animal sanctuary. She looked after Peluso until his death. The abuse and neglect the dog had suffered caused kidney failure, distemper and deafness, and he sadly died five days before the statue was unveiled on 20 July 2008.

As there were an estimated 3 million stray dogs in the city at the time, the statue was intended to raise awareness of the responsibilities of keeping a pet.

The statue, which is sited at a road junction, has been vandalised and restored several times. On one side of the junction there used to be a plaque – this has now disappeared, leaving Peluso alone once more. The inscription read as follows:

Mi único delito fue nacer y vivir en las calles o ser abandonado.
Yo no pedí nacer y a pesar de tu indiferencia y de tus golpes, lo único que te pido es lo que sobra de tu amor.
¡Ya no quiero sufrir, sobrevivir al mundo es solo una cuestión de horror!
¡Ayúdame, ayúdame, por favor!
Peluso.

(My only crime was to be born and to live on the streets or to be abandoned.
I didn't ask to be born and despite your indifference and your blows, the only thing I ask is whatever is left of your love.
I don't want to suffer any more, survival in this world is just dreadful!
Help me, help me, please!
Peluso.)

MONUMENTO AL BARRENDERO

Popular figures recycled from Bordo Xochiaca junk

Avenida Renato Leduc at junction with Calle Chimalcóyotl
Tren ligero: Huipulco; Metrobus: Fuentes Brotantes

Protected by padlocks and plantpots, the *Monumento al barrendero* (Monument to the Street Sweeper) forms a mini-park on the central reservation of Avenida Renato Leduc. Its distinctiveness lies in the fact that everything is made from recycled materials – from passers-by to dogs to trees, even a little chipmunk.

The work is officially called *Haciendo historia, reciclando el pasado* (Making History, Recycling the Past), by artist Rafael Payró. It was conceived as a nostalgic tribute to popular figures of the past and includes a cymbal-banging monkey, a barrel organ, a postman, an old man sitting on a bench and some roadsweepers at work. All the statues were made from materials culled from the Bordo de Xochiaca dump.

Payró had hoped to add many other elements, including a tram stop in memory of one that used to stand here, but he ran out of time. For a while there was a horse at the entrance to the park, but it trotted off into the street, so only its hoofprints remain, embedded in the concrete.

NEARBY

Along Avenida Renato Leduc, you can still follow the tracks of the tram that served the city centre from 1900. They lead to number 84 Avenida San Fernando, a government building with a concrete arch at the entrance that marked the tram terminus. The renovation of the street in 1969 linked the San Fernardo track with Renato Leduc. The blocks of cement along the avenue that were used by the tramway until the 1980s are now home to curious works of modern art.

'Monuments and busts are only there for dogs to piss on and pigeons to shit on'

Renato Leduc, a foul-mouthed and cynical poet, was born in Tlalpan where he worked as a telegraph operator for Pancho Villa. When out and about, he liked to leave poems at places he'd visited, whether they were brothels, newspaper offices or cafes. In particular, he is credited with this colourful quote: 'Monuments and busts are only there for dogs to piss on and pigeons to shit on.' Ironically, in 1992, former President López Portillo installed a bust of the poet in a park between Renato Leduc and Industria.

TLALPAN MINARET

Mudejar-style tower in the backyard

Only visible from Casa Frissac
Plaza de la Constitución 1, junction with Calle Moneda
Centro Histórico de Tlalpan
Monday to Friday 9am–2pm, Saturday and Sunday 11am–3pm
Metrobus: Fuentes Brotantes

At the end of the main garden of Casa Frissac, outlined against the sky, you'll see a minaret. It belongs to the nuns who live in Casa Ramos, at number 2 Calle Moneda, and who unfortunately don't allow access to the premises.

The neo-Mudejar style minaret has a balcony at mid-height, as well as a disused interior staircase. By adopting this style, the architects unconsciously reproduced Muslim symbols. The repetition of geometric painted figures represents the infinite – the All created by Allah. The perfect circles (here in blue) represent Allah.

The roof has an elegant wind rose surmounted by a crescent moon. An Islamic symbol, the moon is also associated with Ramadan, the ninth month of the Islamic lunar calendar, during which the Quran was revealed.

The Casa Ramos minaret dates from the end of the 19th century. The villa's façade was renovated later (probably during the 1920s or 30s) in the same architectural style. In the 19th century, a fashionable trend

among the wealthy was to have at least one 'exotic room' whose Chinese, Arabic or Indian motifs were reminiscent of the Orient. Only the most eccentric – see, for example, Casa Serralde at number 6 Rubens, Mixcoac – could afford the luxury of building their entire home in this style.

There isn't enough historical background to determine who designed the villa, although in the 1930s it was the home of the Ramos family – Manuel and Rafael Ramos, Tlalpan's first delegates. In 1928 the Constitution was amended, leaving the municipalities outside the Federal District and creating the devolved *delegaciones*.

EL ÁRBOL DE LOS AHORCADOS (THE HANGING TREE)

⑭

The tree where those who plotted to assassinate the Emperor Maximilian were hanged

Plaza de la Constitución, south-east corner
Centro Histórico Tlalpan
Metrobus: Fuentes Brotantes

In a corner of Tlalpan's Plaza de la Constitución there stands a half-dead tree. Unsuccessful attempts have been made to preserve it by encircling it with iron bands and even reinforcing it with cement. It's known as El Árbol de los Ahorcados (The Hanging Tree).

The tree dates from the time of the Second French Intervention in Mexico (1861–67), when the Second Empire was in the hands of Maximilian von Habsburg. At that time, Tlalpan had seen two of its officials assassinated by guerrillas: Colonel Falcón in 1864 and Juan Becerril in 1865. They were succeeded by General Tomás O'Horán, who had deserted from the colonising army just as it was gaining ground in the battle.

While Maximilian was preparing for his last trip from his home in Cuernavaca to Mexico City, O'Horán organised an assassination attempt in Tlalpan. But the plan was denounced and Austrian hussars were posted on the road where it was supposed to take place.

When O'Horán learned that the attack had been foiled, he decided to execute all the conspirators, including his secretary, to ensure his own safety. As an example to others, they were strung up in public on this tree, as was customary for criminals.

The following lines are inscribed on the plaque at the foot of the tree: 'Names of the patriots who were hanged on this tree: Dr Felipe Muños, Vicente Martínez, Mayor Manuel Mutio, Capitán Lorenzo Rivera, Teniente HC José Mutio. Tlalpan D.F. 1865–1940.'

When the Republic prevailed in 1867, Tomás O'Horán was condemned to death and shot.

FAÇADE OF HOSPITAL MIGUEL GEA

The world's first building faced with a material that absorbs city smog

Calzada de Tlalpan 4800
Colonia Sección XVI
Metrobus: El Caminero

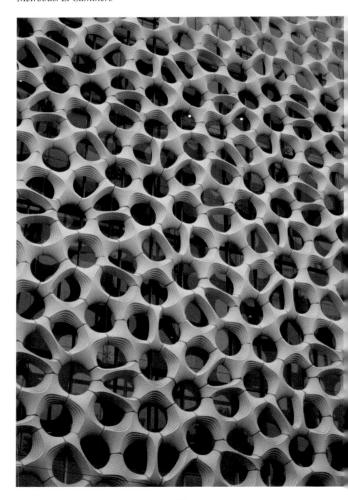

At first glance, the enormous white coral-like design on the façade of Miguel Gea González Hospital seems to be simply decorative. Actually it's a smart filter that converts smog into other chemical components. This is the first site in the world to be equipped with this system, which was installed in 2012.

The material used, called 'Prosolve370e', is a type of ceramic coated with titanium dioxide that reacts to ultraviolet light: the blocks absorb nitrogen oxide and volatile organic compounds, and convert them into tiny amounts of water and carbon dioxide.

When Mexico City was declared the world's most polluted metropolis in 2005, a number of public policies were developed to deal with the problem. Since then, Mexico's position on the list has improved, albeit slowly.

As the hospital was opened in 1946 specifically for patients with advanced tuberculosis – a disease made worse by pollution – the coral-like material was installed here.

Although the process by which titanium dioxide works is questioned in the scientific world, it's part of a new direction in the fight against pollution.

The material was invented by the German company Elegant Embellishments and the façade consists of 500 separate blocks, covering a total area of 2,500 square metres. Currently, cells made from this same material have been installed on a smaller scale on buildings in Australia, the United Arab Emirates and Germany.

The structure covering the hospital can neutralise the pollution produced by 1,000 vehicles a day.

MUSEO MISIONEROS DE GUADALUPE

A shrunken head and a spirit doll, souvenirs from Catholic missions

Insurgentes Sur 4135
Premises of Universidad Intercontinental
mg.org.mx/museo
Guided tours: call (+52) 5573 3000
Monday to Friday 8am–4.30pm
Admission free
Metrobus: La Joya

When the Guadalupe Missionaries (a Roman Catholic society in Mexico) began to devote themselves to foreign missions in 1949, a number of them brought gifts and souvenirs back to Mexico City. These are now displayed at the Intercontinental University, where each showcase contains a diversity of objects organised by country.

Although the exhibition doesn't have documentation to explain every detail, the museum provides leaflets describing the most representative objects. In addition, the guided tours (highly recommended) are very informative.

The visit begins in Latin America, where the Brazil showcase presents blowpipes and darts that hunters used to smear with frog venom. There's also a dissected piranha and a *tzantza* (shrunken head) from the Amazonian Shuar tribe. In the Cuba showcase, small *orisha* dolls represent just three of the 401 deities of the Yoruba religion, together with a *santero* (spirit) doll. The highlight of the Peru showcase is the *cushma* garment, made from local cotton yarn and remarkable for its beautiful patterns.

In the Mozambique display, look out for the small *mbira*, a curious musical instrument that produces a delicate sound when metal keys are pressed together.

All the costumes in the Africa section are unique: Kenya, for example, uses the colours of the earth. The dolls and paintings have the colours of Africa – orange earth and yellow sun, blue sky and black night. Don't miss the little Ikoku doll, a deity whose presence alone guarantees fertility for the Turkana tribe.

The Asia section is the most elaborate, with fine Hong Kong porcelain, Korean silk embroidery used to decorate homes, and a magnificent Hina-Matsuri (Doll Festival) altar exactly as found in Japan. Each doll represents a different member of the imperial family from the Heian period (9th–12th centuries).

The museum also has a space for temporary exhibitions and a small section dedicated to Monsignor Alonso Escalante, founder of the Missions Seminary. Two displays stand out: Bibles in different languages, ranging from Masai to Quiché (a Mayan language) and from Mandarin to Hebrew; and a series of Virgin Marys from different parts of the world, dressed according to the traditions of each country.

HOLY COMMUNION AT THE SANTUARIO DE LA SANTÍSIMA HOSTIA SANGRANTE

A miraculous host on display once a month

Calle Zoquipa, junction with Cucurpe - Colonia El Parque
Eucharistic Adoration on the 23rd of each month
Daily 7am–8pm
Metro: Fray Servando

The lavish shrine of Our Lady of Guadalupe of the Most Holy Bleeding Host, open every day, is well worth a visit. Decorated with millions of little golden angels, the *tezontle* (volcanic rock) church with its gilded mosaics stands opposite a statue of the Virgin on the sidewalk. The altar is entirely covered with gold and cherubim adoring Our Lady of Guadalupe. This profuse ornamentation might well be described as postmodern Spanish Rococo. During religious festivals, the statues of saints all along the interior and exterior passageways are decked out with thousands of flowers.

However, the main attraction of the church is not its decoration but the consecrated host in its crystal glass.

The story goes that during Holy Thursday Mass of 23 March 1978, the sacramental host began to bleed after it was consecrated. Following this phenomenon, a number of studies were carried out and the host was placed in a glass filled with water to avoid natural deterioration. When the Roman Catholic clergy of the archdiocese refuted the idea of a miracle, the church turned to the Mexican Catholic Apostolic Church, a Christian denomination founded in 1861. Ever since, the host has been scrupulously guarded and released from its glass container only on the 23rd of each month.

Inside the church is a display case of miracles in the shape of a Sacred Heart, with a photograph of the host in its crystal glass. On the right wall are pictures of the many studies of the host, accompanied by a letter from the Curia of the Archdiocese of Mexico City written in 1978, describing the precautions to be taken to preserve it.

The shrine's nuns are dressed in red garments in reference to the blood of the Eucharistic miracle.

BIBLIOTECA VIRTUAL TLATOANI

Surf the web from a plane

Delegación Venustiano Carranza esplanade
Francisco del Paso y Troncoso 219
Colonia Jardín Balbuena
Monday 1pm–7pm, Tuesday to Sunday 9am–7pm
Admission free
Metro: Moctezuma / Fray Servando

The Tlatoani Virtual Library, in the Venustiano Carranza district, has an extremely unusual location – the interior of a former passenger plane. The government, in collaboration with several companies, opened this library in a McDonnell Douglas DC9-14 airliner donated by Aerovías Caribe in 2005.

To enter the plane, where you can browse the internet for a set time, all you have to do is show an ID and sign in.

Until a few years ago the plane had its original seating, but after an accident when some Christmas trees left inside caught fire, the seats were replaced by desks and chairs. You can still see the cockpit at the entrance.

Nowadays the old plane is simply a computing centre, with a flight simulator program on several machines for the use of visitors. Sadly, it has lost its original function as a virtual library. This is particularly regrettable because when it opened in 2005 it was the first of its kind in all of Latin America.

LA FÁBRICA

Second World War weapons factory turned into artwork

Avenida Viaducto Rio de la Piedad, s/n, Colonia Granjas
Inside Deportivo Magdalena Mixhuca (Gate 6)
Monday to Friday 7am–8pm, Saturday and Sunday 7am–5pm
Admission free
Metro: Ciudad Deportiva

La Fábrica (The Factory), at one end of the parking lot of Gate 6 in Magdalena Mixhuca sports complex, is a very unusual sculpture park featuring 18 huge machines. They have been turned into artworks

by Vicente Rojo, a member of the Generación de la Ruptura (Breakaway Generation) movement that turned away from Mexican muralism.

There is a splendid contrast between the oxidised orange of the mechanical monsters and the red, blue and gold pieces that the artist has added to each of the sculptures.

The way they are placed between palms, concrete paving and lawns gives the impression of visiting a reinvented factory. Each machine has a plate with the name of the manufacturer and its weight in tonnes. But apart from their aesthetic value, these machines were chosen for their historical interest, which may not be immediately evident.

In the final years of the industrial era (apparently in 1911), the machines were manufactured in Chicago for delivery to the neighbouring town of Toledo, Ohio (USA). Toledo was severely affected in 1929, during the Great Depression, and when the Second World War broke out the factories turned to arms manufacturing. Toledo made cones for missile heads, industrial glass, protective coatings for warplanes, tank engines, uniforms, and in the case of the machines on display here, bullets and missiles.

These steel monsters were witness to the time when the women were keeping their families alive by working in factories, while their men were fighting in Europe. When the war ended (and with it the demand for arms), some factories went bankrupt. This is how these machines – bought by La Vasconia factory in 1949 – arrived in Mexico.

La Vasconia (located in the industrial zone of Azcapotzalco) manufactured aluminium kitchen utensils. In 2000, when these machines were taken out of service by the factory, the idea arose of reviving them for posterity.

Where does the name Estadio Palillo come from?

Jesús 'Palillo' Martínez was the only comedian who dared to criticise the Mexican government during the harshest periods of censorship. His worst experiences were under the Regente de Hierror (Iron Regent), Ernesto Uruchurtu, who governed Mexico City from 1952 to 1966. With his earnings from the theatre, Palillo had bought and was financing the construction of the sports complex, but Uruchurtu boycotted this project whenever he could by imprisoning the comedian or refusing permits. When President Ruiz Cortines inaugurated the stadium in 1958, the sporting authorities installed a plaque in the main building (opposite La Fábrica) bearing the name 'Palillo'. Uruchurtu ordered the plaque to be removed the same day. The present plaque has been there since 1983.

SANTUARIO DE FELIPE DE JESÚS

Relics of Mexican martyrs in a Japanese-style templ

Calle Peyote, s/n
Colonia Infonavit, Delegación Iztacalco
Monday to Friday 8am–6pm, Saturday 8am–7pm
Metro: Iztacalco

San Felipe's shrine, despite its huge pagoda and Japanese architecture, is a Roman Catholic church built on the initiative of Father Nicolás Álvarez Casillas in memory of the country where the first Mexican saint, San Felipe de Jesús, was martyred.

The story goes that the young Brother Felipe, who was born in New Spain, travelled to Japan during the imperial government of Shogun Toyotomi Hideyoshi. In 1587 the shogun published an edict to expel foreign missionaries. In 1597 he ordered the crucifixion of Felipe, and 25 others, on Nagasaki hill.

On 5 February, Brother Felipe was allotted the central cross, number 13, and hung up on five rings. His feet weren't attached properly and slipped, so the ring around his neck began to strangle him. The soldiers, seeing his agony, stuck two spears in his ribs, which formed a cross in his chest cavity. Thus Felipe acquired his status of martyr, and later of saint.

His martyrdom is depicted on the huge stained-glass windows and small glazed ovals with oriental motifs on the church doors.

Although the site has housed the saint's relics for some time, it isn't well known as a shrine. Father Nicolás, in memory of San Felipe's martyrdom, has brought together the relics of 25 martyrs of the Cristero War – the persecution of Catholics in the early 20th century. They now rest around the crucifix inside the church, while the façade bears the names and portraits of each of them.

When the church was built in 1994, the parishioners organised charity fairs and raffles, and made a small path from peso coins. The shrine now has a restaurant and community hall.

Muere el Bienaventurado
Felipe de Jesús, el primero de
sus compañeros crucificados,
y es atravesado por tres lanzas,
logrando por esto la Palma
de Proto=Mártir, entre
aquellos mismos
Proto=Mártires

CAPILLA DEL DIVINO SALVADOR DEL CALVARIO

A cave transformed into a shrine

16 de Septiembre, s/n
Barrio de San Antonio Culhuacán
Daily 6am–6pm
(Passage open Sunday 9am–3pm allows a closer view of the statue)
Admission free
Metro: Culhuacán

In one of the most traditional districts of the city, backing onto the slopes of Cerro de la Estrella (Hill of the Star), is the Divino Salvador del Calvario (Divine Saviour of Calvary) chapel. It was built in the early 20th century to welcome pilgrims wishing to venerate the statue of the Señor del Santo Entierro (Lord of the Holy Burial), discovered in a cave. Few know that the cave shrine is still there near the porch, at the end of the corridor on the right.

The Señor del Santo Entierro is a legendary image of Christ's Entombment from the colonial era. Versions of its discovery vary, but most agree that some workmen about to finish for the day came across a small cave. Inside they found the statue, so vowed to build a shrine in its honour on that very spot.

To reach the cave, go down a few small steps – but watch your head! Here you'll see all that remains of the ancient shrine: a 16th-century stone column and a brief inscription with the date 1672. On one side is a plaque dating from 1953 recording the names of those who restored the site and made the mosaic on the floor. At the back is an urn marking the spot where the statue was discovered.

Research on the remains found here suggests that this site has been used as a temple since pre-Hispanic times.

A grand *fiesta patronal* (local holiday) is still held in honour of the image, usually on 6 August.

A rogue image

To the left of the porch is a large wooden door that is opened on Sundays to allow a closer look at the statue and the stained-glass windows at the back of the chapel.

The security guards warn that you must ask permission before taking photos: if not, the image of Christ could come out blurred!

REMAINS OF A PAPER MILL

Latin America's first paper mill

Avenida Tláhuac, Cerrada 15 de septiembre
Culhuacán
Metro: Culhuacán

In a small enclosed plaza in the Culhuacán neighbourhood, which is used as a pedestrian route between Tláhuac and 15 de septiembre, two arches and the ruins of a stone wall are all that remain of Latin America's first paper mill, dating from colonial days.

Before the frantic urbanisation that is now devouring Culhuacán, this was an unpaved square with a few houses. The ruins of the mill were used during the Mexican civil war by Carranza partisans as an execution block for enemies of the revolution.

No one suspected the historic value of the site until Señora Teresa Ambriz, who inherited the land in 1957, discovered its story and came to the rescue.

In 1982, the Centro Comunitario Culhuacán was built in the former convent of San Juan Evangelista. The plaza was paved, the ruins restored, and the paper mill found to be the first on the continent.

This is how the mill worked: water from a nearby source flowed through a raised conduit, and when it was necessary to halt the mill wheel, a valve was closed to obstruct the flow. The water passed through the lower arch while the upper arch concentrated the power of the wheel to retain the water. The mill is thought to have been used for fulling: the cleansing of cloth to eliminate impurities and make it thicker.

Paper for the preachers

As paper took too long to arrive from Europe and Mexican *amate* bark paper couldn't be produced quickly enough, the Augustinians of San Juan convent and seminary built the mill to help in the rapid evangelisation of the new villages. The first traces of the building's existence were discovered in the book *Relación geográfica* (1580), although the mill is believed to have been operating for several years by then.

RESCATE HISTÓRICO TLALTENCO ㉓

Hair 168 cm long, Doña Lugarda's parties, Zapata's secret courier ...

Village of San Francisco Tlaltenco
Most panels are around the square bordered by Avenida Tlahuac, Morelos and Miguel Hidalgo
Metro: Tlaltenco

In the 1990s, on the initiative of the Rescate Histórico Tlaltenco association, plaques telling of community life, from picturesque anecdotes to unusual news items, were installed in the streets of San Francisco Tlaltenco.

From the history of Tlaltenco's first store and details of its range of products, to that of the temazcal (sweat lodge / sauna that originated in pre-Hispanic Mesoamerica) on Independencia, the village streets are filled with memories of the indigenous peoples of Mexico.

Some of these plaques are in front of houses where famous Tlaltenco people lived, such as Don Nicolás Rioja, who is thought to have been Emiliano Zapata's secret courier; Doña Lugarda, who organised lavish house parties in the 1920s; landscape artist Francisco Torres; and Gregoria Leyte, whose hair (according to the plaque) was 168 cm long – her photo was used in France to advertise a soap encouraging hair growth.

Other plaques tell how Empress Carlota of Mexico (Charlotte of Belgium, wife of Maximilian of Austria) distributed bread in the street accompanied by the Imperial Guard, or how men abused their wives when they didn't finish grinding the flour.

Carnival of San Francisco Tlaltenco

The village's greatest pride is its carnival, first held in 1945 in Hildago, as recorded on the largest plaque.

During the carnival (between February and March), participants parade through the main streets dressed in traditional *charro* costumes embroidered with gold thread worth more than 80,000 pesos, accompanied by allegorical floats.

IGLESIA DE LOS 100 SANTOS

All the saints in the world

Juan de Dios Peza, junction with Lucio Blanco
Colonia La Era, Iztapalapa
Parish of Santa María de San Juan
Monday to Saturday 8am–3pm
Metro: Constitución de 1917

The sober façade of Santa María de San Juan parish church doesn
do justice to its magnificent interior. On the beams, between th

walls, on the columns and even on the ceiling are thousands of oil paintings with scenes from the lives of the Catholic saints. Hence the name by which it is popularly known: 'Church of the 100 Saints'.

One of the wooden beams is dedicated to all the saints of royal descent, such as St Stephen, St Constance, St Edward and St Edith, all dressed in royal garments from the Middle Ages and wearing their respective crowns. The 20th century saints are on the first beams at the entrance. Saints from some unexpected places are also depicted: St Kateri (Catalina) Tekakwitha in her indigenous Mohawk costume, St Andrew Kim (Korea's first Roman Catholic priest) in Korean dress and with his Asian features …

But the portraits are not only of saints. On the right side of the altar are various Mexican figures associated with Catholicism, from the first Archbishop, Juan de Zumárraga, to the mystic Concepción Cabrera. Also Sister María Angélica, whose heart, found with a hole in it when her remains were exhumed, showed that it had been pierced by Divine Love. And finally, Blessed St Sebastian of Aparicio, whose body has remained incorrupt and can be viewed in the Church of St Francis at Puebla.

The left-hand wall shows the hierarchy of angels: seraphim, cherubim, thrones, dominations, virtues, powers, principalities, archangels and angels.

On the rear walls of the church are the biblical prophets, as well as Adam and Eve in the Garden of Eden.

The columns at the entrance are dedicated to the virgins: Our Lady of La Salette, a Marian apparition in France; Our Lady of Aránzazu, with shrines in Spain and the colonies; Our Lady of Fátima, revered in Portugal; and the Virgin Mary as Our Lady of Refuge, worshipped in Italy.

As if all that wasn't enough, the side beams have paintings of all the popes as head of the Church, the only portraits whose names are missing from the frames. Not to mention the stained-glass windows showing the 12 apostles.

The wood-panelled church, with the detailed engraving of the Last Supper on the altar, were the idea of a priest called Humberto Jiménez, who wanted to decorate the recently built church with portraits instead of the usual sculptures. Thanks to the collections at Mass, he was able to commission one painting a week. The church acquired so many paintings that when they ran out of saints (the first to be portrayed in the parish), the spaces were filled with flower paintings before any new characters were added to such a splendid church.

AJEDREZ CERVANTINO CHESSBOARD

University life around a chessboard

Calle del Puente 222
Colonia Ejidos de Huipulco
Instituto Tecnológico y de Estudios Superiores de Monterrey, Ciudad de México campus
Only open to students and their guests, and members of the university
Tren ligero: Periférico

Sheltered by the vast buildings of the Monterrey Institute of Technology and Higher Education (ITESM), the *Ajedrez Cervantino* (Cervantes Chessboard) is a fibreglass and granite work by sculptor Miguel Peraza.

The university – colloquially known as TEC de Monterrey, or simply TEC – is famous for its competitiveness. The chessboard is inspired by this mission, like a strategy game with no chance of cheating. The board is laid out in the university gardens in such a way that a game can be played – the first move was made in 1993 by TEC's former chancellor, businessman Eugenio Garza Lagüera.

Each piece has a different symbolism; on the back is a reference to the work of Cervantes. The horse symbolises total dedication; on the back is a sunlit landscape. The bishop is a man emerging from an obelisk; the back looks like Sancho Panza, 'down-to-earth' without lowering standards. The king represents man's momentous achievements in the service of Mexican development. The tower is also known as the Torre de la Excelencia.

In 2003, the pieces were reproduced on a large scale and placed at several strategic points as monumental sculptures, in order to bring harmony to the campus. The symbolic weight of the chessboard was such that the university identified its buildings with the pieces: the lecture halls as 'towers', the offices as 'bishops', the technological development centre as 'horse' and the library as 'king'. A curious work of art, considered one of the biggest chessboards in the world.

A city within the city

Work on the TEC Ciudad de México campus began in 1989, designed on golden ratio proportions to be aesthetically pleasing. In order to blend in with the city, each building was given its own identity, alluding to the time of the viceroys and the neocolonial style. This can be seen in the lecture halls with their church-like cupolas, and the neoclassical student centre. From the outside, TEC gives the impression of a city within the city.

CASTILLO DE XOCHIMILCO

Straight out of a fairy tale

By land: Callejón Tlalchitongo, Barrio de San Diego
By water: the nearest jetties are Puente de Urrutia (Calle Puente de Urrutia y Apatlaco) and Fernando Celada (Avenida Guadalupe I. Ramírez, s/n)
Boat operating times change frequently

Once upon a time, most of the *chinampas* (floating islands) of Xochimilco had small houses surrounded by gardens. One of the householders gave up crop-growing to build a white castle that still stands today, hidden among the canals and alleyways some distance from the jetties. It takes over an hour to reach the castle in one of the traditional *trajinera* boats.

By road, just follow a series of zigzags along Callejón Tlachitongo until the canal blocks the way. There stands the white castle on its island, complete with towers, ramparts and even guard dogs. Trees obscure part of the building, while enhancing the view.

This is no medieval castle, or even one from the colonial era: it's only an eccentric 1930s construction by a man named Eduardo Ramírez.

His wife is said to have always dreamed of a castle by the sea, and to grant her wish he built this little castle at Xochimilco. An amusing but probably apocryphal story.

Despite plans to turn it into a cultural venue, the castle was long abandoned before being acquired as a private residence.

The monster of Xochimilco

According to an Aztec legend, Ahuizotl was a huge sea creature, the lord of all freshwater fish. Some locals had heard that it was a huge fish that whipped up storms with its tail and grew enraged when fishermen violated its territory. So in 1975, when locals found a dead 'fish' with similar characteristics, they panicked.

When the authorities arrived to restore calm, they explained that the fearsome beast was none other than a manatee (sea cow) that had died of pneumonia. Four manatees were found dead, all belonging to the municipality. Introduced to control the spread of water lilies, they had escaped and not been seen since. Nicaraguan poet Ernesto Mejía invented a story that the manatees had been sacrificed and eaten by local people. In the collective imagination, the legend persists that even today manatees and monsters live in the Xochimilco canals, and that they can still be seen in the most isolated spots.

PETROGLYPHS AT CAPILLA DE TLATEUHCHI

27

Pre-Hispanic remains on a chapel wall

Plazuela de San Juan
Junction of Nicolás Bravo and Sabino y Josefa Ortiz de Domínguez
Colonia San Juan
Tren ligero: Xochimilco / Francisco Goitia

Although the San Juan Tlateuhchi chapel was built in the 17th century, some of the petroglyphs on its pink walls clearly date from a much earlier period: the flowers on the bell tower, a snail and a Cross on the side door, another more elaborate flower on a buttress and even a human face on the side wall.

These carvings were probably taken from the central pyramid of the village of Xochimilco, now gone, when these great pre-Hispanic monuments were pillaged and destroyed during the Spanish conquest and the creation of the Viceroyalty of New Spain. Some decorative elements were however preserved to maintain a link between the ancient pre-Hispanic rites and Roman Catholicism.

Although the flowers and snails were only harmless engravings to the evangelists, to the indigenous peoples they had a supernatural meaning.

The symbol of a snail in cross-section was worn as a necklet by Aztec gods of the night sky such as Tezcatlipoca or Tecciztécatl, because as well as resembling a star, the snail was linked to agriculture and the underworld. This symbol could also signify the presence of the deity himself, and only priests could use it.

Flowers were generally used in herbal cures, such as *yoloxochitl* to treat heart disease. Rituals commonly included hallucinogenic plants such as tobacco, *ololiuqui*, or a magic mushroom sometimes also shown in cross-section. The similarity with the human features on the side wall of the chapel has given rise to the belief that the face represents a pre-Hispanic priest or chieftain.

PARADE OF ALLEGORICAL *TRAJINERAS* (CANAL BOATS)

28

Take a floral trip along the canals of Xochimilco

Embarcadero Nuevo Nativitas, Calle Mercado
Xochimilco
Once a year, Viernes de Dolores (Friday of Sorrows, date varies), from 9.30am
(advisable to arrive an hour before) – parade starts 10am
Free trips on the boats that accompany the parade
Tren ligero: Xochimilco

The allegorical *trajineras* event, held once a year as part of the Fiesta de la Flor más Bella del Ejido (Festival of the most Beautiful Flower of the *Ejido*) to commemorate ancient Xochimilco, is well worth a visit. (In the traditional Indian system of land tenure, *ejidos* are communally held agricultural lands).

This is a competition for the best *trajinera*, in which members of other docks or boat owners take part. The main criterion is that the boats should be decorated with fresh flowers, mostly grown in the greenhouses of Xochimilco, and sewn together by hand.

The boats are strewn with carpets of petals (made only 24 hours earlier so that the flowers don't wilt), floral arches, and sculptures of animals, people or objects in the Mexican rural tradition. The event begins when the competitors take to their boats and speed off to Caltongo lagoon, where the route ends and the judging takes place. Afterwards they return to Nuevo Nativitas dock.

To enjoy the parade, you can wait for the *trajineras* to come back to the dock, but the best option is to travel alongside them.

Very early in the morning, a procession of competitors' families and friends crosses the bridge to choose from a selection of boats available free of charge to accompany the *trajineras*. If you'd rather stay on land, you can sample *antojitos* (Mexican appetisers) and traditional music sessions along the canal banks. Once the spectators are seated in the boats, the parade begins.

This event was launched in colonial days to celebrate Viernes de Dolores and has been held in different neighbourhoods over the years: Centro Histórico and La Viga while there were still canals, Míxquic, and currently Xochimilco. In the early 20th century, the *trajineras* were smaller and all decorated with floral arches – a tradition gradually abandoned as being too expensive and too wasteful of flowers. But watching this parade is a rare chance to imagine what the canals must have looked like over a hundred years ago. Despite some two centuries of celebrations, this event is still little known in the city.

ZONA ARQUEOLÓGICA CUAHILAMA

The old woman who tried to protect the petroglyphs

Entrance on Calle 2 de Abril, at Prolongación 2 de Abril
Tuesday to Sunday 10am–5pm
Admission free

The important but forgotten set of petroglyphs of Monte Cuahilama, behind its metal barrier, is worth a visit.

The little-known entrance that leads to some steps may look unpromising, but once at the top you'll understand the significance of the site.

The first petroglyph, hidden in the undergrowth with a circular metal railing to protect it, depicts a pyramid and a human profile.

A little further on you'll see a coyote, the god Tonatiuh and the legend of the Fifth Sun, an allusion to Quetzalcóatl, and a hand raised in a three-finger salute.

Although the origin of the petroglyphs is unknown, some theories suggest that they could represent the points of the compass, the seasons of the year that were part of a calendar, or were simply for ceremonial rituals. The place used to be called Acapilxca but is now known as Cuahilama, meaning 'the old woman who protects the forest'.

The summit gives onto a plain where a pre-Hispanic track was found and which is still used for solstice ceremonies. There is also a Nahualapa ('stone map') almost 2 metres in size that shows the canals, water sources and springs around the site, which was the first settlement of the Xochimilca people (one of the seven Nahua tribes that migrated into the valley of Mexico).

There are historical accounts of up to 17 petroglyphs on this hill, as well as other sculptures and archaeological relics. Now only seven are left. In the 1950s, a sculpture of the mother goddess Cihuacóatl at the entrance was dynamited. Despite some vandalism by local students, the carvings are still magnificent.

Some of the people living nearby built the steps to protect the site and encourage visits. A plaque at the entrance is dedicated to one of them for their custodianship of the site in the 1980s.

We recommend exploring the area around the hilltop, taking care not to disturb the fauna and flora. Here you'll see traces of pre-Hispanic foundations as well as being able to admire the beautiful landscape from the various viewpoints.

'CANTOYA BALLOONS'
AT SAN AGUSTÍN OHTENCO

Calling out the dead with flying lanterns

Avenida Niños Héroes, junction with La Pradera
1 November 2pm to 12am, 2 November 5am to 12am
Admission free

The Días de Muertos (Days of the Dead, 1 and 2 November) are celebrated in an unusual way at San Agustín Ohtenco. So that the dead may find their way back to their homes and feast on the offerings laid out for them, instead of scattering flower petals, their loved ones call them with paper balloons, lanterns hung on the doors of houses, or fires that families stoke throughout the night.

Since the launch of the Cantoya balloon competition, this local custom has turned into a festival. The balloons have become bigger and bigger, more and more spectacular, every year. They are released throughout the day to entertain the crowds and call out the dead, then guide them back to their loved ones.

According to tradition, when dead children arrive from the underworld on 1 November, small balloons are launched at Ohtenco. Then, on 2 November, when the adult dead arrive in their turn, bigger balloons go up. In truth, what matters is not so much the size as the shapes created – stars, crosses, animals and countless other figures rise into the sky. Some people make beautiful paper models, while others stick on hand-painted canvases, which can only be seen once the balloon is aloft.

The spectacle is even more impressive at night when the balloons are lit. There are even street traders selling little balloons that are easy to assemble, so just ask the way to the field and someone will help you launch your own. Don't miss a nearby shop full of graffiti featuring local culture. Inside, you can find out how the gigantic balloons are made with over 500 sheets of paper.

These Mexican flying lanterns, called *Globos de Cantoya* [or *Cantolla*] (Cantoya balloons), are hot-air balloons made from paper, so called in tribute to balloonist Joaquín de la Cantolla. He made several flights from 1863, and although not the first balloonist in Mexico, he's still the best known. He died in 1914, following his last flight, when the Zapatistas tried to ground the balloon by firing at it. Even though the balloon didn't burst and Cantolla landed safely, he died on his way home from a stroke brought on by the terrifying experience.

TECÓMITL CEMETERY MUD SCULPTURES

Sculptures of the dead in the cemetery mud

Panteón de San Antonio Tecómitl
End of Calle 12 de Octubre
1 and 2 November, 24/7

The small cemetery of San Antonio Tecómitl is rather gloomy at night, but every 2 November (All Souls' Day), it fills with light, music and food, like many other graveyards around the country.

Unlike other cemeteries, where people only spend the night and leave a few offerings for the dead, here the local residents use the graveyard earth to make mud sculptures in their honour. Strangely enough, this tradition is little known, although the cemetery is only 2 kilometres from Mixquic, the most visited place in Mexico City on the Day of the Dead.

Although some mourners begin work on 1 November, the best time to appreciate this curious ritual is during the night of the 2nd, when the whole place is illuminated by candlelight and becomes even more fascinating.

Along Calle 12 de Octubre, street vendors sell all kinds of flowers to be used in the sculptures, while people collect water from an inside tank to start work with. Many of the graves are decorated with

geometric shapes and complex floral arrangements, others are covered with religious images or pre-Hispanic figures made from a mixture of flowers and sawdust. The most striking designs are real sculptures, representing human skulls, offerings, TV personalities, or things the dead person liked during their lifetime. Everything is designed to welcome the deceased relatives.

Little is known about the origin of this extraordinary tradition, although some people believe it dates from the time of the viceroys.

Tecómitl cemetery is divided into two sections, one for adults and the other for children. On one side are the adults' earth and mud graves; on the other are small, colourful fairy-tale castles, holding the remains of the little ones. For the Day of the Dead, the sculptures in this section include toys, windmills and characters from children's books.

At the far end of the cemetery, another unusual grave has a *narco-corrido* (drug traffickers' ballad) inscribed on the cement that might well relate to the life of whoever is buried there.

Monuments to Death and to shamans who turn into animals

Avenida José López Portillo / Sur del Comercio
RTP bus: route 148 or 141 (destination San Antonio Tecómitl); Tasqueña metro exit

Some of the 13 works created in 2009 by Salvador Jaramillo for Milpa Alta – the *delegación* with the greatest number of indigenous peoples in the city – stand along a sculpture walk that bears witness to the mythical past of its original inhabitants.

In addition to the statues of the *Pulquero* (maker of *pulque*, a Mexican liquor), the *Nopalera*, a woman cooking *mole* (the ultimate ranchero dish) and historical figures such as Luz Jiménez (see below), the two most impressive pieces are those on Paseo López Portillo: *La Muerte* (Death) and *El Nahual* (Spirit).

La Muerte, half-woman, half-corpse, is shown seated, wearing a cloak and extending a welcome to the slope that leads to Tecómitl, one of the 12 indigenous villages of Milpa Alta, gateway to the famous Mixquic where there is an altar dedicated to Mictlantecuhtli, Aztec god of the dead.

A little further along is *El Nahual* – according to indigenous beliefs, *nahualism* is the ability of some humans to turn into animals or natural elements, or to practise witchcraft. It's said that from birth everyone possesses the spirit of an animal responsible for protecting and guiding them throughout their life. These spirits generally manifest themselves in a dream or as an affinity with the guardian animal. Some Mesoamerican witch doctors and shamans could create such a strong link with their *nahuales* that they took on attributes such as a sparrowhawk's sight, a wolf's sense of smell or an ocelot's hearing. It's even said that some can take the form of an animal (therianthropia) for purposes that are not always benevolent.

Doña Luz Jiménez: local woman and artists' model

Doña Luz Jiménez, from Milpa Alta, was forced to flee after the massacre of her family on 15 October 1916. As a way out of poverty, she applied for a job vacancy at the Academia de Artes de San Carlos. When she asked what the job involved, she was told that all she had to do was to keep quiet, and so she became one of the first Mexican indigenous models. Painted by artists such as Siqueiros, Orozco, Tamayo, Rivera, Modotti, Fernando Leal and Jean Charlot, she fought prejudice by posing nude. As a Nahuatl speaker, she also collaborated with anthropologists and linguists such as Benjamin Lee Whorf and Stanley S. Newman, and told traditional stories for a book published by *indigenismo* (local culture) promoter Anita Brenner. Jiménez was knocked down and killed by a car in 1965, and is buried in the Iztapalapa district of the city.

ALPHABETICAL INDEX

ALPHABETICAL INDEX

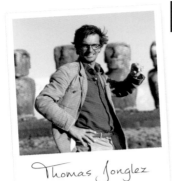

Thomas Jonglez

It was September 1995 and Thomas Jonglez was in Peshawar, the northern Pakistani city 20 kilometres from the tribal zone he was to visit a few days later. It occurred to him that he should record the hidden aspects of his native city, Paris, which he knew so well. During his seven-month trip back home from Beijing, the countries he crossed took in Tibet (entering clandestinely, hidden under blankets in an overnight bus), Iran and Kurdistan. He never took a plane but travelled by boat, train or bus, hitch-hiking, cycling, on horseback or on foot, reaching Paris just in time to celebrate Christmas with the family.

On his return, he spent two fantastic years wandering the streets of the capital to gather material for his first 'secret guide', written with a friend. For the next seven years he worked in the steel industry until the passion for discovery overtook him. He launched Jonglez Publishing in 2003 and moved to Venice three years later.

In 2013, in search of new adventures, the family left Venice and spent six months travelling to Brazil, via North Korea, Micronesia, the Solomon Islands, Easter Island, Peru and Bolivia. After seven years in Rio de Janeiro, he now lives in Berlin with his wife and three children.

Jonglez Publishing produces a range of titles in nine languages, released in 40 countries.

ACKNOWLEDGEMENTS:

Antiguo Templo de Cristh Church, Museo Franz Mayer, Museo del Calzado 'El Borcegui
Templo Metodista de la Santísima Trinidad, Fundación para Ancianos Concepción Béistegu
IAP, Museo Casa de la Memoria Indómita, Patronato del Hospital de Jesús, Dirección Genera
de Promoción Cultural y Acervo Patrimonial de la Secretaría de Hacienda y Crédito Públic
Instituto Nacional de Antropología e Historia, Instituto Nacional de Bellas Artes, Toallas L
Josefina, Museo Pinacoteca del Oratorio de San Felipe Neri 'La Profesa', Archivo Históric
de la Ciudad de México 'Carlos Singüenza y Góngora', Secretaría de Cultura del Gobiern
de la Ciudad de México, Secretaría de Educación Pública, Secretaría de Medio Ambiente
Recursos Naturales, Secretaría de Cultura, Suprema Corte de Justicia de la Nación, Museo d
Tatuaje, Sistema de Transporte Colectivo, Instituto del Fondo Nacional de la Vivienda para l
Trabajadores, Casa Fortaleza de Emilio 'El Indio' Fernández, Casa de la Cultura Jesús Reye
Heroles, Museo del Automóvil México, Patronato Universitario de la Universidad Nacion
Autónoma de México, Mapoteca Manuel Orozco y Berra, Dirección General del Bosque c
Chapultepec, Panteón Civil de Dolores, Capilla Alfonsina, Parroquia de la Sagrada Famili
Museo del Padre Pro, Taller Tlamaxcalli, Centro Cultural Estación Indianilla, Instituto d
Ciencias Forenses, Instituto Mexicano del Seguro Social, Herbario Medicinal del IMSS, Panteó
Francés de la Piedad, Asociación Franco Mexicana Suiza y Belga de Beneficencia IAP, Parroqu
de Nuestra Señora de la Piedad, Parroquia del Perpetuo Socorro, Coordinación del Patrimoni
Artístico y Cultural de la Secretaría del Gobierno de la Ciudad de México, Centro de Coinversió
Social y Cultural Juan González y García, Museo de Arte en Azúcar, Casa Museo Benita Galean
Fundación María y Héctor García, Museo Ídolos del ESTO, Sindicato Mexicano de Electricista
Sindicato de Trabajadores Ferrocarrileros de la República Mexicana, Comisión Nacional para
Desarrollo de los Pueblos Indígenas, Museo Indígena, Museo Legislativo 'Los Sentimientos d
la Nación', Los Baños del Peñón, Instituto Politécnico Nacional, Dirección General de Siti
y Monumentos de Conaculta, Museo de Figuras de Cera de La Villa, Tecnológico de Estudi
Superiores de Ecatepec, Universidad Intercontinental, Universidad del Claustro de Sor Juan
Santuario de Nuestra Señora de Guadalupe y la Santísima Hostia Sangrante, Capilla del Divin
Salvador del Calvario, Instituto Tecnológico y de Estudios Superiores de Monterrey.

Personal thanks:

Mario Torres Madrid, Leonor Santamaría Ibarra, Thomas Jonglez, Anna Cetti, Roxan
Elvridge–Thomas, Abril Edsel Ceja Curiel, Scarlett de la Torre, Daniela Rico, Álva
Santillán, Jazmín Juárez, Dulce María de Alvarado, and to all Mexico City residents, wh
make it a magical and otherworldly place.

PHOTOGRAPHY CREDITS:

All photos were taken by **Mario Yaír T.S.** with the exception of:

Edsel Ceja: Plaza Capuchinas altarpiece, El monolito de 1968, O'Gorman's first mural, Parque Margain Pool, Prehistoric pyramid, Hand-cranked car, Archivo general de suenos y utopías, Madonna of mercy, 'Wonder room' at museo Idolos del Esto, The last 'Vigilante del Chopo', History trail in Parque Tezozomoc, Mazatepetl maquette

Scarlett de la Torre: Jardin de los Perros, Los Talavera tiles depicting Don Quixote, Monument to Rockdrigo, Memories of El Halconazo, Ajedrez Cervantino chessboard

Daniela Rico A.: Holly relics in the cathedral (right page)

Reuters: Virgin of Hidalgo metro station (right page)

Casasola México: Red Houses of the Gallas (right page)

Fundación María y Héctor García: *Niño en el vientre de concreto*

Fabrizio León / La Jornada: Monument to Rockdrigo (right page)

Carlo Ardán Montiel J.: Mammoth at Talisman metro station (right page)

Biblioteca Lerdo de Tejada: Plaza de Etiopia (right page)

Maps: **Cyrille Suss** – Layout Design: **Coralie Cintrat** – Layout: **Stéphanie Benoit and Emmanuelle Willard Toulemonde** – English Translation: **Jeremy Scott, Caroline Lawrence and Jane Bonnin** – Proofreading: **Matt Gay, Eleni Salemi and Kimberly Bess** – Publishing: **Clémence Mathé**.

© JONGLEZ 2024
Registration of copyright: January 2024 – Edition: 02
ISBN: 978-2-36195-543-4
Printed in Bulgaria by Multiprint